A More Perfect Military

A More Perfect Military

How the Constitution Can Make Our
Military Stronger

Diane H. Mazur

OXFORD
UNIVERSITY PRESS
2010

OXFORD
UNIVERSITY PRESS

Oxford University Press, Inc., publishes works that further
Oxford University's objective of excellence
in research, scholarship, and education.

Oxford   New York
Auckland   Cape Town   Dar es Salaam   Hong Kong   Karachi
Kuala Lumpur   Madrid   Melbourne   Mexico City   Nairobi
New Delhi   Shanghai   Taipei   Toronto

With offices in
Argentina   Austria   Brazil   Chile   Czech Republic   France   Greece
Guatemala   Hungary   Italy   Japan   Poland   Portugal   Singapore
South Korea   Switzerland   Thailand   Turkey   Ukraine   Vietnam

Copyright © 2010 by Oxford University Press, Inc.

Published by Oxford University Press, Inc.
198 Madison Avenue, New York, New York 10016

www.oup.com

Oxford is a registered trademark of Oxford University Press

Library of Congress Cataloging-in-Publication Data
Mazur, Diane H., 1956–
A more perfect military : how the constitution can make our
military stronger / Diane H. Mazur.
    p. cm.
Includes bibliographical references and index.
ISBN 978-0-19-539448-1 (hardcover : alk. paper)
1. Military law—United States. 2. Civil-military relations—United States. I. Title.
KF7209.M39   2010
343.73′01–dc22   2010003112

1 3 5 7 9 8 6 4 2

Printed in the United States of America
on acid-free paper

Contents

A More Perfect Military

Introduction

There is no more delicate subject in America today than the fitness of the all-volunteer military. Thirty-five years after Congress dismantled the military draft at the end of the Vietnam War, we find it difficult to have serious, honest conversations about the meaning of military service or the wisdom of military policies. Any discussion of who should be serving in the military, and whether this special responsibility and privilege is fairly shared among all Americans, is extraordinarily sensitive. The subject becomes even more difficult, almost untouchable, when we ask whether the military might be more effective if we made different choices. Maybe we should rethink who should be allowed to serve in the military, or who should volunteer to serve, or perhaps who should be required to serve as an obligation of citizenship. Maybe we should, but we probably won't. Any suggestion we could have something less than the very best people serving in the military today is one of the most taboo subjects of national security debate.

The lesson we have learned all too well is that there is very little to be gained by asking whether the military could in some sense be better, because someone will inevitably interpret the question as an insult meant to convey there is something wrong with the military. We don't consider whether young people joining the military could be better in terms of education, maturity, experience, or temperament, whether the military's professional leadership could be better, whether civilian government's management of the military could be better, or whether the relationship between the military and the rest of America could be better. In the last thirty-five years, certainly few people have been rewarded for thinking creatively about the military. No one wants to go down that road, because no one, of course, ever wants to be accused of not supporting the troops. The most effective conversation stopper ever invented in contemporary American dialogue is the charge that someone doesn't respect the military or those who serve in the military.

There is an uneasy and sometimes unbearable tension between appreciation and critique whenever we discuss the all-volunteer military and the people who serve our country in uniform. Surveys show that the military is the most respected and trusted institution, public or private, within our society.[1] We hail our servicemembers as heroes and hold them out as the best of what America has to offer. However, contrary to what most of us assume to be true, the civil-military relationship in America since the Vietnam War has drastically deteriorated, to a degree that would be frightening if anyone paid attention to the warning signs. But we don't. Our optimism about the fundamental rightness of our military hides a considerable amount of fear, ignorance, disinterest, resentment, and guilt dividing those who have served in the military from those who have not. We fear or avoid what we don't understand; we ignore or forget what seems so distant from our daily lives; we withdraw from issues we are told we know nothing about; and finally, we feel resentful, or guilty, when we suspect responsibility for military service is not shared fairly among us.

We seem to have reached a tense compromise that tolerates only the most stilted and artificial debates about matters involving the military. For example, we often discourage those who have not served in the military from taking part in ongoing national debates about military issues, even though grassroots, everyday discussion among citizens is an important part of the process of civilian control of the military under the Constitution. We assume that civilians who have never served cannot understand the military well enough to offer constructive suggestions, even on policy matters that have nothing to do with professional questions of weaponry and tactics. Perhaps we also believe nonveterans have not earned the right to speak because, in an era of voluntary service, they made the choice to let others carry the burden for them.

We also enforce informal restrictions on what people are safely allowed to say about the military. We tend to be skeptical about opinions that differ from what we think is the accepted "military" viewpoint on an issue, even if our level of understanding is closer to military fantasy than military reality. In this instance, it doesn't seem to matter if someone has military experience. If veterans tell us something that steps too far outside our comfortable assumptions, their opinions are suspect because they fail to support what we have convinced ourselves is the correct "military" way of seeing the world. But if civilians without military experience wrap themselves in the false facade of the military's endorsement, their opinions are likely insulated from criticism. Political correctness is usually assigned to those of a liberal persuasion, but in the military arena it is definitely an equal-opportunity disease. Too often we look for what is billed as the "militarily correct" answer, only to miss the literally correct or smarter one.

Inflexible rules of discussion tend to fossilize current views on military issues and make it extraordinarily difficult to think in new ways about policies that are important to all Americans, both inside and outside the military.

They lead us to disregard actual military judgment when it is "different" and instead defer to those who are much less knowledgeable about military affairs—but who at least confirm all our old assumptions. The rules also encourage persistent but inaccurate myths related to military service, since anyone who dares to suggest conventional wisdom is wrong is painted as unsupportive of the military. We have made it impossible to point out the emperor is wearing no clothes in the land of military affairs.

Our inability to talk constructively about the military makes it less likely that professional military expertise will play its proper role in the decisions civilians make about military affairs. When knowledgeable military voices can be crowded out of the conversation, civilians can hide behind assertions of military necessity and use the military in ways that exceed constitutional bounds and for reasons that are corrosive to military professionalism and military effectiveness. These odd little rules of military debate invite constitutional mischief by civilian actors who would misuse the military for purposes far outside the military's traditional function and role.

We have become unusually comfortable with discussions about military issues that are incomplete, misleading, or even dishonest. We have been willing to accept the idea that supporting the military means we should not ask questions, we should not make ourselves more knowledgeable about military affairs, and we should look the other way whenever we vaguely suspect something is wrong with the relationship between the military and civilian America. We obediently follow all the unwritten rules of conversation about the military, accept all the conventional wisdom about the military, and take no responsibility as citizens for the process of civilian control of the military envisioned by the Constitution.

The purpose of this book is to change all the rules that limit the way we talk about the military. It will speak with candor about the military and the future of our civil-military relations even when—especially when—the conventional wisdom has been altered and stretched to fit in order to reach our favorite answers. It will tell the rest of the story conveniently left out in all the partial, misleading discussions we have had in recent years on subjects such as military recruiting and the shared obligations of citizenship; the nature of the relationship we want to have between the military and civilian America; the meaning of the Constitution for members of the military in the areas of equal protection, free speech, religious freedom, and respect for the rule of law; the proper scope of military influence in civilian society and the proper scope of civilian influence in military society; the cultural flash point of women in military service; and, finally, the post-Vietnam drift toward a politically partisan military and the impact it has had on civilian control of the military. Years of tightly scripted, superficial, and empty conversations about the military have left many important facts unsaid.

I wish it did not matter so much whether those who write about the military out of respectful appreciation for its role in our constitutional design were themselves veterans of military service. But it does matter, and until the rules of conversation about the military change, there is perhaps no other area of study in which personal credentials matter more. I am a law professor at the University of Florida who specializes in constitutional law, military law, and civil-military relations. I am also a former officer in the United States Air Force, one of the relatively few military veterans among faculty members in law schools today who have served in the all-volunteer era. As for women who are tenured law professors and also former military line officers or enlisted persons, as far as I know I am one of only two nationwide.[2] I am also deeply concerned about the direction that civil-military relations in the United States have taken since the end of the Vietnam War. What follows next is but one example of the many ways we have been encouraged to misunderstand something vitally important about the military and its place in America.

The civil-military divide has been especially sharp on university campuses—or at least the conventional wisdom pushes us to see it that way. Universities are irresistibly easy targets when making arguments about military service. Everyone assumes that universities turned their backs on the military and on people in uniform during the Vietnam War, and everyone assumes they have continued to be hostile, or at best aloof and distant, ever since. As the *Wall Street Journal* observed in an article about Reserve Officer Training Corps (ROTC) programs at Ivy League campuses, "Few debates better demonstrate America's cultural divide."[3]

Unfortunately, few debates are as ridden with myths, misunderstandings, and misrepresentations as the one about how badly universities have treated the military. The myth of academia's fierce opposition to the military is just one example of how our inability to have meaningful discussions about the military has led us to rely on increasingly skewed and convenient versions of reality. It is also a powerful example of the kind of willful ignorance that too often characterizes the civil-military relationship today and goes unchallenged because we have learned it is not our place to question accepted understandings about the military. If an understanding as widely accepted as the one about universities and the military actually has no basis in reality, at the very least we would have to seriously question what else we don't understand about civil-military relations today.

A search of newspaper and magazine articles published after September 11, 2001, will reveal hundreds of references to the claim that some universities—usually elite Ivy League institutions—have either banished, banned, barred, exiled, or expelled ROTC military training programs from their campuses.[4]

Most of the reports explain that ROTC was "kicked out" or "thrown off" as an undeserved consequence of pervasive animosity against the military, and the military seems to agree with that assessment. The official journal of the Army War College published an article entitled "Storming the Ivory Tower: The Military's Return to American Campuses,"[5] leaving little doubt about the author's perspective on the size of the cultural divide between universities and the military. He looked forward to the possibility that changing attitudes at elite universities like Harvard and Yale—he was a graduate of both—might lead to "the reintroduction of the military to schools that have been hostile to the military since the Vietnam War."

Given how often universities have apparently slammed the door on ROTC, one might wonder why it is that not one of these unpatriotic educational institutions has been punished for violating the federal law that says universities cannot exclude ROTC from their campuses, at least not without facing serious financial consequences. Why hasn't this law been enforced by either Democratic or Republican administrations? Under the law, universities must forfeit federal funding if they have "a policy or practice" that prevents any of the military services from "maintaining, establishing, or operating" an ROTC unit on their campuses.[6] The requirement is no secret. Candidates in the 2008 presidential race promised to enforce the law and pull federal funding from resistant universities, and they called on universities to end their bans on ROTC.[7] No one, however, asked the candidates why they thought the law was not currently being enforced.

The answer to the puzzling question of why these universities have not been punished by the federal government is that the eviction of ROTC from university campuses amid antiwar protest and antimilitary attitudes is nothing more than an urban myth. These universities have not, in fact, banned ROTC from their campuses, and they never did. This conventional wisdom about the military and academia is no more true than the breathless, frightening stories told around campfires about homicidal intruders or menacing hitchhikers. But how could a myth so easy to disprove become such an unshakable part of our national understanding?

The only research investigation of ROTC's history on university campuses was published in *Making Citizen-Soldiers: ROTC and the Ideology of American Military Service*, a book written by Michael Neiberg.[8] Professor Neiberg is by no means an antimilitary zealot bent on insulting the military or covering up the antimilitary sentiment of universities. Now the codirector of the Center for the Study of War and Society at the University of Southern Mississippi, he taught future military officers as a professor at the United States Air Force Academy for seven years. If anyone knows the truth behind the assumption that some universities have banned ROTC from their campuses in violation of federal law, he does. As a good historian, he based his conclusions on records and documents from the time in question and not on today's opinions or recollections about what happened in the past.

Contrary to what almost everyone assumes to be true, Professor Neiberg's comprehensive study of both university and ROTC records revealed that universities have actually been strong supporters of shared civil-military ties and military education for more than a century. He found that universities have been consistent advocates for the traditional concept of "citizen-soldier" that was so respected by our nation's founders. As a general rule, universities have been attentive and loyal to the role higher education should play in maintaining good civil-military relations and in developing competent citizen-soldiers for our defense, much more so than either Congress or the military. Professor Neiberg concluded that ROTC's biggest critics have been "in uniform, not on campus."[9]

What led ROTC to leave some university campuses at the close of the Vietnam War was the convergence of two powerful trends, one of them academic in nature and the other entirely military. First, for decades the military and the program's host institutions had been battling back and forth over a handful of university policies. The two most important were whether ROTC courses should qualify for full academic credit without having to meet regular standards for academic content, and whether ROTC military instructors should be awarded the rank of professor even if they did not have the advanced academic degrees required for other faculty members.[10] Second, when the military draft changed, ROTC changed along with it. In the later years of the Vietnam War the federal government adopted a lottery selection mechanism that restored some predictability to the military draft, but it also eliminated the need for male students to enroll in ROTC as a means of managing their exposure to the war. Before the move to a lottery, enrollment in ROTC was an effective way to limit the possibility of being assigned to combat in Vietnam, or at least to postpone it.[11]

Rather than adapt the content of some less academic ROTC courses to meet university requirements or, alternatively, accept a program in which cadets enrolled in ROTC more for the military training and benefits and less for the academic credit, ROTC chose to leave some schools—especially if ROTC enrollment had already plummeted because it was no longer needed to avoid the draft. Articles appearing in the *Harvard Crimson* newspaper at the time explained matter-of-factly how these events caused Harvard and ROTC to go their separate ways, without the false reinterpretation of history, such as "Harvard kicked ROTC off campus," we would see in the typical report written today.[12] Harvard did not by any definition evict ROTC; instead, ROTC believed it should not have to comply with the same rules applicable to other academic departments on campus, and so it opted to leave.

It is no doubt true that opposition to the war led some faculty members to become more impatient and less forgiving in the long controversy over ROTC's compliance with academic requirements. But the important point is that universities, with extremely rare exception, did not want to end their affiliation with ROTC, even during the Vietnam era, and they did not force ROTC off their campuses. This doesn't mean there weren't some students with more radical perspectives who used ROTC as a punching bag for opposing the war, because there were. It does mean, however, that these students were not at all representative of their universities, or even of most students.[13] Universities did want to alter their academic relationship with the military, but ROTC made its own choice to leave for greener pastures. There was already a long line of other colleges standing by, hoping to entice new ROTC programs to their campuses with promises of greater local funding and assurances they would not be as demanding in applying regular academic standards to questions of course credit and professorial rank.[14]

So why do we, thirty-five years later, happily assume that black is white, square is round, up is down, and ROTC does not exist at some elite universities because antimilitary academics have thrown the military off campus? There are two reasons. First, this historical myth comfortably fits the way our society has chosen to frame the civil-military dynamic. The military and those who are perceived to be its supporters are the good guys; universities, professors, and others in the business of academia find themselves on the elite, unpatriotic, and ungrateful side of the divide. It is very difficult to dislodge such a fundamental way of viewing the world. Information supporting the assumption tends to be remembered, and information that doesn't tends to be ignored or rewritten to match expectations.

Granted, some recent developments have dovetailed perfectly with the myth of how the academic community despises the military, and they have helped to feed the stereotype. A very small segment of the academic world—law schools, and only a small minority of law schools overall—made an unfortunate decision to protest "Don't Ask, Don't Tell" by interfering with the military's recruiting of new Judge Advocate General's (JAG) Corps candidates on their campuses. ("Don't Ask, Don't Tell" is the federal law that attempts to bar gay people from military service, and the acronym "JAG," shorthand for a military lawyer, became well known through the title of a popular television series.)

These law schools took their case all the way to the Supreme Court in 2006 and were handed a spectacular loss in *Rumsfeld v. Forum for Academic and Institutional Rights*.[15] Although by then their position had been remolded into a respectable claim about academic freedom and the rights of free speech, for many years the law faculty members driving the protest concentrated their efforts on petty acts of disrespect toward members of the military's legal corps when they arrived on law school campuses to interview interested students. I've heard law professors trading tips at conferences on the best ways to be rude and unkind to military visitors as an expression of displeasure with "Don't Ask, Don't Tell." Their proposed array of personal slights included denying military officers the friendly cups of coffee or lunches that were routinely offered to other legal recruiters and assigning the military the most inconvenient and distant interview rooms. On several occasions, law professors acted immaturely and unprofessionally in attempting to disrupt interviews with students.[16] These professors were certainly unaware of the long tradition of the university community as an important player in developing the traditional "citizen-soldier" who is a leader in the civilian community and also a defender, if needed, of national security.[17]

Keep in mind that a small minority of law professors translates into a microscopic, insignificant percentage of academics overall. However, their protest against "Don't Ask, Don't Tell" and their eventual loss in the Supreme Court received tremendous publicity. Their public resistance to military recruiting over the past fifteen years has given Congress a platform to rail repeatedly against supposedly antimilitary universities by enacting progressively harsher financial penalties for schools that do not cooperate with military recruiters. This ill-chosen course of action by law schools only made it easier to teach another generation of Americans the myth that universities are intrinsically hostile to the military and the people who serve our country in uniform. In essence, we believe the myth because it fits so neatly with the polarized way our culture has come to characterize our military and our universities.

The second reason we have become so comfortable in accepting and relying upon myths about the military and military service—like our universal misunderstanding about what happened to ROTC on college campuses during and after the Vietnam War—is right at the center of what this book is about. Something quite serious has happened to the state of our civil-military relations during the three decades we have had an all-volunteer military. We have apparently reached a point at which truth, fact, and reality are much less relevant to the way we make decisions involving the military, and worse yet, we haven't even noticed the change.

I have strong allegiances on both sides of the cultural divide between the academic community and the military community. As a law professor, my academic work focuses on how the Constitution affects the military, the civilian institutions of government that oversee the military (Congress, the president, and the courts), and the people who choose to join the military. As an Air Force officer, I received training as an aircraft maintenance officer and served at Grand Forks Air Force Base, North Dakota, and at Incirlik Air

Base, Republic of Turkey. After leaving the Air Force, I attended law school, practiced law for a few years, and then began an academic career as a law professor. My interest in the military and its connection to civilian society, to government, to law, and to political dissent is a product of both allegiances.

Things have certainly changed since my 1979 arrival at Grand Forks Air Force Base. The base was then under the control of the Strategic Air Command, the airborne component of our Cold War nuclear deterrence that was so dramatically depicted in the classic Henry Fonda film *Fail-Safe*. I was assigned to an aircraft maintenance squadron that repaired B-52 Stratofortress long-range bombers and the KC-135 Stratotankers that refueled them in midflight; at the time, any women working outside the traditional fields of medicine and administration were still rare enough to be the subject of mild curiosity. The woman who would one day become the first female B-52 pilot, Lieutenant Kelly Flinn, was still working her way through elementary school. You may remember the name. In 1997, less than two years after she first climbed into the cockpit of a B-52, she was threatened with court-martial by the Air Force for adultery and other offenses and quickly became the infamous symbol of the military's stumbling efforts to integrate women and control sexual misconduct.[18] Today, we no longer place bombers on nuclear alert, and the Grand Forks refueling mission has shifted to include airlift and medical evacuation.

Incirlik Air Base, located a few miles from the Mediterranean Sea near Turkey's border with Syria, has also seen its share of changes as its role has shifted from a relatively sleepy installation for training, support, and storage during the Cold War to a crucial air hub for current military operations in the Middle East.[19] Following the first Gulf War in 1991, aircraft enforcing the no-flight zone against Saddam Hussein's Iraqi air forces flew out of Incirlik Air Base, and after the attacks of September 11, 2001, the base became a busy transit center for air traffic to both Afghanistan and Iraq. Incirlik has come a long way from the tiny American air base that was almost deactivated in the 1970s.

The military has undergone many significant changes in the thirty-five years that have passed since the end of the Vietnam War. The most fundamental change is probably the transition from a draft-assisted to an all-volunteer, recruited force. The military has also shifted its tactical focus. As a result of the second war in Iraq, Operation Iraqi Freedom, the military has increased its emphasis on training in counterinsurgency techniques (winning a "hearts and minds" campaign) in comparison to conventional methods of warfare. Operational tempo has increased to the point of raising periodic concerns that we risk breaking the military through repeated deployments with insufficient resources.

Even military culture has evolved, effectively disproving the common argument that the military must always remain exactly the same as it has been, because change or "experimentation" will put the mission at risk—a convenient position, of course, to take in support of the status quo. Today, for example, the military makes far more effective use of the female half of the population than it did at the beginning of the all-volunteer force in the 1970s. The military has changed fundamentally for men as well as for women, although we tend to be less concerned about changes involving men. Today, the military struggles to manage a huge array of social services for male servicemembers, 85 percent of the total force, who are now much more likely to have wives, children, and a need for extensive family support programs than they did during the Vietnam era.

Although the way the military fulfills its mission requirements can undergo substantial change in the course of a single generation, other, more fundamental, aspects of the institution should remain constant. The constancy of military professionalism that our nation relies upon is principally grounded in a foundation of law and, more specifically, in the structure of our Constitution and the guidance it provides for civil-military relations. The Constitution is the common denominator that ought to control the military's relationship to the civilian society it serves, to the civilian branches of government that oversee its operation, and to the constitutional ideals its members have all sworn to support and defend.

The title of this book, *A More Perfect Military*, is a phrase borrowed from the Preamble to the Constitution of the United States, which declares our constitutional purpose "to form a more perfect union." The comparison is much more than just a turn of phrase. The foundation of strong civil-military relations and an effective military is built on faithfulness to the Constitution and its vision for our armed forces and the civilians who lead them. This foundation, unfortunately, has deteriorated since the end of the Vietnam War, in part because we no longer have a military draft to circulate a more representative range of citizens—privileged and nonprivileged, liberal and conservative—through the experience of military service. However, the transition to an all-volunteer military would not have caused the same decline without some underground assistance from the United States Supreme Court. Over the last thirty-five years, the Supreme Court has consistently undermined the military's traditional relationship to law and the Constitution. Ironically, the Court has managed to weaken the military at the same time it insists it is only protecting and defending the military from harm.

In a series of court cases that never became household names, the Supreme Court developed a new standard for evaluating the constitutionality of government policies involving the military. Under this new doctrine, for example, if someone were to challenge a federal law or a military judgment as violating constitutional protections of equality under law, free speech, or religious freedom, the government would no longer be asked to explain specifically why military necessity required such an intrusion on constitutional rights. It would be enough for the government to assert that it had good military reasons for disregarding the usual constitutional expectations, but it would not be asked to substantiate that those reasons were valid in the same way that other functions of government would normally be required to do. The justification for the Court's new doctrine was that the military was different from the rest of us. It had less reason to be faithful to the Constitution than the rest of America because the military's moral standards were already higher than civilian standards. In any event, the Court believed that civilian judges were incapable of understanding military issues, and so it made little sense to have courts play any important role in ensuring that military-related decisions were faithful to the Constitution. What the Court failed to understand, however, was that it was unraveling the military's traditional connection to the rule of law.

A decline in civil-military relations can be subtle in appearance while significant in effect, for two reasons. First, it is easy to confuse healthy civil-military relations under the Constitution with a high level of respect and admiration for the military, but the two concepts are unrelated. In fact, sometimes civil-military relations can be the most fragile when our respect and admiration for the military is the greatest, because we are least attentive to indications of possible problems—and most reluctant to be so rude as to mention them. Second, it is easy to confuse healthy civil-military relations with our confidence that the military will never engage in a coup against civilian government, or anything even remotely close to a coup. We assume that civil-military relations are good when the military follows the orders of its civilian leaders.

While civil-military relations certainly have failed, and failed spectacularly, if the military refuses to follow civilian direction, this is much too blunt a measure to use in assessing constitutional health. It identifies only the complete disaster that is overwhelmingly unlikely to occur. Not only is military obedience the wrong measure, the military itself is usually the wrong focus. In the case of the American military, some of the most telling signs of civil-military decline can be seen in the actions of civilians, not servicemembers. When civilians are able to use the military for nonmilitary purposes—for political advantage or convenience—there is a civil-military problem. When civilians are able to use the military to evade the limitations of domestic law, or when civilians encourage the military's influence outside traditional constitutional bounds, there is a civil-military problem. When civilian control of the military is distorted to mean that only some civilians have the right to speak on military issues, or that only one or two of the three branches of government have the right to participate in civilian control, there is a civil-military problem.

Civilian misuse of the military, of course, will always have a correspondingly corrosive effect on the military itself. We tend to assume the military and its culture are constant and unchanging, channeled by a focus on military necessity. We underestimate the effect that civilian society has on the military and forget that it is well within our ability to change the nature of our military, for better or for worse. Over the last thirty-five years, civilian influences—primarily from institutions of law, and especially from the Supreme Court—have without doubt changed the nature of the military for the worse.

A More Perfect Military begins with the story behind the Supreme Court's most recent pronouncement on the constitutional relationship between the military and civilian society. Chapter 1 takes a civilian perspective, explaining why law schools squared off against Congress and the military in an attempt to bar military recruiters from their campuses and why the Supreme Court ruled unanimously against them. Although most observers were comforted by the Court's apparent success in protecting the military from the misguided efforts of academics, *Rumsfeld v. FAIR* was only the most recent in a line of cases in which the Court undermined the military's constitutional health. Chapter 2 assesses the damage from the military side by digging beneath the surface of one of the dozens of briefs filed in the case. The arguments in this brief, which came from law students who were also military veterans, revealed ominous signs of deterioration in civil-military relations and civilian control of the military.

Chapters 3 and 4 will then take a step back in time to uncover the history of how the Supreme Court began to chip away at the military's professional bond to law and the Constitution. Three post-Vietnam decisions by the Court, all authored by former chief justice William Rehnquist, were primarily responsible for distorting our traditional understanding of the military's relationship to civilian society under the Constitution. Not coincidentally, these cases involved three of the most divisive issues in civil-military relations today: politics and the military, women and the military, and religion and the military.

Chapter 5 returns to the present and examines the current crisis of political partisanship in the military, one of the most telling symptoms of a constitutionally fragile military. Implicit in the Constitution is a bargain between the military and civilian society: for civilian control to be effective, the military must remain politically neutral. However, over the last thirty-five years, the military's professional ethic of political neutrality has eroded. The military has become more comfortable with open political partisanship and extreme social conservatism, and its political allegiances have affected a range of military concerns, including the candor of advice given to the president and to Congress. At the same time, the transition from a draft to an all-volunteer military has made the military less politically and culturally representative of civilian society.

Chapters 6 and 7 reveal more of the unintended consequences that follow from the military's frayed connection to law. The Supreme Court has negligently fostered a military culture in which servicemembers are encouraged to be resentful of civilians and civilian influence, which weakens our domestic civil-military relations and also undercuts our military operations abroad. When the Court taught a generation of servicemembers to disrespect or disregard law in the presumed interest of military necessity, it helped to ensure the failure of the military's legal system for detention and prosecution of suspected terrorists, and it also set the stage for the military's complicity in torture and abuse of prisoners.

Chapters 8, 9, and 10 explain how this fundamental change in civil-military relations has affected three of the most difficult social challenges the military faces today: the hidden crisis of military recruiting, the uncomfortable controversy over "Don't Ask, Don't Tell," and the uncertain status of women in the armed forces decades after their service should have been accepted and routine. Almost every difficult issue faced by the military today has been made more difficult, unfortunately, by the Court's deep erosion of the military's relationship to civilian society and to law.

Chapter 11 finally circles back to the unimaginable prospect of a military coup—the one disaster of civil-military relations we assume is overwhelmingly unlikely to occur. It recounts the untold story of how close we came to civil-military disaster during the 2000 presidential election. As much as we are concerned about our civil-military relations and how they affect a number of contemporary debates, nothing has more gravity than the prospect that civilians will deploy military votes in an effort to swing a presidential election. The full story will surprise you.

A More Perfect Military closes with a chapter that offers three specific suggestions for reversing this post-Vietnam trend and restoring the military's constitutional health. We may not need to return to a draft—although it is much more difficult to have a constitutionally healthy military without one—but we do need to take decisive actions that return the military to its original constitutional foundations.

Chapter 1

Slam-Dunked Law Professors

How could a bunch of smart law professors have been so wrong about the law? In *Rumsfeld v. Forum for Academic and Institutional Rights*,[1] a case decided by the United States Supreme Court in 2006, they had the professional advantage. The law professors' organization, Forum for Academic and Institutional Rights, was an association of thirty-six law schools joining together for the sole purpose of challenging the constitutionality of a federal law known as the Solomon Amendment. First enacted in 1994 and named for its congressional sponsor, Representative Gerald Solomon of New York, the Solomon Amendment took federal funding away from universities if they prevented the military from interviewing students during school-sponsored career-placement events.[2] In this unusual lawsuit, the law professors were the plaintiffs, not the legal advisors, and collectively they probably knew more about the law than anyone else in the room.

The defendants in *Rumsfeld v. FAIR* included Secretary of Defense Donald Rumsfeld and several other cabinet members who controlled funding affected by the Solomon Amendment. The plaintiffs, however, were more difficult to identify specifically. Individual law schools joined the litigation under the group banner of *FAIR* so they would have the option of remaining anonymous, although two-thirds eventually revealed their identities. They were concerned the government might retaliate against schools by cutting their funding and, less persuasively, they said they feared political criticism for their challenge to military recruiting. Incidentally, my law school, the University of Florida, did not join the *FAIR* group of law schools. This was a position consistent with that of other law schools in the South and, at least at the University of Florida, it was a position taken without any deliberation or debate by faculty or students. It was always assumed that we would welcome military recruiters to interview on campus, just as our parent university did. Solomon Amendment protest is, for the most part, a Blue State phenomenon.

The *FAIR* law schools said they opposed military recruiting on their campuses as a matter of principle. In their brief to the Supreme Court, they stated their long-held view that "discrimination is morally wrong and fundamentally incompatible with the values of the legal profession."[3] Consistent with that belief, they sought to promote an educational atmosphere of fairness and equality for *all* law students, not just some or even most of them. Law schools took the position that all employers—military or civilian, public or private—were welcome to interview their future lawyers, provided they were also willing to abide by a nondiscrimination agreement to hire without regard to factors such as sex, race, religion, or sexual orientation.[4] Anything less, they believed, would be unfaithful to their students and to values of equality. Of course, the intractable problem was that the Judge Advocate General's (JAG) Corps, the military's employer of lawyers, could not agree to the terms of the nondiscrimination policy. The JAG Corps, like the rest of the military, had a legal obligation to comply with "Don't Ask, Don't Tell," the federal law that bars—or at least attempts to bar—gay people from serving in the military.[5]

The law schools believed they were doing the right thing in protecting an academic environment that was inclusive and supportive of all students, but they also argued they had the right to make their own educational policy choices, right or wrong, under the First Amendment to the United States Constitution. According to the law schools, the Solomon Amendment's funding restriction allowed the government to interfere with their expression of a strongly held viewpoint about the importance of equality in legal education. They believed the law forced them to host and assist military recruiters who voiced a distinctly different and unwelcome message—one of discrimination, not equality—under the threat to deny federal funding both to the law school and its parent university. *FAIR's* Complaint in the United States District Court opened with the following statement:

> This case is about the freedom of educational institutions, specifically law schools, to shape their own pedagogical environments and to teach, by word and deed, the values they choose, free from government intrusion. It is about whether the government may compel law schools to lend their resources, personnel, and facilities to propagate a message they abhor—a message of discrimination that violates the core values they inculcate in their students and faculty.[6]

The Solomon Amendment was a particularly powerful weapon against law schools because it threatened to withdraw federal funding from entire universities even if only a small college or department within the larger university, such as a law school, did not welcome military recruiters, and even if the law school agreed to operate entirely without federal funding. The federal funding at issue was not only for defense-related programs but also included unrelated grants and contracts for science, medicine, and other fields of research. Therefore, if a law school excluded military recruiters from its career-placement program, the entire university would lose federal funding for projects as distant from military affairs as, for example, cancer research. Clearly, the Solomon Amendment was a serious proposition for universities.

Rumsfeld v. FAIR promised to be a fascinating case for those who follow developments in First Amendment law and the Court's treatment of the constitutional right to freedom of speech. Law schools marshaled a wide variety of legal arguments in support of their position that the Solomon Amendment violated their constitutional rights, and each argument was based on earlier decisions of the Supreme Court that construed the meaning and scope of the First Amendment. For the most part, their contentions were perfectly standard fare. In fact, the plaintiffs' arguments against the Solomon Amendment offered an unusually comprehensive tour, all in a single case, through many of the important legal doctrines underlying the First Amendment's protection of free speech.

I doubt many people realized that *Rumsfeld v. FAIR* had anything to do with the First Amendment. The free speech concerns at the core of the case became almost invisible in public debate, crowded out by something far more emotional and intriguing. *Rumsfeld v. FAIR* had the potential for initiating thoughtful discussion of the Constitution and the limits of public debate and protest, or of the role that universities should play in shaping public policy on matters of national security. Instead, the case was transformed into a crude marker of allegiance to the military. *Rumsfeld v. FAIR* was the accidental but perfect story line of deep cultural conflict between people we assume are strong supporters of the military and people we assume are not, and this tempting cultural drama easily overshadowed any constitutional nuance of free speech law.

Law schools and their professors were cast in the classic role of the liberal, overeducated, and clueless elite who reflexively expressed contempt for the military, for servicemembers, for patriotism, and presumably for America itself. The government, in contrast, defended the Solomon Amendment and its denial of federal funding to universities from a post–September 11, war-fighting stance. They argued that the efficient recruitment of the very best law students for service as military lawyers was vitally important for reasons of national security, particularly, they said, "in a time of War," dramatically showcased with a capital W.[7]

The Supreme Court ruled against the law schools in *Rumsfeld v. FAIR*, finding that the First Amendment offered them no protection from cuts in federal funding if they refused to allow military recruiting on their campuses. The decision was uncontroversial because it seemed to protect the military and strengthen national security. For many people, it made intuitive sense to let the military recruit lawyers in whatever way it thought was most effective, even if it upset the wishes of a few law professors who, after all, knew next to nothing about the military and probably resented what it stood for as well. Public reaction to the ruling seemed to suggest a general sense of relief along the lines of "thank goodness the Supreme Court protected the military," accompanied by a generous helping of self-righteous ridicule aimed at law schools for pushing the issue as far as they did.

It all seemed to make sense, except for the fact that all the assumptions were wrong. The Supreme Court didn't protect the military in *Rumsfeld v. FAIR*, and it hasn't protected the military at any time during the thirty-five years we have had an all-volunteer force. The reality is that the Supreme Court has worked—unintentionally, I believe, but consistently—to undermine the constitutional strength of our military and the health of our civil-military relations, all the while hiding behind superficial expressions of support no more helpful than plastering a "Support Our Troops" decal on your car. Professor Charles Moskos, who for many years was considered the dean of academic military research, often ridiculed such casual and meaningless statements of support for the military as "patriotism lite."[8] Unfortunately, unlike the innocuous car decal, the Supreme Court's own version of "patriotism lite" causes real harm.

Many of the difficult issues the military struggles with today can be traced back to the damage courts and law have caused to civil-military relations since the end of the Vietnam War. *Rumsfeld v. FAIR* was only the latest indicator of fundamental weakness in the way institutions of law and the military interact to ensure constitutionally healthy civilian control of our armed forces. If one digs beneath the surface of what appeared to be an easy decision for the Court, what emerges is a warning of constitutional decline in the relationship between the military and the civilian society it serves. The case is but a symptom of significant problems in the constitutional vitality of the all-volunteer military.

The *FAIR* law schools relied on three separate strands of Supreme Court doctrine in arguing that the Solomon Amendment's financial penalty violated one of the First Amendment's fundamental commands: "Congress shall make no law . . . abridging the freedom of speech." These three rules are, in short: (1) the government cannot compel someone to speak; (2) the government cannot impose unconstitutional conditions on the right to speak; and (3) the government cannot interfere with the right to join together with others in sending a message or making a statement—the right of "expressive association."

First, the government cannot compel people to sponsor, support, or accommodate a message with which they disagree. A classic example is *Wooley v. Maynard*,[9] in which the Supreme Court held that New Hampshire could not punish a driver who had covered up the state's "Live Free or Die" motto on his car license plate. New Hampshire officials thought that displaying the motto promoted "proper appreciation of history, state pride, and individualism," and no doubt many citizens of the state agreed. However, the Court held that "where the State's interest is to disseminate an ideology, no matter how acceptable to some, such interest cannot outweigh an individual's First Amendment right to avoid becoming the courier for such message."

Second, the government cannot grant or deny financial benefits based on the recipient's willingness to sponsor a message with which he or she disagrees. If the government was allowed to use financial incentives as leverage in shaping the content of what people say, it could accomplish indirectly what the Constitution prohibits by more direct means. In *Speiser v. Randall*,[10] the Court invalidated a California law that required military veterans to sign a declaration disavowing violent overthrow of the government in order to qualify for the veterans' property tax exemption. The Court explained its decision by comparing the government's use of financial incentives to encourage the "right" kind of speech to its use of punishment to discourage the "wrong" kind of speech, because both measures lead to the same unconstitutional effect. In the Court's words, "To deny an exemption to claimants who engage in certain forms of speech is in effect to penalize them for such speech."

Under this principle, known as the "unconstitutional conditions" doctrine, a state could not award property tax breaks on the condition that homeowners fly an American flag in the front yard, and it could not take away tax breaks from homeowners who refuse to do so. The state could not defend the law by arguing that taxpayers are free to choose whether to fly the flag or not, or by claiming that taxpayers want to have their cake and eat it too when they expect to receive the tax break without flying the flag. The "have your cake and eat it too" criticism is irresistible, of course, especially when it is not your cake being taken away. A prominent federal judge who was not involved with the *FAIR* case used this phrase to belittle the *FAIR* law professors even though he surely knew it was not an all-purpose excuse:

> Of course a law school (and its university) would prefer to have federal money given to it without strings attached, especially strings that will get it in trouble with students and faculty members who are strongly hostile to the military's policy on homosexuals. The law school merely wants to have its cake and eat it—and who doesn't?[11]

One can't forget, however, as this judge did, that the "strings" of government still have to respect the Constitution. The First Amendment prohibits government from forcing people to make this kind of choice.

Third, the government cannot intrude upon the First Amendment's freedom of expressive association by forcing an organization to accept or tolerate the presence of unwanted "outsiders" who communicate an inconsistent message on behalf of the group. This last doctrine explains why, according to *Boy Scouts of America v. Dale*,[12] the Boy Scouts are not required to accept gay scoutmasters even in states that prohibit public organizations from discriminating on the basis of sexual orientation. The law schools in *Rumsfeld v. FAIR* took special ironic satisfaction in relying on *Dale*—a symbol of the exclusion of gay people from public life—in support of their attempt to exclude the military from law school recruiting events.

For all these reasons, law schools believed the government had overstepped its constitutional limits by threatening to deny federal funding to universities who refused to sponsor military recruiters in the same way as other prospective employers. Law schools never objected to their students joining the military as JAG Corps officers, although the government certainly suspected their policies were motivated by a distaste for military service. Law schools only objected to being forced, on pain of significant financial penalty, to serve as hosts, aides, and administrative assistants for military recruiters on their own campuses. They noted the military was free to contact or interview students in any way it would like, as long as it did so without the law schools' help.

The bitterness of the contest involving law schools and military recruiting was intense. Interestingly, however, in a struggle that was most often billed as "law schools versus the military," Congress was by far the most committed combatant. Defense and military officials did not support the Solomon Amendment, finding it "unnecessary, duplicative, and potentially harmful to defense research initiatives."[13] From a military perspective, the new law could require cancellation of funding for mission-critical defense research even if, in the military's professional judgment, the university's Solomon offense had little or no impact on military recruiting.

Both Congress and law schools have at times used the military as a convenient forum for airing opinions about patriotism or about unjust discrimination. Neither institution, unfortunately, is particularly interested in the actual military issues underlying the Solomon Amendment. Congress has never studied whether excluding the military from campus programs has any effect on the recruitment of military lawyers, and law schools have never engaged the military in discussions of military law and its justifications for regulating sexual conduct. As later chapters in this book will show, Congress often finds it convenient to use military law as a means of making more sweeping statements on cultural, moral, or social issues of the day. Congress does so primarily because it can. Courts have been extremely reluctant to judge the constitutionality of military law even under circumstances in which the law being challenged has little or no connection to actual military concerns. Law schools are creatures of convenience on this score as well. It is much easier to summarily banish the military from campus as an expression of protest against "Don't Ask, Don't Tell"—out of sight, out of mind—than it is to become a knowledgeable and active participant in military legal reform.

Rumsfeld v. FAIR was the culmination of more than a decade of dueling speech and expression between Congress and law schools, both using the military as a means of "making a point" about strongly held beliefs. Congress enacted "Don't Ask, Don't Tell" in 1993, codifying in federal law exactly the same rule excluding gay people from military service that was already in effect as a matter of executive policy. An important part of the reason Congress did so was to make a public statement against legal equality for gay people. The military served as a convenient platform for a socially conservative response at a time in which the developing trend in some states was to treat sexual orientation discrimination as a violation of civil rights.

Law schools strongly opposed hiring practices that discriminated on the basis of sexual orientation. They wanted to make a public statement about their commitment to values of equality and their opposition to discriminatory hiring practices like "Don't Ask, Don't Tell," and so law schools adopted rules that had the effect of excluding the military from sponsored recruiting events for as long as the military excluded gay people from national service. The proviso "had *the effect* of excluding the military" is important because the interviewing rules never mentioned the military at all. Any employer—not just the military—who refused to abide by a nondiscrimination policy would similarly be barred, but generally the military was the only employer who failed the test.

The primary purpose of the Solomon Amendment, in turn, was to make a pointed congressional statement to universities that their educational policies were unpatriotic and insufficiently respectful of the military. One congressional champion of the bill urged Congress to "send a message over the wall of the ivory tower of higher education":

> It is nothing less than a backhanded slap at the honor and dignity of service in our nation's armed forces, at those who have worn our nation's uniform before, and at this Congress, which has set in law military personnel standards.
>
> These colleges and universities need to know that their starry-eyed idealism comes with a price. If they are too good—or too righteous—to treat our Nation's military with the respect it deserves, to allow ROTC units to operate, or to afford our military the same recruiting opportunities offered to private corporations, then they may also be too good to receive the generous level of taxpayer dollars presently enjoyed by many institutions of higher education in America.[14]

The spiral of dueling messages between Congress and law schools did not end there. In 2005, United States District Court Judge William M. Acker announced he would not hire Yale Law School graduates as judicial clerks in order to make a statement of protest against Yale's legal challenge to the Solomon Amendment.[15] Apparently the only remaining opportunity for retaliation would have been, hypothetically, for Yale Law School to exclude Judge Acker from attending law alumni events. Then the spiral of shunning would be complete, because (1) law schools would have excluded judges (2) who excluded clerk applicants (3) from law schools that excluded recruiters (4) for a military that excluded gay people from service. One of the perverse benefits of retaliatory shunning is that it gives everyone an opportunity, deserved or not, to complain they have been discriminated against.

Law schools, however, were optimistic they would eventually have the last word on the issue of discrimination. In *Rumsfeld v. FAIR*, they were the home team. The plaintiffs challenging the Solomon Amendment were backed by hundreds of experienced and talented law professors ready and able to help craft the most compelling legal arguments. They were already on a roll, defending an earlier legal victory instead of challenging a loss. In the Third Circuit Court of Appeals, a federal court below the Supreme Court, a majority of the judges had already agreed with the law schools' constitutional arguments and issued an order prohibiting the government from enforcing the Solomon Amendment.[16] Even the name of their organization, Forum for Academic and Institutional Rights, seemed to signal optimism for an eventual win. Each time the cleverly conceived acronym *FAIR* appeared in the case name *Rumsfeld v. FAIR*, it artfully framed Donald Rumsfeld, then the secretary of defense, as the stubborn opponent of all that was fair and right in the world.

None of it, however, would make a difference. It is difficult to lose a Supreme Court case as thoroughly as the law schools and their professors lost *Rumsfeld v. FAIR*, but they did, and spectacularly. The vote was 8-0, and it would have been 9-0 had Justice Sandra Day O'Connor not retired before the decision was handed down. The conservatives of the Court voted in the government's favor; the liberals voted in the government's favor. (New justice Samuel Alito was appointed to the Court after the parties made their oral arguments, and he did not participate in the Court's decision.)

The unanimous vote was not even the worst insult. The opinion condescendingly lectured the law schools on all the simple points of constitutional law the Court thought they failed to understand. The Court cracked jokes at their expense; it laughed as much as courts can laugh while writing a formal judicial opinion. For example, it made fun of the law schools' concern that if forced by the Solomon Amendment to host military recruiters, they would be seen as condoning the very discrimination that "Don't Ask, Don't Tell" requires and that law schools strongly oppose. The Court responded to their serious question with a bit of a smirk, observing that even high school students can tell the difference between speech a school sponsors because it agrees with the message and speech the school permits only because the law requires it to do so. "Surely students have not lost that ability," the justices wrote, "by the time they get to law school."

After the Court's ruling, there was more than enough smug amusement to go around. Even the *New York Times*, a longtime critic of "Don't Ask, Don't Tell,"[17] injected some humor into this crushing rejection of law schools and law professors with the headline "Supreme Court Smackdown!"—mocking punctuation included.[18] The law schools' fundamental miscalculation was in failing to realize the Court would see *Rumsfeld v. FAIR* as a case primarily about the military, not about the First Amendment. Perhaps their miscalculation was understandable because the center of Solomon Amendment controversy was Congress's effort to control what it believed was an intolerable level of sass and disrespect from law schools toward the military. When the stated purpose of a law is to "send a message" or to force a display of respect toward government institutions, then generally a nugget of a First Amendment claim lies somewhere within.

The military's role in *Rumsfeld v. FAIR* was, in comparison, an attenuated one. At worst, it would suffer some administrative inconvenience if the government lost the case. The military would have to contact students directly instead of relying on law schools to pass on information about military legal careers. Military recruiters would have to call students to schedule interviews instead of relying on law schools to arrange interviews for them. The military would have to find a place to meet with students other than in campus rooms reserved for nondiscriminating employers. However, it is also possible these inconveniences would have been small in comparison to the current frustration of trying to extract administrative cooperation from law schools that were not inclined to provide it willingly. The controversy only emphasized the existence and persistence of "Don't Ask, Don't Tell," a policy that seems rather ludicrous to most young adults of law school age. In this instance, military recruiters might have been better off somewhere other than law school campuses. Either way, the result in *Rumsfeld v. FAIR* would probably have had little practical impact on the military.

Framing *Rumsfeld v. FAIR* as a case primarily about the military, however, would change everything in legal terms. There were earlier hints this was the direction the Court would take. During oral argument, Justice Antonin Scalia asked Solicitor General Paul Clement, the lawyer representing the government (and ostentatiously called "General Clement" by the justices even though his job has nothing to do with the military),[19] why he was bothering to argue that the Solomon Amendment's funding restriction was consistent with similar laws found constitutional under the First Amendment. Why not,

Scalia asked, simply defend the law as an exercise of Congress's power to raise armies under Article 1 of the Constitution, and forget about the First Amendment? This was a "softball" exchange in which Scalia tried to guide "General" Clement toward a more superficially appealing way of making his argument.[20]

Scalia strongly signaled his belief that the First Amendment would not apply at all, or at least would mean much less, if the Solomon Amendment were evaluated under Congress's constitutional power to raise military forces instead of its authority to spend federal dollars "for the common defense and general welfare of the United States."[21] Putting aside for the moment whether Scalia's suggestion made any sense as a matter of constitutional law, it was extremely telling of how he and his colleagues on the Court would ultimately decide the case. In the final written opinion of the Court granting victory to the government, the justices began their analysis by observing that Article 1 of the Constitution gives "broad and sweeping" powers to Congress to do what is necessary "to raise and support armies."[22] The Court acknowledged, barely and reluctantly, that Congress was still subject to the rest of the Constitution, including the Bill of Rights, when acting under this power, but then immediately discounted this limitation. In a strangely awkward phrase, but one that has a significant history in Supreme Court opinions after the end of the Vietnam War, the Court asserted: "judicial deference is at its apogee when Congress legislates under its authority to raise and support armies."

What is "judicial deference," and what does it mean for "judicial deference" to be "at its apogee"? With this statement, the Court signaled its intention to do something more than simply give Congress the benefit of the doubt in deciding whether legislation it had enacted violated the Constitution. Instead, the Court would take a significant step back from its normal responsibility for judicial review and give Congress "deferential treatment" to the greatest extent possible. ("Apogee" is a phrase normally used to describe the highest point of an object's orbit above the earth, and so in a legal context it seems fairly dramatic.)

For Justice Scalia, when "judicial deference" is "at its apogee," it means the government should not be asked to answer difficult questions. In fact, it means the government need not explain itself at all. During oral argument, Justice Scalia was clearly irritated at the plaintiffs' suggestion that the government be asked to explain—just explain—why it needed sponsorship from law schools in order to recruit effectively. He snapped off a quick retort:

> JUSTICE SCALIA: Here's a need. How about this? We have said in our
> opinions—and I am quoting from Rostker versus Goldberg—"judicial
> deference is at its apogee when legislative action under the
> congressional authority to raise and support armies and make
> rules and regulations for their governance is challenged." And
> that's precisely what we have here.[23]

Scalia's comment was the judicial equivalent of the impatient parent who responds to a child's desire for explanation with an exasperated "Because I said so." It doesn't provide any useful information, and it doesn't explain the decision in any reasoned way. Its purpose is only to stop the child from asking more questions. Similarly, the primary purpose of judicial deference in the area of military affairs is to protect the government from having to answer questions or offer justifications for its decisions. In *Rumsfeld v. FAIR*, the government may very well have been able to explain convincingly why a particular way of recruiting for JAG officers—in a format sponsored and assisted by law school personnel—was important enough to justify some limits on free speech and expressiveness by law schools. Under the policy of judicial deference, however, the government never had to answer the question.

The consequence of this special deference in *Rumsfeld v. FAIR* was to dial back the meaning and scope of the First Amendment when deciding whether the right of law schools to speak freely had been infringed. Put more bluntly, the Court believed the First Amendment provided less protection for free speech when the speech had something to do with the military, even when all the speakers were civilians. As far as the Solomon Amendment was concerned, the Court cut off the discussion and concluded, in effect, "This is for Congress to decide, not the courts or the Constitution." The law schools' First Amendment claims were minimized with the briefest of discussion, or at least what passes for brief discussion in the often ponderous and long-winded opinions of the Supreme Court. The Court summarily distinguished prior cases in which the government had unconstitutionally compelled speech or had unconstitutionally conditioned receipt of government benefits on speech, finding they did not apply to the Solomon Amendment. According to the Court, the Solomon Amendment did not infringe on rights of free speech because the law did not force law schools to say (or prevent them from saying) anything at all—or at least not anything that was constitutionally relevant.

Even though the Solomon Amendment required law schools to speak in limited instances on behalf of military recruiters—sending e-mails to students, posting notices on bulletin boards, distributing JAG Corps materials, and scheduling interviews—the Court decided their words did not count as protected speech under the Constitution because law schools routinely provided the same administrative assistance to all employers. Therefore, placement services provided by universities were not, in the Court's words, "inherently expressive." Neither did the forced presence of military recruiters infringe on the law schools' right to expressive association. By the Court's reasoning, military recruiters were only occasional visitors to the law school community, not members of the community, and so their presence did not affect the law schools' ability to craft and express a message as an organization.

The law schools did not lose because they misjudged how the Court would balance rights of free speech under the First Amendment against the military's need to participate in sponsored recruiting events. They lost because the Court believed the law schools were not even speaking, in a constitutional sense, and so therefore their right to speak freely could not possibly have been infringed on. Their chosen method of protesting against "Don't Ask, Don't Tell"—exclusion of the military from on-campus interviewing—did not qualify as expression under the First Amendment. According to the Court, law schools were free to complain and they were free to protest, but they were not free to physically exclude military recruiters from their campuses unless they convinced their parent universities to give up federal funding for the entire institution, something that, as a practical matter, was never going to happen.

The significance of *Rumsfeld v. FAIR*, however, was never as neat and clean as the law professors, Congress, the military, or even the Court portrayed it to be. What they all overlooked was the way in which the case exposed the current state of decay in our civil-military relations. To see that decay, however, one had to look beyond the arguments made by the parties in the case.

Chapter 2

A Canary in the Civil-Military Mine

In *Rumsfeld v. FAIR*, many *amicus curiae* ("friend of the court") briefs were filed with the Third Circuit Court of Appeals and the Supreme Court. Amicus briefs are written by individuals and groups who are not parties to the case, but who can offer the court some helpful knowledge or experience that the parties may not have. These outside contributors included even more professors (law and otherwise), military officers, university career-placement professionals, advocacy groups of every political stripe, gay law students, veterans' organizations, and, oddly, the Boy Scouts of America, who were concerned the case might affect their policy of excluding gay people from scouting. Amicus briefs are not part of the official record of evidence in the case, but they may bring a different perspective to the controversy between the parties. For example, on the intensely polarized issue of military recruiting on law school campuses, the perspective of persons with experience in both settings, in military service and in the study of law, could have been especially illuminating.

One of the amicus briefs in the Third Circuit was filed on behalf of three groups of military-affiliated law students, representing law schools at the University of California, Los Angeles ("UCLAW Veterans Society"); Washburn University in Topeka, Kansas ("Veterans Law Association"); and the College of William and Mary in Williamsburg, Virginia ("Military Law Society").[1] Similar extracurricular groups exist at many law schools, and at the University of Florida College of Law, I am one of the faculty advisors for our Military Law Students Association. Law students who join these organizations are typically military veterans, members of reserve units, or active-duty officers attending law school as a military assignment. Also welcome would be law students who are considering a military career, have an interest in military issues, or come from military families. The primary mission of military law student organizations is to promote mutual support among law students sharing common interests, but they also may engage in service activities on behalf of servicemembers deployed overseas or their family members on the home front. Sometimes these organizations serve as an academic resource on military or national security issues for the law school community.

The Third Circuit did not mention the military law students' amicus brief in its ruling in favor of law schools. There is no way to know whether their brief influenced the court in any way, positively or negatively, and also no way to know whether it influenced the Supreme Court in later reversing the holding of the Third Circuit. However, for reasons that have so far escaped the attention of the courts, the parties, the media, and even the military law students themselves, their brief may have been one of the most revealing filings in the entire case. Quite unintentionally, and quietly, it opened a window on the future of civil-military relations, the weakening bond between law and military professionalism, and the declining strength of our civilian control of the military. If the content of the military law students' brief is an accurate measure of civil-military relations today, the view is a bleak one.

Two important themes emerged from their arguments. First, their brief was built on the assumption that military-related decisions should not have to be explained or justified under law to the same degree as other choices made by government. It didn't matter whether the military itself was making the choice or, like in *Rumsfeld v. FAIR*, civilians in Congress were making a choice on the military's behalf. In either circumstance, if someone were to challenge the decision as unconstitutional, the government should not be required to explain its reasoning or reveal the facts underlying the decision. The government would only need *to assert* the decision was made for the military's benefit, and that claim alone should automatically outweigh any interest in preserving constitutional rights. In cases involving the military, these law students believed that courts should have no role in forcing information about military decisions into public view.

The second basic theme of the military law students' brief was one step removed from the litigation between the parties, but it was equally insidious as a matter of civil-military relations. This theme—one of distance, division, and distrust between servicemembers and civilians—said more about the general relationship between the military and civilian society than it did about the specific disagreement between Congress and law schools in *Rumsfeld v. FAIR*. What came across very clearly in the military law students' brief, more than anything, was their deep resentment that the military was being challenged or second-guessed by civilians. From the perspective of the military law students, a wide gap of military experience, expertise, and morality elevated servicemembers above their civilian counterparts, and the students seemed to have difficulty squaring that sense of superiority with civilian criticism. To say the least, they took it personally. Their brief suggested there was a sphere of military prerogative that civilians should enter only at their own risk, because their interference would be interpreted as hostility or discrimination against individual law students affiliated with the military.

Perhaps this is a good time for a few more words of disclaimer and disclosure. Because I have a foot in both camps, my personal views do not line up neatly on one side or the other of the expected divide between academic and military communities. For example, I believe that the legal exclusion of gay citizens from military service reflects poor judgment by the military and by Congress. I believe "Don't Ask, Don't Tell" was motivated by discomfort with gay people and not by concern for national security, and that the policy significantly impairs military effectiveness. I also believe the Solomon Amendment's effort to coerce law schools into supporting military recruiters was ill considered and unhelpful. I also believe, however, that law schools exercised very poor judgment in barring military recruiters from their sponsored career-placement programs, and they compounded that poor judgment by filing suit against the government to preserve their discretion to exclude the military. Law schools do not understand that their efforts to shun military recruiters from the law school community contribute to a weakening of civilian control of the military. They will never enjoy a seat at the table of military legal reform if their means of expressing opposition is to wash their hands of institutions whenever they disagree with them.

If I could have written the final story of *Rumsfeld v. FAIR*, the Supreme Court would have struck down the Solomon Amendment as a violation of the First Amendment, and then law schools, free from financial coercion, would have made their own decision to welcome military recruiters back into the law school community. Without the distractions of having to fight the Solomon Amendment and constantly posture at the presence of military recruiters, law schools could have channeled their commitment to values of equality in a much more productive direction. They could perhaps *do* something about "Don't Ask, Don't Tell" rather than just *say* something about "Don't Ask, Don't Tell." Unfortunately, the chances of the *Rumsfeld v. FAIR* scenario playing out in this way were always less than zero.

Particularly because the participants in *Rumsfeld v. FAIR* were so stubbornly locked into their positions, the observations of law students affiliated with the military held the promise of something different. They had the potential to see the case in a way that cut through the legal partisanship of the opposing parties. Their perspective was an important one, because conversations about the military too often swing from one extreme to the other. Sometimes we fail to listen to the earned wisdom of people who have served in the military, and as a result we lose the benefit of their experience. At other times, far more frequently, we credit the opinions of veterans exclusively, without reservation or examination, and as a result we discourage those who have not served in the military from actively participating in our constitutional tradition of civilian control. Most rare of all is the circumstance in which we actually consider the value of what military opinions bring to the conversation and decide how much weight, standing on their own merits, they deserve.

The perspective of military law students was also important because it represented both the future of our armed forces and the future of our civilian control of the military. It is no exaggeration to say that law students who return to duty as JAG officers will someday serve as a window into the soul of the military. As military legal advisors, they play a central role, in consultation with the commanders they advise, in maintaining the historical connection between the military and law. On the other hand, for veterans whose term of military service is complete, their combined assets of legal training and prior military service will give them great influence, at times even undue influence, in the ongoing conversation among citizens that forms the foundation of healthy civilian control of the military.

For all these reasons it was disappointing to discover how well military law students have already learned the artificial and dysfunctional way we typically discuss military-related subjects in a legal setting. Without doubt they had assimilated the point of view reflected in Justice Scalia's comments during oral argument in which he all but closed the door to any discussion. For Scalia, it was as simple as this: if the subject was the military, the discussion was over. He believed courts should have little or no role in deciding whether a law related to military service violated the Constitution, and that once Congress had spoken, Congress should not be second-guessed. The military law students anticipated his lead by citing all the cases that featured the strange but standard Supreme Court language specially reserved for military issues: "judicial deference is at its apogee when Congress legislates under its authority to raise and support armies." They neatly set out a position that the needs of the military served as an across-the-board justification for disregarding the Constitution. Assertions of military necessity, they argued, should prevail over individual constitutional rights such as free speech, equal protection for men and women, or the free exercise of religion.

The problem was not that the military law students relied on the Supreme Court cases that best supported their position in favor of the Solomon Amendment. This is exactly what lawyers, and lawyers-to-be, are trained to do. The problem was in their assumption that "judicial deference" meant something far more extreme: that legal arguments involving the military, unlike other government agencies, need not be faithful to fact, reality, or truth. In short, these military law students had somehow learned the lesson that "judicial deference" means that you can simply "make stuff up." Facts did not need to be proved, or even provable. They did not need to be accurate, or even plausible. They could be ridiculous or absurd on their face, and that would be good enough if the subject at hand related to the military, particularly if the speaker has served in the military.

Reasonable people can disagree on the question of whether military recruiters are significantly disadvantaged—or disadvantaged at all—when they don't participate in sponsored recruiting events. The military has taken the position that sponsored recruiting is important, and that it matters a great deal. This argument, however, fails to take into account the fundamental differences between the JAG Corps and the legal employers who most typically rely on the sponsored recruiting process within law schools. First, the face of the military is everywhere: in the news, in national television advertisements, and in the windows of local recruiting offices, not to mention in the mailboxes of law students if the military chooses to send them information. No one is unaware of the military's existence as a potential employer, but individual law firms across the nation do not have the same visibility. Second, one of the weaknesses of sponsored recruiting programs in law schools (and a common subject of complaint by law students) is that they are designed to support the needs of large private law firms, not the needs of government or public-interest legal employers. Law students whose interests lie somewhere other than the standard law-firm treadmill have always had to do more of the legwork themselves in searching for job opportunities. The process of finding legal jobs in government service, or of finding qualified applicants for those positions, happens mostly outside the typical law school recruiting apparatus.

I've never heard district attorneys, public defenders, or lawyers for the federal government complain they can't hire quality law students without participating in sponsored interviewing programs. They often opt out because they don't believe it serves their different needs. Perhaps they want to set themselves apart from the pack that law students tend to mindlessly chase. Perhaps they believe their candidates will be better suited to the work when students must show some initiative in seeking the job, rather than sitting still while the job chases the student. Whatever reasoning may explain the choices of most government agencies, however, the military is the only one to claim it is always disadvantaged if it cannot have its interviews arranged in exactly the same manner as private law firms.

It might have been possible to determine once and for all whether the military did, or did not, benefit from sponsored recruiting assistance, but Congress failed to hold any hearings on military recruiting in law schools before it enacted the Solomon Amendment, and the government did not offer any evidence in *Rumsfeld v. FAIR* to support its allegations of disadvantage. In the end, the Supreme Court dispensed with the problem of not having any information by simply assuming that a difference in treatment between two employers meant that one of them had to be at a disadvantage.

If the military's recruiting options were different from, or fewer than, those available to nondiscriminating employers, the Court would automatically assume the military had been harmed, whether or not those different options actually had any discernable effect on recruiting success.

In the military law students' brief, I expected to find information concerning why, from their perspective, it was important for the military to take its place next to civilian law firms in the typical law school recruiting process. Instead, they offered an incredible level of exaggeration and misrepresentation, and they made clear their belief that they were entitled to push the boundaries of truth and candor because they were military veterans speaking on what was, at least in part, a military subject. This is an unmistakable sign of looming problems in the future of civil-military relations: that legally trained military veterans have learned that they need not, and should not, treat military facts with the same care and respect they would give to any other information offered in a legal proceeding.

It is one thing to avoid knowledge of inconvenient facts, as the government consistently attempted to do in enacting and defending the Solomon Amendment. Congress never wanted to find out whether JAG recruiters were really disadvantaged by law school recruiting policies, because those facts were unrelated to the real purpose of the Solomon Amendment—to compel universities to display respect for the military. It is another thing, however, to misrepresent, exaggerate, or confuse those facts. In their amicus contribution, the military law students made factual allegations, supposedly based on their military experience, that they had no reason to believe could possibly be true. For example, they told the Third Circuit that if the military had to recruit lawyers outside of sponsored career-placement events, it would be "*next to impossible* to recruit the best military lawyers." They said it was "*nearly certain* that military recruiters would fail to meet recruiting goals for new Judge Advocates by a wide margin." (The emphasis is mine.)

Perhaps their certainty about disastrous consequences for JAG recruiting was grounded in their equally absurd assumption that the military would have no way of contacting law students without career-placement events hosted by law schools. From the statements in their brief, it appeared the military law students did not consider the possibility that the military might call law students by phone, send them recruiting information by mail, or even schedule face-to-face meetings with students, all tasks that could be accomplished without the assistance of law school personnel. Taking what they wrote at face value—because I do not think they actually believed what they wrote—the students encouraged the court to assume that, if the plaintiffs in *Rumsfeld v. FAIR* prevailed, the military would be hopelessly unable to recruit any student who attended a law school subject to the AALS non-discrimination policy:

As soon as the gavel sounds, 166 AALS member law schools would shut their doors to military recruiters. The armed forces would immediately lose access to 92% (166/181) of their potential applicant pool, at a time when our nation is at war and under attack.

The drama continued. Having assured the court that JAG officer recruiting would be fatally undermined by lack of law school assistance, the military law students then spun another tale—again, supposedly based on their military experience—of the specific harms that would certainly befall a military with a shortage of JAG officers. In their view, the actions of career-placement professionals on law school campuses would leave military criminals running loose, deny servicemembers their constitutional rights, and ultimately put the military and our national security at risk:

> In criminal cases, Staff Judge Advocates (the military's prosecutors), faced with severe personnel shortages, would be forced to triage military justice cases, perhaps dropping many non-violent prosecutions, thereby harming unit discipline. Trial Defense Services offices, facing similar personnel shortages, would face overwhelming caseloads, resulting in less time being devoted to each case, pressure to plea-bargain, and a loss of rights by accused servicemembers. The decline in the efficacy of the military justice system would lead to plummeting unit effectiveness, the very downward spiral the current military justice system was enacted to address.

This fictional shortage of military lawyers might have international ramifications as well. The military law students warned the court that a ruling in favor of law schools might mean the military would be less likely to comply with the law of war. They wrote the following in their amicus brief in February 2004:

> A lack of military lawyers could increase the likelihood of law of war violations by soldiers and unacceptable civilian collateral damage during military operations. This, in turn, could have strategic ramifications because of the way that any such incidents would be viewed by the world. The perception of American military operations around the world depends, in no small measure, on our military's adherence to the law of armed conflict.

Ironically, they gave this warning just a few months before the first reports of torture at the American-run Abu Ghraib prison in Iraq would drain their statements of all credibility. It clearly wasn't a shortage of military lawyers that caused the Abu Ghraib abuses to occur. At a fundamental level, the military law students failed in their responsibility as *amici* to provide facts as they knew them to be—based on their military experience and expertise— and not as they speculated, guessed, or feared them to be for purposes of propping up the Solomon Amendment. Even if one is inclined to forgive an excess of heated advocacy on behalf of the government—in a situation, remember, that called for professional expertise, not advocacy—there is no justification for statements that directly mislead the court.

One of the problems the government had in litigating *Rumsfeld v. FAIR* was that JAG recruiters themselves said the competition for positions was still "very keen" despite Solomon protest, even at the nation's top law schools.[2] The military law students might have explained that this keen competition no longer existed (if that was true) or that it was irrelevant to the questions before the court. Instead, they attempted to hide unhelpful facts. They cited a series of sources documenting the difficulty of recruiting *new enlisted personnel*—not lawyers, and not even officers—in support of their contention that law schools were putting JAG recruiting at risk. It seemed they were particularly annoyed that law schools had quoted the JAG recruiters' own words, because the military law students made a sarcastic, unprofessional reference to the "rosy picture of military recruiting that the plaintiffs seek to paint." It was inappropriate, however, annoyed or not, for the military law students to misrepresent the distinction between two unrelated recruiting tasks—the enlistment of tens of thousands of teenagers and young adults each year versus the commissioning of a tiny, select handful of law school graduates—and hope the court would not notice the difference.

It was also inappropriate, as a matter of both legal and military professionalism, to seek sympathy points by giving the court a false impression of the combat risk faced by JAG lawyers. The military law student *amici* took an almost comical turn in their brief when they suggested law schools must be stopped from interfering with military recruiting because JAG lawyers may soon "be called upon to lead enlisted servicemembers in combat." In support of that far-fetched assertion, they lifted one small sentence from an unrelated Army training booklet designed for enlisted members, which read: "We must prepare all our Soldiers for the stark realities of the battlefield." Although one can never predict the exigencies of combat, and I do not intend to do so here, Army lawyers were not the intended audience for this booklet, and it was absurd to suggest they were. Even the JAG Corps recruiting web site assures applicants that, although they may be assigned to combat areas in time of war, they typically are not involved in active combat.[3] To be fair, the military law students did accurately state in their brief that all Marine officers, including lawyers, attend the same basic officer training. However, the students apparently could not resist expanding the facts to make a larger, more misleading point.

It may seem I am being unnecessarily harsh in my evaluation of the military law students' amicus effort. If so, it is because the consequences for civil-military relations are so severe. These law students are not just students or "the kids," as law professors sometimes slip and call them. Most of them are former and present commissioned military officers, and they are well aware that their professional expertise carries enormous weight. They also know they have a professional obligation to apply that expertise with care and in an ethical manner. If veterans who represent the future of military law and the future of civil-military relations no longer feel particularly tethered to law and fact in matters involving the military, there is a significant problem. If they have learned this dysfunctional means of discussion and discourse from the Supreme Court, which I believe they have, the problem looms even greater.

The military law students' brief opened with an odd observation that may have been more revealing than they intended it to be. Instead of stressing how the exclusion of military recruiters from school-sponsored placement programs causes harm to the JAG Corps and the military practice of law, they chose to underscore instead how important it was that law schools be punished for their actions. According to the military law students, "allowing law schools to exclude military recruiters without facing the consequences provided for in the Solomon Amendment would cause serious harm to the Nation." The distinction is important. The problem, as they described it, was not that serious harm would result from the exclusion of military recruiters; rather, they thought serious harm would result if law schools did not face consequences for their disrespect to the military. This statement must have been a Freudian slip, because it was surely not the point military law students intended to make. It did reveal, however, a tip of the hidden iceberg of resentment and bitterness that infects our civil-military relations.

My role as a faculty advisor for the Military Law Students Association at the University of Florida College of Law unexpectedly gave me an inside look at the motivations underlying the military law students' brief. Before the brief was filed and open to public view, military law students involved in the *Rumsfeld v. FAIR* project—not students at my own law school at the University of Florida—sent a draft version of the brief[4] to a number of military law student organizations at other law schools, seeking their comments and suggestions. One of my students at the University of Florida forwarded the draft brief to me. It surprised me greatly, and not in a good way.

The draft brief was laden throughout with a disturbing level of resentment and anger toward civilian law schools, civilian law professors, civilian classmates, and civilians in general. The military law students vividly painted themselves as by far the most victimized participants in the entire Solomon Amendment controversy. Never mind the gay people serving in uniform, or those who had been discharged, or the gay law students hoping to become military lawyers. If there was unfair discrimination, according to the military law students, it was against *them*. Their speculation about what would happen if law schools prevailed in *Rumsfeld v. FAIR* was so bizarrely over-the-top that it brought into question whether they were ever speaking on the basis of professional military experience and expertise. From the wildly speculative content of their draft brief, it seemed much more likely they were speaking with self-centered annoyance at having been disagreed with:

> This would add to an already hostile learning environment many veterans face at AALS member schools. . . . Already, members of the *amici* organizations have experienced blatant discrimination from professors, employers, and fellow students, as a direct result of current AALS policy. The discrimination these students would face would certainly grow exponentially as a result of military exclusion.
>
> That law schools exclusively target the military as a result of its legally-mandated hiring practices, but not other federal agencies, further stigmatizes law students interested in JAG service as pariah members of an outcast group.
>
> The essence of the plaintiffs' political message is that the military is an odious institution for its enforcement of discriminatory policies against gays and lesbians.

Law schools are a "hostile learning environment" for military veterans? Veterans are victims of "blatant discrimination" from professors, classmates, and employers? They are stigmatized as "pariah members of an outcast group"? The essence of career-placement policy is that the military is "an odious institution"? My first reaction to these statements was to laugh because, in my experience as a professor, visitor, or invited speaker at a number of different law schools, the problem with civil-military relations in law schools is much more likely to be undue worship of military law students, not prejudice against them. My second reaction, however, and one I shared with the military law students working on this project, was concern that the brief would put military veterans in an unprofessional light, based on its tenuous connection to fact and its strong expression of resentment for civilians. The final version of the amicus brief filed with the court dropped much of the language quoted here and softened the overall level of bitterness and offense.[5] I have no way of knowing whether my objections had anything to do with the change. Regardless of the reason for revising the brief, however, there should be tremendous concern that resentment of civilian policy was such a powerful motivating force for these highly educated military veterans.

The military law students seemed to take particular offense at any suggestion the military might share some moral responsibility for the existence of "Don't Ask, Don't Tell," the policy that triggered the long Solomon Amendment spiral involving Congress, law schools, and the military. Of all the things the military law students might have chosen to concede, one would think the military's close involvement in the creation of "Don't Ask, Don't

Tell" would be an easy, uncontroversial option. Right or wrong, good policy or bad policy, "Don't Ask, Don't Tell" exists because the military vehemently insisted in testimony before Congress in 1993 that it could not possibly do business without it.

In their draft brief, however, the military law students disavowed any military responsibility whatsoever for the existence of "Don't Ask, Don't Tell." They were irritated, and seemingly baffled, that anyone would choose to target the military itself when protesting against the law that made gay citizens ineligible for military service. "Don't Ask, Don't Tell," they thought, should be considered a product of Congress and the president, not the military, and any disgruntled law school protest should be directed accordingly. They wrote:

> By indirectly communicating that the military is less deserving of law school support than all other law-abiding employers, law schools will perpetuate the erroneous and biased message that the military is morally blameworthy for its discriminatory hiring practices, without reference to the Congress that passed the law of "Don't Ask, Don't Tell" or the President who signed it—to say nothing of the courts which have upheld it.

The military law students did have half a point. They were correct that "Don't Ask, Don't Tell" is now a federal law that will remain in force unless it is amended or repealed by Congress, ruled unconstitutional by a court, or suspended by presidential executive order under "stop-loss" authority.[6] They were also correct that the military is the only institution law schools have ever targeted for protest of "Don't Ask, Don't Tell." It would never occur to law schools to deny sponsored recruiting assistance to members of Congress who voted for the policy, judges who denied constitutional challenges to the policy, or even the federal Department of Justice that has so tenaciously defended the policy in court. Sometimes people in each of these categories have been viciously antigay in their defense of "Don't Ask, Don't Tell." Nonetheless, law schools would never exclude them from career-placement events provided they promised, with a wink or without, to hire law students without regard to sexual orientation. These employers would be welcome to continue to work on behalf of antigay discrimination in military service, and welcome to use law school resources for restocking their personnel. The military does appear to be the only employer actually held responsible by law schools for playing a role in creating and maintaining "Don't Ask, Don't Tell."

However, it is also important to understand why the military law students were more wrong than they were right. When they disclaimed any military accountability for "Don't Ask, Don't Tell," they were not only misrepresenting history but also undermining a professional obligation requiring servicemembers to accept responsibility for their actions. People tend to forget how

cruel and ignorant much of the military testimony was during the congressional debate on "Don't Ask, Don't Tell" during the summer of 1993. When
military witnesses justify the policy with nonchalant, callous predictions
that gay servicemembers will be killed by their colleagues and there was
little the military could, or would, do about it,[7] the military's moral responsibility for the policy is at least equal to that of Congress or the president. The
military law students knew very well that the policy was originally justified
on the basis of military necessity. If the military were now to take the position that, in its professional opinion, the policy was hurting the military
more than it was helping, it would be much more difficult for courts to
uphold it or for Congress to resist repeal.

Even though the military law students decided to tone down the level of
resentment in their final submission, their bitterness at civilian disagreement still came through. Amazingly, they told the court that, in their professional opinion, some veterans would choose not to attend law school at all if
the federal government could no longer coerce law schools into sponsoring
military recruiters. At the very least, the military law students believed that
even if veterans were resourceful and brave enough to attend law schools
that did not sponsor military recruiting, they would be inhibited from joining
in the academic exchange among professors and students that is so important to legal education.

It seems odd to hear students with military experience argue that they
may lack the fortitude as civilians to debate military policy with other law
students or with their professors. For that matter, it seems odd to hear gay
law students argue, as they did in *Rumsfeld v. FAIR*, that they may lack the
fortitude to participate fully as law students if military recruiters are visible
on campus and allowed to join in sponsored recruiting events. I believe both
groups of students—military law students and gay law students, not to mention military law students who are gay—are made of stronger stuff and are
fully capable of carrying on despite an issue that divides us not only on law
school campuses, but in the real world. Americans disagree about whether
gay citizens should serve in the military and, rightly or wrongly, this uncertainty is now memorialized in federal law. Part of becoming a lawyer is
learning how to cope with and respond to controversial laws. The answer is
not to take the ball and go home.

There was no shortage of irony in the military law students' brief, and if
the issue wasn't so important, it would have been amusing. They devoted an
inordinate amount of space to reminding the court that the Solomon Amendment was a necessary part of finding and keeping high-quality personnel
(including the authors, who described themselves as "a unique and distinguished group"). They repeated again and again the self-evident fact, with
which no one disagrees, that military effectiveness depends on recruiting

and retaining the best people possible. Of course these statements are correct, although they are so general as to be nearly meaningless. No profession, including the military, ever hires all the best of any group of people. It's a competitive world, and highly qualified people will always have a variety of career interests, goals, and options. However, it does seem to have escaped the *amici*'s attention that some of the best law school graduates are gay, and that "Don't Ask, Don't Tell" hinders military recruiting a great deal more than law school career-placement officials do. The policy, of course, prevents the best law school graduates from joining the military if they are gay, but the effect of "Don't Ask, Don't Tell" on military recruiting is much greater than that. Some of the best heterosexual law school graduates would never seriously consider a position that may require them to defend a policy they feel is unnecessary and unjust.

The brief filed by military law students was an accidental, yet powerful and painful statement on the state of our civil-military relations today. It is essential that we stop and consider why legally trained veterans assume the government need not justify or explain itself in the usual way when its decisions involve the military, or why these veterans would act as though they had a license to deal in facts—"making stuff up"—they had no particular reason to believe were true. It should be an eye-opener that military veterans who have sworn to "support and defend the Constitution of the United States against all enemies, foreign and domestic," and to "bear true faith and allegiance to the same,"[8] have learned to treat the Constitution with dismissive disregard whenever someone claims a military personnel policy is unconstitutional. Why does the brief suggest there is a line that civilians may not cross in second-guessing military assertions?

The most disturbing question of all may be why the brief reflects such deep resentment and bitterness for civilians who disagree with military choices. These veterans seem to have taken policy disagreement quite personally, as if it constitutes a direct affront to servicemembers. Where does this sense of the military's moral superiority in comparison to the civilian world come from, and why would military law students be so reluctant to accept that the military shares some moral responsibility for its role in the Solomon Amendment controversy, even if, as they argue, the military's actions were intended to strengthen military effectiveness?

The answer, interestingly, does not lie within the military. Before the end of the Vietnam War, I don't believe military law students would have submitted a brief to a court with the same tone of detachment from law and fact or the same tone of distance, division, and distrust. What has changed since that time, only thirty-five years later, is the way the Supreme Court defines the proper constitutional relationship between the military and civilian society. Largely through the opinions of a single justice of the Supreme

Court, we have experienced a complete reversal in our understanding of civil-military relations, one that has eroded our military's constitutional strength, diminished our civilian control of the military, interfered with necessary public debate, and even discouraged citizens from military service. The next two chapters take a step back in time and trace the unprecedented development that began just a few decades ago.

Chapter 3

Inventing the Civil-Military Divide

Many Supreme Court cases are fairly pedestrian in terms of public interest. Although each one must have been distinctive in some way to draw the Court's attention and become one of the small number of cases it decides, that distinctiveness is no guarantee of notoriety. For example, a 1953 decision written by Justice Robert Jackson, *Orloff v. Willoughby*,[1] was a short and conclusory opinion destined for the dusty shelves of forgotten cases. The case did not involve anyone of fame or celebrity, the legal issues at hand were not matters of intense public debate, and the final result affected no one beyond the parties themselves. The court's reasoning was very straightforward, the result uncontroversial. No law professor or law student would write an article about *Orloff* and argue that it was or wasn't correctly decided, or that it would or wouldn't affect how other cases were decided in the future—it just wasn't that interesting.

More than twenty years later, however, a future justice (and later chief justice) of the Supreme Court, William Rehnquist, would use *Orloff's* casual generality to change the direction of civil-military relations and set in motion a steep decline in the constitutional health of the military. Justice Rehnquist would not have to dig very deeply to find *Orloff*. On March 9, 1953, the day the *Orloff* opinion was handed down, Rehnquist was working as a law clerk for Robert Jackson, the justice who wrote the opinion. It is possible that Rehnquist himself drafted some of the critical language that turned out to be so handy for him a generation later, but at the very least, Rehnquist would have been familiar with the case and its reasoning.

Stanley J. Orloff, the petitioner, was a medical doctor—a psychiatrist—who was drafted into the Army during the Korean War. But for his medical degree, Orloff would not have been eligible for the draft at all because he was older than the standard age limit of twenty-six under the Selective Service Act of 1948. However, the law had an exception for doctors, allowing them to be drafted up to the age of fifty if there was a military need. Orloff received his medical training during World War II at government expense and had not yet served at least ninety days in the military, and so the priority rules put him at the front of the line for induction.

Members of the Army Medical Corps customarily served as commissioned officers, but Orloff and the Army soon reached an impasse over commissioning requirements. Orloff disclosed some, but not all, of the information the Army requested about his association with organizations designated by the attorney general as "subversive." In short, the government was looking for Communists, and Orloff was not cooperating. He said that he objected "as a matter of conscience" because the commissioning requirements allowed "an inquisition into my personal beliefs and views" and relied on "the principle of guilt by association."

Because Orloff chose to, in the Court's words, "haggle about questions concerning his loyalty," the Army withdrew its promise to commission him as a medical officer. Instead, the Army put Orloff to work as an enlisted man and assigned him duties as a medical laboratory technician. Orloff then filed the petition that eventually led to his hearing before the Supreme Court. He argued that if the Army was not going to assign him duties that required a medical degree, he should be relieved of his military service obligation and discharged. From his point of view, if the only reason he could be drafted was because he was a doctor, but the Army had no intention of using him as a doctor, then the government should not have the power to compel him to serve. The Army, not surprisingly, saw it differently. It argued that Orloff had been lawfully inducted under the Selective Service Act and, once he was a member of the military, the Army had the discretion to assign him to any duties it chose, in the best interests of the military.

The Court had absolutely no interest, understandably, in getting in the middle of an argument between the Army and one disgruntled draftee about his particular work detail. It ruled against Orloff and in favor of the Army, for three reasons. First, if it granted Orloff's request, how many more would there be? It was simply not feasible or practical for courts to decide whether individual soldiers have been assigned duties consistent with their specialty or job classification. Second, the Court was openly contemptuous of Orloff and his behavior, painting him as selfish and ungrateful, especially given the financial assistance he received from the government for his medical training. In this dispute, Orloff would have to bend, not the Army, because, as the Court wrote, "the very essence of compulsory service is the subordination of the desires and interests of the individual to the needs of the service." The Court also commented that someone else must have had to take up the slack while he was busy litigating his dissatisfaction: "Presumably, some doctor willing to tell whether he was a member of the Communist Party has been required to go to the Far East in his place."

The third and most basic reason the Court ruled in the government's favor was that this result was consistent with the structure of the Constitution and its separation of powers among the three branches of government:

> We know that from top to bottom of the Army the complaint is often made, and sometimes with justification, that there is discrimination, favoritism or other objectionable handling of men. But judges are not given the task of running the Army. The responsibility for setting up channels through which such grievances can be considered and fairly settled rests upon the Congress and upon the President of the United States and his subordinates. The military constitutes a specialized community governed by a separate discipline from that of the civilian.

When the majority spoke of a military community that is "governed by a *separate discipline* from that of the civilian," they were referring to the parallel system of law and justice that governs persons who serve in the military. Unlike civilians, who are only subject to "discipline" or punishment by courts of an individual state or by federal courts authorized under Article 3 of the Constitution, servicemembers must also answer to a separate system of military courts and a separate set of rules for proper conduct. The separate courts are military courts-martial, and the separate rules of conduct are part of the Uniform Code of Military Justice.[2] Article 1 of the Constitution authorizes Congress to create this distinctive system of military justice for the purpose of maintaining good order and discipline: "The Congress shall have power . . . to make rules for the government and regulation of the land and naval forces." Throughout our nation's history, civilian courts have been respectful of the military's parallel system of justice and have been reluctant to interfere with disciplinary decisions involving individual servicemembers.

The Supreme Court majority had the better argument in *Orloff*, although the three dissenting justices also raised some fair points. The dissenters' principal argument was that the special "doctor's draft" of the Selective Service Act should be interpreted differently. These justices believed that Congress would not have extended draft eligibility to the age of fifty without very good reason—and the reason was to make sure that doctors were available to the military to practice medicine. There was no similarly extraordinary justification to draft doctors for duties that anyone else could perform just as well. The dissenting justices also expressed some concern that Orloff was being punished for his speech and associations, an issue that raised important First Amendment questions even during the 1950s "Red Scare."

In the end, however, *Orloff* involved exactly the sort of individual, case-by-case judgment about the performance of military duties that should reasonably be left to the Army's professional wisdom. A court would not have been in the best position to judge whether Orloff's duties as a medical technician made "enough" use of his medical education and specialty when translated into a military setting. The Army would also have been in a better position to judge the sincerity of Orloff's grievances. If Orloff was more stubborn than overqualified, which the Court seemed to believe was the case, then that should have been the Army's call to make. The bottom line in

Orloff was that lawfully inducted draftees would have to perform the duties the military assigned them to do. It was as simple as that. Courts were not going to get involved, absent some specific violation of the draftee's constitutional rights by the government. Here, the Court did not see one.

Keep in mind, however, some of the specific statements the Court made in rejecting Orloff's claims. As uncontroversial as they were when applied to the individual circumstances of Dr. Stanley Orloff, they would later come to stand for something very different:

> *Judges are not given the task of running the Army.*

> *The military constitutes a specialized community governed by a separate discipline from that of the civilian.*

> *The very essence of compulsory service is the subordination of the desires and interests of the individual to the needs of the service.*

William Rehnquist was nominated for the Supreme Court by President Richard Nixon in 1971. During Rehnquist's first two years on the Court, his influence on civil-military relations and constitutional control of the military was relatively small, but his ideological allegiance was unmistakable. An influential constitutional law scholar and Harvard Law School professor once described Rehnquist as "preoccupied with the question of the judiciary's proper posture towards the military."[3] That's a fair description, and probably understated. If one were looking for words to capture what Rehnquist had in mind for the "proper posture" courts should adopt in relation to the military, some good possibilities would be "supine," "submissive," or perhaps "subservient." From the beginning, it seemed Rehnquist's intent was to push the military outside our nation's constitutional fold and weaken its connection to civilian courts and civilian law.

Early in his Supreme Court tenure, Rehnquist wrote dissenting opinions in two cases involving constitutional challenges to decisions made by military officials, *Flower v. United States*[4] in 1972 and *Frontiero v. Richardson* in 1973.[5] *Flower* was a case about the Vietnam War and the passionate disagreement it provoked among Americans, both civilian and military. *Frontiero* was a case about the changing economic and legal status of women that was filed by a female military officer who believed she should not be paid less than men of the same rank just because she was female. The cases are interesting because they capture a time of tremendous social upheaval in civilian America and in the relationship of civilian society to the military. The individual stories of the participants are important because they are in many ways timeless. We face some of the same issues today, or at least remnants of the same issues, but strangely we have become less capable of discussing them thoughtfully.

John Flower, a civilian, was convicted in federal court and sentenced to six months of confinement for the crime of entering Fort Sam Houston (an Army post in San Antonio, Texas) and handing out leaflets on the sidewalk in front of the post library. This was not the first time Flower had distributed flyers on the post, and the commander had ordered him not to return, on threat of arrest. Flower violated the order by entering the base, but he didn't do so in the way you might imagine in our security-conscious, post–September 11 world. He didn't have to overpower the guards, climb over fences, or hide himself in the trunk of a car. In 1969, Fort Sam Houston was the type of military installation known as an "open post." Civilians could come and go without restriction through dozens of different entrances, and thousands did each day. There were no entry gates, checkpoints, sentries, or searches that limited the ability of civilians to come and go as they pleased. In fact, a major San Antonio traffic artery, New Braunfels Avenue, ran through Fort Sam Houston, and both civilians and servicemembers used its sidewalks extensively. It was on this avenue that Flower was arrested for leafleting:

> Flower when arrested was on foot, by himself, carrying no picket signs or sound amplifiers, not obstructing anyone and not littering the street. He was not using obscene language or otherwise behaving discourteously. He was simply handing out the described flyer or handbills to passersby, nothing more.[6]

Flower wanted people to come to a "town meeting" about the Vietnam War, and he believed soldiers would be interested in attending. The event organizers took great care to ensure all perspectives would be heard, inviting a variety of speakers of different political stripes from government, politics, the military, and academia. Members of the audience would also be welcome to speak. The event described in Flower's unauthorized leaflet was especially remarkable for its lack of partisanship, especially when viewed from today's perspective in which public "debate" is usually designed to preach to the already converted:

THIS FRIDAY DECEMBER 12
—8:00 PM—
SAMS MEMORIAL GYMNASIUM, TRINITY UNIVERSITY
TOWN MEETING ON THE VIETNAM WAR
—VIET EXPERTS PRO AND CON—
*DAVID CARPENTER, U.S. State Department
*RICHARD SANCHEZ, chairman of the Mexican-American Advisory Committee to
the Republican Party
*JONATHAN MIRSKY, Co-Director of the East Asian Center at
Dartmouth University
*DAVID PLYLAR, a former Air Force officer and now a teacher at
Edgewood High School
ALL PRESENT ALSO GET A CHANCE TO STATE THEIR VIEWS
—sponsored by the trinity university free forum—

The Supreme Court reversed Flower's conviction and held that the commander's order barring Flower from the post was unconstitutional under the First Amendment. While the Court recognized that a military commander generally does have the authority to control activities on a military installation, the commander cannot open the streets and sidewalks for public use and then attempt to control what people say when they are there. That would be a violation of Flower's right to free speech.

Rehnquist dissented, and the reasons he gave were quite telling for the future. He would have upheld Flower's conviction under the assumption there must have been *some* military necessity for barring Flower from the post, because why else would the commander have barred him? Rehnquist complained that the commander was left with only two less-than-perfect options in meeting "the unique requirements of military morale and security." First, the commander could close the avenue to civilian traffic and inconvenience local residents, but also retain his authority over civilian speech on the sidewalk; or second, he could accommodate civilian traveling convenience, but at the cost of his authority to control what people said.

Rehnquist had not the slightest interest or curiosity in the third and best option—having the commander explain to the Court why, under the circumstances, Flower's leaflets caused a problem for military morale or security, justifying some restrictions on free speech rights. I'm sure the commander's explanation would have carried a great deal of weight with the Court, if there was an explanation other than sheer annoyance that his soldiers were being invited to an open discussion of the war they had volunteered for or been drafted to fight. Perhaps the commander barred Flower because he believed soldiers could not be exposed to disagreement about the war without suffering a loss of morale or discipline. But if that was the case, this justification needed to be aired because it didn't make a lot of sense. The commander would have had to rip out the newspaper racks and strip the library of magazines to shield his soldiers from public debate about the war. Furthermore, do we really want to be a country that believes its servicemembers will fight only if they are ignorant? These are important First Amendment questions.

If shielding servicemembers from public debate is what Rehnquist meant by "the unique requirements of military morale and security," then the issue deserved some serious discussion. However, this is exactly the discussion that Rehnquist's dissenting opinion intended to prevent. For Rehnquist, it was good enough that there might hypothetically be some military need important enough to justify a restriction on free speech rights under the First Amendment. He did not see any need for the Court to be told what that need was, let alone examine it. The danger in deciding cases hypothetically, of course, is that anyone can fill in the blanks of what they imagine military needs might be, regardless of whether they line up with actual military needs or with our sense of our constitutional selves.

Rehnquist was even more out on the legal edge in *Frontiero v. Richardson*. Interestingly, *Frontiero* is a case commonly taught in basic constitutional law courses in law schools—not because it involves the military, but because it was one of the earliest cases applying constitutional principles of equal protection to laws that treated men and women differently. Sharron Frontiero, an Air Force lieutenant, challenged a federal law that gave all male servicemembers who were married extra housing benefits and medical coverage for their spouses, but female servicemembers who were married received those benefits only if they could prove to the military that their husbands were financially dependent on their military salaries. Frontiero's husband, Joseph, was attending college with the assistance of veterans' benefits, and so the military concluded he was not economically dependent. It was literally a nickel-and-dime operation: because Joseph's share of marital expenses was calculated to be $354 per month and his veterans' benefits were $205 per month, he did not qualify for spousal benefits because he was not dependent on his wife for at least one-half of his living expenses.

The important point was that Sharron Frontiero did not receive the same military compensation that would have been paid to a married man of equal rank. The military apparently made no effort to discover how many military wives received college financial aid or other government benefits, not to mention how many were earning wages, that might make them financially independent of their husbands under the law. Military men automatically received the extra housing and medical benefits simply because they were men.

The government defended having one rule for men and another for women by pleading "administrative convenience." Because almost all military personnel at this time were male and men were traditionally the family breadwinners, the government believed it was inefficient to require proof of dependency in the hope of uncovering what it assumed would be very few instances in which wives were not financially dependent. In the case of married military women, on the other hand, there weren't that many of them to begin with, and because the government assumed most of their husbands would also be breadwinners—that's what men do—it made sense to deny benefits to women unless they could affirmatively prove their husband's dependency. The Supreme Court struck down this rule, finding that it unconstitutionally discriminated on the basis of sex in violation of the due process clause of the Fifth Amendment. While "administrative convenience" was a sufficient justification for many routine laws, it was not an important enough reason to justify treating men and women differently when they were otherwise similarly situated. Eight of the justices voted to strike down the law.

Rehnquist was the only justice who thought the lower court had gotten the case right. As for Lieutenant Frontiero and other military women who would be paid less than male officers in the same position, Rehnquist endorsed the lower court's vague insinuation that they were somehow greedy, expecting something to which they were not entitled. Family housing and medical benefits would be a "windfall" for Lieutenant Frontiero because her husband was not depending on her salary. However, when men received the same benefits for nondependent spouses, the extra compensation was labeled "incidental" to the larger purpose of administrative convenience, not a windfall.[7] From Rehnquist's perspective, if the men were being paid more than they deserved, it was understandable because the bonus was, in some distant sense, primarily for the military's benefit.

Take note of the subtle aspersions of poor character against those who challenge military policy, because it would become a frequent theme of Rehnquist's later judicial opinions involving the military. Also take note of the breathtaking failures of logic that can take hold where the military is concerned. One of the more ludicrous aspects of the lower court's opinion in *Frontiero*—and of Rehnquist's endorsement of that opinion—was its belief that it was sensible to require military women to prove dependency because husbands were generally the family breadwinners and wives generally the dependent partners. If one stops to think about it for just a moment, it makes no sense to apply general assumptions about marriages with nonworking wives to a situation in which the one inescapable fact we do know is that the wife is a salaried military professional.

Rehnquist was not always in the minority when evaluating military cases during his earliest years on the court, and he did not always vote in ways that upset a healthy constitutional balance in civil-military relations. *Gilligan v. Morgan* arose out of one of the defining events of the Vietnam era, the fatal shooting of four Kent State University students by the Ohio National Guard in May 1970.[8] The petitioners, acting on behalf of all Kent State students, hoped to ensure such a tragedy would never happen again, but what they asked the court to do was extraordinary by any definition. In essence, they wanted a federal court to take command of the Ohio National Guard:

> [Petitioners] continue to seek for the benefit of all Kent State students a judicial evaluation of the appropriateness of the "training, weaponry and orders" of the Ohio National Guard. They further demand . . . that the District Court establish standards for the training, kind of weapons and scope and kind of orders to control the actions of the National Guard. [Petitioners] contend that thereafter the District Court must assume and exercise a continuing judicial surveillance over the Guard to assure compliance with whatever training and operations procedures may be approved by that court.

Not a single justice of the Supreme Court voted to award any part of the remedy sought by the students. The Court explained that Article 1 of the Constitution grants Congress the power "to provide for organizing, arming, and disciplining, the militia," which is the historical ancestor of the modern National Guard units of each state. Identifying the source of government power is often an important step in constitutional cases because the Constitution intended to create a federal government of limited powers. By design, the federal government has no power to act unless that power is expressly granted by the Constitution.

Article 1 of the Constitution grants a variety of powers to Congress, including, for example, the power to collect taxes, coin money, and establish rules for immigration and naturalization, bankruptcy, and patents and copyrights, among other subjects. Article 2 grants powers to the president, including the power to act as the commander in chief of the armed forces, to make treaties, and to enforce the law. Article 3 grants to federal courts a general "judicial power," which extends to all cases "arising under this Constitution, the laws of the United States, and treaties made." The Article 3 judicial power is a blank slate that incorporates *all* cases arising under the Constitution and federal law, and for that reason it does not list specific areas of law or government that fall within its constitutional responsibility, as in Article 1 and Article 2.

Even when the Constitution grants specific powers over particular activities to Congress or the president, courts still have a role to play in ensuring those powers are exercised in accordance with the Constitution and law. The Constitution assigns many specific powers to the elected legislative and executive branches—if it didn't, the federal government would have no power to act—but the judicial branch still routinely decides cases involving, for example, taxes, naturalization, bankruptcy, or patents and copyrights, subjects that the Constitution also expressly assigns to Congress. The military is similarly expected to answer for its decisions or actions in a court of law. The *Gilligan* majority affirmed this understanding, emphasizing that "it should be clear that we neither hold nor imply that the conduct of the National Guard is always beyond judicial review or that there may not be accountability in a judicial forum for violations of law or for specific unlawful conduct by military personnel."

However, the problem with *Gilligan* was that it would have been impossible for the Court to exercise judicial power in the normal way because the questions to be answered were not in any way judicial questions. The Court had no legal tools in its judicial toolbox suitable for deciding how the Guard should arm itself or how it should conduct weapons training, and therefore it ruled that the case was "non-justiciable" or inappropriate for judicial resolution. The students' idea that a federal court should select specific weapons

for the Guard, establish standards for their use, and exercise continuing sur-
veillance of weapons training bordered on the frivolous. The Court's choice
to decline such a supervisory role over the Guard was the only one that reasonably could have been made.

The majority opinion, however, did not stop there. It took the opportunity
to plant a seed that might grow to discourage courts from reviewing constitutional challenges to military decisions under a much broader range of circumstances:

> Moreover, it is difficult to conceive of an area of governmental activity in which
> the courts have less competence. The complex, subtle, and professional
> decisions as to the composition, training, equipping, and control of a military
> force are essentially professional military judgments, subject *always* to civilian
> control of the Legislative and Executive Branches. The ultimate responsibility
> for these decisions is appropriately vested in branches of the government
> which are periodically subject to electoral accountability.

This statement went far beyond the situation at hand and was completely
unnecessary to the result. The Court rejected the students' claims not
because they involved the military but because they would have required
the Court to supervise the Ohio National Guard without the guidance of any
controlling legal standards. The problem was that the requested remedy was
outside the Court's job description, not that the military as a whole was outside its job description. Unlike the unusual circumstances of *Gilligan*, military cases often do involve the application of legal standards, and when they
do, courts have a constitutional obligation to review them in the same way
they review other legal challenges to government policies.

What if, for example, military policies were challenged on the basis that
they infringed on constitutional rights of free speech, equal protection, or
free exercise of religion? In each of these areas, legal doctrines are available
to guide courts in balancing respect for the Constitution with awareness of
the special circumstances of military life. These kinds of cases should be very
different from *Gilligan*, in which the Court declined to supervise weapons
policy for the Guard, or from *Orloff*, in which the Court declined to comment
on the individual duty assignments of disgruntled draftees. The above
language in *Gilligan*, however, suggests that courts and judges should vacate
the entire military field regardless of the nature of the claims.

The Court's italicized emphasis of the word *always*—meaning that Congress and the president *always* control the military, and courts *never* do—was
a very bad sign. As a matter of law it was inaccurate, and as a matter of civil-
military relations it was disastrous. With this statement the Court seemed to
suggest that civilian control of the military involves only two of the three
branches of civilian government, and that military policies, activities, and
decisions should be regulated by majority vote and political partisanship, not

necessarily by law. The only available remedy for military decision making that strayed from the Constitution would be a much-delayed "electoral accountability" for legislators who enacted laws governing the military or for presidents who directed the military as commander in chief. The majority came to the right result in *Gilligan*, but its careless explanations, like the casual generality of *Orloff*, created a real risk for the future. Just two days short of a year later, Justice Rehnquist would pick up these loose threads of imprecise commentary and begin to transform them in an unprecedented way.

Chapter 4

Justice Rehnquist's Vietnam War

Throughout our history, the Supreme Court has often been asked to draw lines separating military law from civilian law. When the Fifth Amendment was ratified in 1791, adding to the Constitution a requirement for grand jury indictment in criminal cases (among other important rights), it included an exception for military courts-martial, which everyone recognized would not use civilian grand juries. The harder question was defining the scope or reach the military justice system should have. Members of the military, of course, were the primary focus of the system, but how far should the scope of court-martial jurisdiction extend? Could former members of the military be court-martialed for offenses committed while they were on active duty? Could civilian family members accompanying the military overseas be court-martialed if there was no other way to punish their criminal acts?

The Constitution also left some open questions for active servicemembers. It seemed appropriate, even necessary, for the military to enforce discipline by court-martial when operating in the field, or when overseas. But what if the alleged criminal offense was committed within a civilian community in the United States, and civilian prosecutors would be equally able to enforce the law and impose punishment? What if the offense had absolutely nothing to do with the servicemember's military duties? Under those circumstances, did the military have the right to proceed by court-martial and deny its members the right to be tried by a civilian court?

The Supreme Court has defined the jurisdiction of the military's court-martial system in ways that are both limited and expansive. It has decided that civilian spouses cannot be tried by court-martial, even if their conduct overseas affects good order and discipline, and even if they would otherwise go unpunished.[1] It has also ruled that once servicemembers leave the military, they are no longer subject to court-martial, even for offenses committed while they were serving.[2] Military status is the key; without it, the Constitution normally requires trial in civilian criminal courts.

In contrast, for those currently serving in the military, the scope of court-martial jurisdiction is potentially infinite. Although the Fifth Amendment seems to define the reach of courts-martial as "cases arising in the land or naval forces," the Court has concluded that all it takes for a case to "arise" in the military is for the defendant to be *in* the military.[3] No matter how distant or unrelated an offense might be from military duty, the military has the authority to prosecute the case within its own system of military justice. Again, military status is the key, but with the added justification of preserving the military's authority and discretion in dealing with matters of good order and discipline.

In addition to separating courts-martial from civilian criminal trials, the Court has also drawn lines distinguishing military-related legal claims from civilian lawsuits. In the civilian community, persons who have been wronged by another generally have access to civilian courts to press claims for compensation or other relief. However, under the *Feres* doctrine, a rule named for a 1950 Supreme Court decision, both servicemembers and veterans have been barred from filing lawsuits against other servicemembers or the government for similar complaints arising during their military service.[4] They have no access to the usual civilian remedies for injuries caused by negligence or the intentional denial of constitutional rights. Instead, *Feres* channels their claims toward military remedies, such as the assistance or protection provided by the chain of command, punishment of offenders by way of the military justice system, or the payment of veterans' or survivors' benefits.

Although it might appear harsh, the *Feres* doctrine has a reasonable justification in most circumstances. Given the importance of the chain of command to military effectiveness and the serious responsibility that rests at all levels of rank to maintain discipline and ensure safety, it would be enormously disruptive if individual servicemembers could bypass the command system and simply file lawsuits against their superiors. Without some limitation on civil lawsuits within the military, we run the risk of encouraging "discipline by lawsuit" instead of the usual discipline enforced by military leadership.

Feres is most controversial today in one extremely narrow circumstance: military medical malpractice. Many have argued that servicemembers should have the right to file regular malpractice claims if they are injured by the negligence of military doctors, at least when the claims arise from routine care far from the battlefield. It is much more difficult to see the justification in barring these lawsuits when the negligence is unrelated to military duty and the doctor is not in the patient's chain of command. In almost all other military situations, however, there are clear advantages when problems are corrected within the chain of command. After all, if we trust military commanders with the lives of the people they lead in war, we need to trust them to rectify misconduct and protect the people who have been harmed. If commanders are unable to perform that duty with care and skill, the solution should be a new leader, not a lawsuit.

If the Supreme Court's primary influence in military affairs had stopped here, limited to defining the proper reach of a court-martial or making rules for when servicemembers could sue for damages, the overall effect on our civil-military relations would have been small. These doctrines do exclude individual servicemembers from the civilian court system in many instances, and this can be a significant consequence if the remedies provided by the military in a particular circumstance are not as protective or favorable as the civilian option might have been. For the most part, however, these doctrines are not tremendously controversial because we accept that the needs of the military may require us to channel criminal prosecutions or legal claims in a military direction rather than a civilian direction.[5] The distinction is not intended, presumably, to minimize the importance of either the claim or the person who brings the claim. The point is to assign the matter to the best forum for resolution, based on the original vision of the Constitution and the institutional needs of the military.

We have always operated with an understanding of two constitutional systems of justice, one military and one civilian, but it has not meant that the military enjoyed any special exemption or exception from the Constitution itself. Imagine, however, if the Court suggested that servicemembers were not entitled to protection under the Constitution at all, a step that goes far beyond a ruling that they cannot have their cases heard in a civilian forum. If the Constitution no longer applied to military decisions or policy in the same way it applied to other exercises of government power, this would raise a fundamentally different question from the more routine task of drawing jurisdictional boundaries between military and civilian criminal courts, or between military and civilian legal remedies. This step could potentially affect civilians and the health of our civilian control of the military as much as it would affect individual servicemembers.

Beginning with the 1973–74 term of the Supreme Court, Justice Rehnquist would finally take control of the Court's most important military opinions. Over the next twelve years, Rehnquist would write a series of three opinions that would sharply change the face of civil-military relations, distance the military from civilian society and from the rule of law, and erode the military's constitutional health. Rehnquist's opinions covered three of the most contentious civil-military issues of the all-volunteer era—politics and the military, women and the military, and religion and the military—and it is no coincidence that these issues continue to bedevil the military today. It is also no coincidence that Rehnquist set these changes in motion just as the Vietnam-era draft was ending. One of the consequences of ending the draft and relying on a force of volunteers is that we are less likely to notice funda-mental change in the relationship between the military and civilian society and, unfortunately, we are also less likely to care whether we do.

Rehnquist intuitively understood that the most effective way to reduce the influence of courts in military affairs was to drive a wedge between the military and civilian society. His opinions would build that wedge on a foundation of four troubling principles:

1. The military should be portrayed as distant, remote, and separate from civilian society. The more different the military is from the civilian society it serves, the less justification there might be for holding the military to the expectations of civilian law.
2. The military should be viewed as morally superior to civilian society and civilian government, and military values should be elevated above constitutional values. If military values were morally superior to constitutional values, it would be much easier to disregard the Constitution when its protections appeared to conflict with assertions of military necessity.
3. Civilians should be encouraged to withdraw from active participation in civil-military relations and civilian control of the military and to see themselves as unqualified and undeserving to question assertions of military necessity. Servicemembers should be encouraged to resent civilians, civilian society, and civilian influence over the military.
4. Judges, courts, and other institutions of law should be reluctant to insert themselves in legal controversies involving the military, creating a vacuum that could be filled by political partisanship and allegiance.

These three cases—*Parker v. Levy* in 1974, *Rostker v. Goldberg* in 1981, and *Goldman v. Weinberger* in 1986—are the most underrated of Rehnquist's thirty-three-year Supreme Court career.[6] No other Rehnquist opinions have changed our nation so fundamentally without ever registering on the public radar. Rehnquist would use them to address the churning culture war of the day and transform the constitutional relationship between the military and the judiciary, giving Congress and the president a wide latitude to use assertions of military necessity to shape not only the military but also the nature of civilian society itself.

Army Captain Howard Levy was, in some respects, the "Hawkeye Pierce"[7] of the Vietnam War, but perhaps even less suited than Hawkeye to the military practice of medicine. Drafted in 1965, he was a dermatologist who deeply opposed the war in Vietnam and the way it was being conducted. He aggravated superiors with his resistance to doing things "the military way," and he found many of the traditional customs and courtesies of an officer's life—saluting, joining the officers' club, and the like—to be silly.[8] Less than two years into his term of Army service, Captain Levy was court-martialed and sentenced to three years at hard labor in a federal prison. It was Levy's opposition to the Vietnam War—and the means he chose to express it—that led him to become one of the most notorious court-martial defendants in Supreme Court history. More than three decades later, his case is still cited today whenever the military punishes servicemembers for what they say.

The charges against Levy were based on statements he made while on duty as chief of the Dermatological Service at Fort Jackson Army Hospital in South Carolina. He spoke out against the war on a number of occasions, both to his military patients and to soldiers he was assigned to train as medical aides for Special Forces units. Levy was apparently not shy or subtle in his opposition to the war. According to the specifications filed by the prosecution in the case, the following statement was representative of the way Levy spoke to lower-ranking personnel:

> The United States is wrong in being involved in the Viet Nam War. I would refuse to go to Viet Nam if ordered to do so. I don't see why any colored soldier would go to Viet Nam; they should refuse to go to Viet Nam and if sent should refuse to fight because they are discriminated against and denied their freedom in the United States, and they are sacrificed and discriminated against in Viet Nam by being given all the hazardous duty and they are suffering the majority of the casualties. If I were a colored soldier I would refuse to go to Viet Nam and if I were a colored soldier and were sent I would refuse to fight.

Levy's appeal to the Supreme Court challenged his conviction by court-martial for crimes committed in violation of two sections of the Uniform Code of Military Justice. The first, Article 133 of the UCMJ, codifies the classic military offense of "conduct unbecoming an officer and a gentleman," and the second, Article 134, sets out a less familiar military offense of "disorders and neglects to the prejudice of good order and discipline in the armed forces."[9] Both are extraordinarily general in their wording, to say the least, and would seem to cover almost any disruptive behavior in a military environment.

Levy first argued that it was unconstitutionally "vague" to punish conduct because it was "unbecoming" or upset "good order and discipline." Criminal laws violate the due process clause of the Fifth Amendment when they fail to give fair warning that certain conduct is a crime.[10] Second, Levy also argued that Articles 133 and 134 were unconstitutionally "overbroad" because they targeted too much speech that should be protected by the First Amendment. The overbreadth doctrine takes into account the First Amendment rights of other potential speakers not involved in the case before the court. If a law is written so broadly that it could discourage or chill a substantial amount of constitutionally protected speech by other people, then the law should not be enforced against anyone, not even against defendants like Levy who was perfectly well aware that his statements could cause a disciplinary problem among lower-ranking soldiers.[11]

It can be difficult to weigh competing concerns of free speech and discipline in a military environment. When the speaker is a servicemember, should spirited disagreement be considered dissent or discussion protected by the First Amendment, or should it be considered insubordination punishable as a breach of military discipline? While this might be an engaging question in some cases, in *Parker v. Levy* it was easy to answer. Captain Levy's statements were more than just expression of a political viewpoint on the Vietnam War. He was also using his authority as a commissioned officer and a military doctor to encourage his subordinates to shirk their duties and disobey orders.

As a legal matter, Levy's appeal was extremely weak. Surely to no one's surprise, including Levy's, the Court held that when a commissioned officer directly urges subordinates to refuse to go to Vietnam and fight as ordered, it falls squarely and unambiguously within a class of misconduct considered "unbecoming" of an officer and also in breach of good order and discipline. *Parker v. Levy* found, not unreasonably, that military personnel understood the military's expectations for discipline and obedience and, therefore, Articles 133 and 134 of the UCMJ were not unconstitutionally vague or overbroad even though their language was extremely unspecific. The opinion could have been, and should have been, a short one. As a general rule, it should be within the military's discretion to determine whether an individual soldier's conduct is unbecoming or harmful to good order and discipline. Throughout our legal history, the Supreme Court has been reluctant to disturb such judgments made by courts-martial as part of the military's constitutionally separate system of justice.

Ironically, it wouldn't have made any difference if *Parker v. Levy* had been a civilian rather than a military case. Many people assume that the military is uniquely restrictive of First Amendment rights, but the military is not the only government institution that limits the speech of its employees. Civilian government employees have never been able to say whatever they please while on the job—anyone who believes otherwise has never been, for example, a public school teacher. *Parker v. Levy* could have arrived at the same result by applying the standard rule for civilian government employees established in *Pickering v. Board of Education*, a 1968 Supreme Court case that allowed restrictions on speech if the government could show the speech interfered with efficient operation of the workplace.[12] In a military context, it would be easy to conclude that officers interfere with military effectiveness when they tell their subordinates to disobey military orders.

Justice Rehnquist, however, used the opinion he wrote in *Parker v. Levy* as a springboard for introducing a new brand of civil-military relations under the Constitution. It was not enough that the Constitution already gave more than adequate discretion to the military to address individual breaches of discipline like Captain Levy's. Rehnquist would use the opinion to build a foundation for separating the military from the expectations and obligations of civilian law, and he would begin by reaching back to the obscure case of his clerkship twenty years earlier, *Orloff v. Willoughby*. Rehnquist would also misrepresent *Orloff* in order to establish the first of the troubling principles necessary to change the course of civil-military relations—that the military should be seen as distant, remote, and separate from civilian society.

The *Orloff* opinion included an offhand, unremarkable observation that the military was "a specialized community governed by a separate discipline."[13] This statement referred to Congress's authority under Article 1 of the Constitution to make rules for the internal governance of the military, including the military's separate system of trial by court-martial. In *Parker v. Levy*, Rehnquist claimed he was relying on *Orloff*, but he did not accurately report what *Orloff* said. Rehnquist instead twisted the statement to read that the Supreme Court "has long recognized that the military is, by necessity, a specialized society separate from civilian society" and "a society apart from civilian society."[14] He took *Orloff*'s casual mention of the military's separate disciplinary system of courts-martial and recast it as a statement that military society as a whole should be separate from the larger civilian world it serves.

The distinction may seem trivial on the surface, but the change was significant and deliberate. Rehnquist did not simply declare that the military's system of law, courts, and justice was separate from the judicial system used to prosecute civilians, which is entirely uncontroversial and all that *Orloff* meant to say. Rehnquist's new and different point was that *military society as a whole is separate from civilian society*, and therefore the Constitution does not apply to the military in the same way it does to the rest of the government. He gave a brief nod to the Constitution, but then turned away:

> While the members of the military are not excluded from the protection granted by the First Amendment, the different character of the military community and of the military mission requires a different application of those protections. The fundamental necessity for obedience, and the consequent necessity for imposition of discipline, may render permissible within the military that which would be constitutionally impermissible outside it.

The Supreme Court has not "long recognized" that the military is "a society apart" from the rest of American society. At most, it has long recognized that civilian courts should not second-guess the result of a court-martial proceeding when it concludes, like in *Parker v. Levy*, that an individual servicemember's behavior has disrupted military discipline or morale. This kind of decision is squarely within the core of disciplinary discretion the Constitution has given to Congress, and Congress has in turn given to the military justice system. Federal civilian courts generally have not interfered with the military's parallel system of justice, in the same way they have not interfered with the separate systems of justice that operate in each of the fifty states of the United States.[15] It does not mean that states should therefore be treated as separate societies from the United States, less connected to the Constitution or less subject to federal law, just because they also operate their own local systems of justice.

As for the proposition that the entire military should be considered distant or separate from civilian society in some way that is constitutionally or legally significant, that time, if it ever existed, is long gone. Much earlier in our nation's history, service in the armed forces might have been considered a peculiar, almost monastic profession, with its members living in isolation from civilian society.[16] However, a geographically distant, frontier military, one without a presence or relevance in the lives of civilian citizens, is now a century in the past. As a result, Rehnquist tried to justify his "separate society" rationale with a series of citations to cases involving the frontier military of the 1800s, the most recent decided in 1897.

Rehnquist's insistence on identifying the military as a separate society is especially difficult to understand, given that Congress would never have enacted the UCMJ in 1950 if not for the near-universal military service of qualified male citizens during World War II. The shared experience of millions of citizens who were returning to civilian life helped to identify the weaknesses of military justice and motivate Congress to modernize military law.[17] In *Parker v. Levy*, however, Rehnquist was able to take a case that should have been resolved on the basis of accepted, uncontroversial principles about the scope of military discretion and turn it into something that could be used to inflame and exacerbate the cultural division of the Vietnam era.

Parker v. Levy also set in motion the second of the troubling principles necessary to change the course of civil-military relations—that the military should be viewed as morally superior to civilian society, with military values elevated above constitutional values. Separatism by its very nature tends to encourage a sense of moral superiority. A society apart is necessarily a society either above or below another, and Rehnquist's opinion in *Parker v. Levy* made clear his belief in the military's moral superiority in comparison to civilian society. As we learned from the shameful practice of "separate but equal," separatism under law is never neutral in its effect.

According to Rehnquist, the military had "overriding demands of discipline and duty" that justified a departure from the usual protections for free speech. By implication, he must have believed civilian society lacks the same commitment to discipline and duty in its various professions and trades, an assumption that seems unfair and simplistic. Even more importantly, however, he apparently believed that the demands of military discipline and duty overrode the longstanding values and principles found in the Constitution. He thought those values made sense in the context of the lesser expectations of civilian life, but not under the higher standards of the military. Civilians had the moral latitude, for example, to be "disrespectful and contemptuous"; servicemembers did not.

One need not defend Captain Levy's conduct to be concerned when the Supreme Court defines military values as inherently higher or better than civilian values, particularly when those civilian values are the ones enshrined in the Constitution. One need not discount the gravity of the military's responsibility to fight our wars to be concerned when the Supreme Court defines military values in an exaggerated and stereotypical way, seemingly at the personal whims of the justices. For example, Justice Rehnquist repeatedly argued that the First Amendment is less relevant to the military because servicemembers live only by the law of obedience. Why, then, would they need any constitutional protection for criticism or questions? He cited an 1827 Supreme Court case that criticized soldiers who paused to consider the appropriateness of orders, adding his own "military" opinion that hesitancy helps the enemy prevail. It is telling that Rehnquist had to go back almost 150 years to find such an inaccurate statement of a servicemember's professional obligation. As a matter of actual military law, Rehnquist's argument hasn't been correct since the Nuremberg trials, if not well before.[18] Military law in fact requires servicemembers to disobey the orders of superiors if they "knew the orders to be unlawful or a person of ordinary sense and understanding would have known the orders to be unlawful."[19]

Remember, of course, that all this judicial improvisation on the nature of military values, and how they were better than civilian values, was unnecessary to uphold Captain Levy's conviction. Few people are going to seriously contend that a military officer should be allowed to urge lower-ranking personnel to disobey lawful orders, and the Constitution would not have changed that conclusion. Rehnquist, however, believed it was important to go beyond what was necessary to decide the case. He used *Parker v. Levy* to lay a foundation that would allow courts in the future to withdraw from their constitutional responsibility to take part in civilian control of the military. The disturbing promise of *Parker v. Levy* would fully come to pass just seven years later.

The Supreme Court's evolution in civil-military relations finally became clear in Justice Rehnquist's 1981 majority opinion in *Rostker v. Goldberg*,[20] the most important case of the twentieth century on the constitutional relationship between the military and civilian society. It was in *Rostker* that the doctrine of judicial deference in military cases was first stated plainly, without reservation—and as if it had always existed, even though it was without precedent. In *Rostker*, we had finally arrived at the legally bulletproof "apogee" that a generation of lawyers would rely on to argue that courts had no place in constitutional control of the military:

> Nor can it be denied that the imposing number of cases from this Court previously cited suggest that judicial deference to such congressional exercise of authority is at its apogee when legislative action under the congressional authority to raise and support armies and make rules and regulations for their governance is challenged.

Rostker was a case about the military draft and whether young women, like young men, should be required to register for potential service. In 1980, President Jimmy Carter, an Annapolis graduate and former naval officer, reactivated the draft registration process in response to the Soviet invasion of Afghanistan, and Carter encouraged Congress to amend the Military Selective Service Act to require the registration of women as well as men. Congress refused to do so, and this lawsuit eventually worked its way to the Supreme Court.

Interestingly, the lawsuit was originally filed years before, while the Vietnam War was still being fought. At first it seemed the lawsuit would be dismissed when the general military draft ended, but a new plaintiff—Robert Goldberg, the Goldberg of the case title *Rostker v. Goldberg*—joined the case and kept it alive. Goldberg was a male medical student, and at that time doctors were still subject to the draft even though regular, combat-eligible troops were no longer being drafted or even registered for the draft. He was attending medical school with women, and he saw no reason why his female classmates shouldn't have the same responsibility for practicing medicine in the military. Once President Carter reactivated the requirement that all males coming of age register for the draft, however, the issue became a much larger one.

The plaintiffs in *Rostker* argued that a male-only draft registration system denied both men and women equal protection of the law, in violation of the Fifth Amendment. By the 1980s, the Supreme Court had devised a standard method for deciding equal protection claims. Run-of-the-mill laws that regulated business matters or health and safety concerns—the vast majority of all laws—would almost always be upheld following only a cursory review by courts. These kinds of laws invariably made difficult choices that resulted in some people or businesses being treated more or less favorably by the government than others, but as long as the government offered some legitimate reason for doing so and the law seemed rationally related to achieving that purpose, courts would not take a hard look or second-guess whatever choices were made.[21] Almost all laws in the "rational basis review" category of cases will be upheld even if the government makes only a superficial effort to explain them.

At the other end of the spectrum, laws that explicitly distinguish between people on the basis of race, for example, will be upheld only if the government carries an extremely heavy burden of explanation. Under this "strict scrutiny" standard, the government must show it has a compelling reason for using race to treat people differently under the law, and it must justify why the racial distinction is necessary to achieve that compelling purpose. Government policies that make distinctions on the basis of race are strongly disfavored, with the exception of some narrowly targeted affirmative action programs.[22] In these cases, the government was able to explain to the court's satisfaction why there was no other way to maintain significant diversity within law and medical schools other than to consciously consider race as one factor in the admissions process.

Somewhere in the middle between rational basis review and strict scrutiny lies the standard of "intermediate scrutiny," which puts less of a burden on the government to explain its choices than strict scrutiny does, but still a great deal more than under rational basis review. This is the standard that applies to the relatively few remaining laws that discriminate on the basis of sex and openly treat men and women differently under the law. In cases applying intermediate scrutiny, the government has the burden to show that it has an important purpose in mind for distinguishing legally between men and women and also that discrimination on the basis of sex is substantially related to achieving that purpose.[23]

Intermediate scrutiny is a more forgiving test than strict scrutiny because the government purpose at issue need only be "important," not necessarily "compelling," and because any legal distinctions drawn between men and women must only be "substantially related" to that purpose, not absolutely "necessary" to that purpose. Intermediate scrutiny affords more flexibility to government decision makers because we assume that on occasion there could be good reasons (normally having something to do with biological imperatives) to treat men and women differently under the law, whereas there are almost never good reasons to treat persons of different races differently under the law. In both intermediate scrutiny and strict scrutiny cases, however, unlike in rational basis cases, we definitely want to hear the explanation to ensure that outdated and unfair stereotypes are not the driving forces behind the law.

Under intermediate scrutiny, the court will expect the government's explanations to be honest and candid. The reasons offered to justify sex discrimination in law have to be the real reasons, not merely hypothetical possibilities made up after the fact for purposes of litigation. The government also has to be acting for legitimate purposes. Some purposes are plainly illegitimate under the Constitution and cannot be used to justify the law. For example, the government cannot treat men and women differently for the purpose of maintaining traditional gender roles, and it cannot justify discrimination against women (or in favor of women, for that matter) on the basis of "archaic and overbroad generalizations" about how most women behave or what most women are like, or should be like. Government cannot use maleness and femaleness as a crude proxy for evaluating the qualifications or interests of individual people. These are the rules of equal protection on the basis of sex, and by the time of *Rostker*, the rules were extremely clear.

This three-tiered system for reviewing equal protection claims—rational basis review, intermediate scrutiny, and strict scrutiny—works fairly well in practice because it matches the level of explanation required to the likelihood the government is acting for constitutionally improper purposes. In essence, the system is designed to "smoke out" improper motives or actions by the government in the situations in which they are most likely to occur. Sex discrimination falls somewhere in the middle of the spectrum of suspicion because there might be some situations—not a high number, but some—in which there could be sufficient justification to treat men and women differently.

In *Rostker*, therefore, all the government needed to do was explain why Congress believed only men should register for, and be subject to, a military draft. Everyone would have accepted that military effectiveness or national security was a sufficiently important purpose, but the key question was why Congress thought it needed to exclude women from draft registration in order to have a strong military, or why registering women would weaken the military. If there was such an explanation—something more than the desire to preserve traditional general roles or the proper "place" of women in society—the intermediate scrutiny standard would be satisfied and the male-only draft registration system would be upheld.

Rostker v. Goldberg should have been a difficult case for establishing a new and sweeping doctrine of judicial deference in matters involving the military. It was very different from previous cases in which the Court gave the military a strong benefit of the doubt in reviewing decisions related to military discipline or military operations. First, the scope of *Rostker* was far larger. In earlier cases, the Court deferred to military judgments about individual servicemembers, but in *Rostker*, the relevant judgment was made about all women as a group, without any information concerning their individual qualifications or interests. Second, in earlier cases the Court had declined to second-guess military judgments when they were made on the basis of professional expertise and experience. The Court was reluctant to insert itself in decisions made by military experts about military professionalism, military duty assignments, or military tactics and training. In *Rostker*, in contrast, the decision to exclude women from draft registration and reserve this important obligation of citizenship only for men was made by Congress, not the military. It should have been more difficult to justify why civilians who served in Congress were qualified and competent to understand military personnel policy, but civilians who served as judges were not.

The third difference is counterintuitive and has been misunderstood by a generation of law students studying *Rostker*. In earlier cases in which the Court based its decision on a principle of deference to military decisions, the final result of the case was consistent with military advice. Most people assume that Congress resisted including women in draft registration because the military did not want them. In *Rostker*, however, *all four military services wanted to register women for the draft*, but Congress and the Court said no. I don't mean to suggest the military should have the authority to overrule civilians, or that the military's opinion should necessarily carry more weight than the judgments of Congress, the president, or the Supreme Court. There is something wrong, however, with a legal doctrine that is justified on the basis of respect for military expertise, but then used for the purpose of ignoring military expertise when the military fails to provide the "right" answer.

There is something about military cases in the all-volunteer era that causes Supreme Court justices to say things that are truly bizarre, as if they had forgotten much of what they learned in law school. Justice Rehnquist began his opinion in *Rostker* by noting that the Constitution mentions military governance and regulation only in Article 1 (the article setting out congressional powers) and not at all in Article 3 (the article setting out judicial powers). Although Rehnquist tossed the plaintiffs a tiny bone, assuring them that "none of this is to say that Congress is free to disregard the Constitution when it acts in the area of military affairs," a few sentences later he reversed course and all but said that Congress was in fact free to disregard the Constitution. This was not by Rehnquist's own choice, he insisted, but because he thought "the Constitution itself requires such deference to congressional choice."

As a matter of constitutional law, his position didn't make a lot of sense. Just because a congressional power to enact laws on a particular subject is mentioned in Article 1, it doesn't mean that courts therefore lack the authority to decide if Congress is using that power properly under the Constitution.[24] All it means is that Congress has the power to act within constitutional limits. An express grant of power was never intended to exempt Congress from challenges that it might be acting beyond the scope of its power or acting in violation of other parts of the Constitution. Yet Rehnquist found it significant that in limiting draft registration to men, Congress was "acting under an explicit constitutional grant of authority." He seemed to have forgotten the basic constitutional lesson that Congress *always* acts under an explicit grant of authority.

If Rehnquist had it right, it would mean courts should automatically defer to congressional choice in any area not specifically mentioned in Article 3 of the Constitution as being within the special province of courts. But, of course, that would mean courts should defer in *every* area of government, because Article 3 doesn't mention any specific areas of law. It describes the judicial power much more generally as including "all cases" arising under the Constitution and the laws of the United States. If Rehnquist had it right, it would mean that federal courts should excuse themselves not only in cases involving the military but also in cases involving taxation, commerce, or bankruptcy—all powers of legislation expressly granted to Congress in Article 1 but not specifically mentioned in Article 3. The Supreme Court would not have a lot to do.

Rehnquist also decided that the military context of the case meant that the usual standard of intermediate scrutiny in sex discrimination cases did not apply. Instead of asking the government to explain why it believed the registration of women would substantially interfere with building an effective fighting force, he turned the standard on its head and asked only if it was possible to build an effective force without registering women—which of course it was.[25] In other words, Rehnquist believed that Congress could exclude women from any responsibility for national service provided the military could manage to get along without them.

Rehnquist had the constitutional analysis exactly backward. When laws explicitly discriminate on the basis of sex, it is not the plaintiffs' burden to show why it is important to treat men and women the same; rather, it is the government's burden to explain why it is so important to treat them differently. According to the established rules of equal protection, the default presumption is that sex discrimination is unlawful unless there is a good explanation for why it is helpful, not that sex discrimination is lawful unless the plaintiffs show it is especially harmful. Under the Constitution, distinctions in law drawn on the basis of sex are considered harmful in and of themselves.

All this constitutional evasion—ignoring the basic structure of the Constitution, disregarding the usual standards of equal protection—was apparently justified because *Rostker v. Goldberg* involved the military and not some other function of government. In *Rostker*, the legal seeds that had been planted in cases like *Orloff v. Willoughby*, *Gilligan v. Morgan*, and *Parker v. Levy* finally developed into an all-encompassing doctrine of judicial deference to military decisions that would completely remove courts from any serious role in civilian control of the military. Rehnquist trotted out all the best lines from earlier cases, seemingly unaware that the circumstances were now very different. Rehnquist stressed how incompetent he believed the Court was to

consider questions of a military nature, citing *Gilligan* for the twin proposi-
tions that it is "difficult to conceive of an area of governmental activity in
which the courts have less competence" and the "complex, subtle, and professional decisions as to the composition, training, equipping, and control of
a military force are essentially professional military judgments." He cited
Orloff for the proposition that "judges are not given the task of running the
Army." *Parker* was useful for its reminder about "the different character of
the military community" that required "a different application" of the Constitution.

He overlooked the fact, however, that *Rostker* was of tremendously broader
scope than any of the earlier opinions. It made sense for the Court to defer
to military judgment and discretion when the issue was whether an individual soldier had been placed in the right duty assignment (*Orloff*) or
whether an individual soldier was a disciplinary problem (*Parker*). It also
made sense for the Court not to get involved in matters far beyond its job
description, such as choosing the weapons used by the Ohio National Guard
or supervising their training on an ongoing basis (*Gilligan*). It was another
question entirely to defer to Congress when it decided, for reasons it did not
explain very thoroughly or convincingly, that half the population of the
United States would be of little use to the military in time of war and therefore should have no obligation for national service.

During the congressional hearings held on the question of registering
women for the draft, military leaders testified they could use eighty thousand female draftees (12.3 percent of the total call of draftees) in the first six
months of a draft, over and above the number of women expected to volunteer.[26] From the military's point of view, the most sensible course of action
was to register the maximum number of potentially qualified persons in the
event there were not enough volunteers for military service. The relatively
high number of potential female draftees was especially striking because
it had been less than a decade since the military began assigning women
in significant numbers to jobs outside the traditionally female fields of
medicine and administration.[27] There was a substantial need for women
even if one assumed, as the Court did, that it was constitutional to bar them
from serving in combat or even in combat-support positions. Rehnquist
disregarded this information. He concluded, in direct contradiction to the
statements of military leaders, that a military draft would call only combat-
eligible troops, and since women were barred from combat duty, there was
no point to registering them for the draft.

It might seem odd that Congress was so insistent in refusing to follow the
recommendations of both the president and the military services that all
young Americans, male and female, should register for the draft. It becomes
less odd only if Congress had some purpose in mind other than military

effectiveness. Rehnquist's opinion in *Rostker v. Goldberg* made little attempt
to conceal that Congress's primary purpose was to preserve traditional ideas
about the role women should play in American society. He justified the
exclusion of women from what has historically been an important obligation
of citizenship by noting that Congress was "fully aware . . . of the current
thinking as to the place of women in the Armed Services" and that their
limited military role "enjoys wide support among our people."

If *Rostker v. Goldberg* had been decided in a civilian context, there is no
question that a similar law discriminating on the basis of sex would have
been found unconstitutional. It is clear under the Court's own precedent
that laws treating men and women differently cannot be justified by a desire
to preserve traditional gender roles in society or by generalizations about
what most women would be able to do or would want to do. There must be
some better reason, one that does not exclude women only because they are
women.

Congress, however, was well aware it would not be asked to provide a reason and could act as it pleased without interference from the Court or the
Constitution. It could use the Military Selective Service Act for the very purpose of affirming traditional gender roles, even though equal protection
principles would not have allowed it in any other context. Three Yale Law
School professors (including Robert Bork, who in 1987 would fail to win confirmation to the Supreme Court) wrote a letter to Senator Sam Nunn assuring
him that Congress would answer to no one in its decisions about the military
draft. In matters involving the military, they concluded, anything goes, and
it doesn't matter whether we call it prejudice or chivalry: "Whether this conviction is a moral judgment or a prejudice, a felt necessity or an echo of earlier, chivalric beliefs about the proper role of women in life, the existence of
the belief is a fact reflected in statutes no group in Congress would now
change, and no court would declare unconstitutional."[28]

In *Rostker v. Goldberg*, Rehnquist proved their prediction to be correct,
and the impact of his opinion would be monumental in two respects. First,
it cemented a sweeping doctrine of judicial deference on military issues
that would lead courts to withdraw from any serious role in ensuring that
military personnel policies respected constitutional principles. Second,
and more insidiously, the new doctrine of judicial deference would make it
possible for Congress and courts to hide behind a facade of deference to
professional military advice while disregarding the same advice. Ironically,
the effect of the doctrine of judicial deference would be, in many instances,
to diminish the importance of military values and expertise, making it possible to use military policy to achieve goals that were not necessarily consistent with military effectiveness. It allowed civilians to construct a
fantasy military from which they could draw whatever make-believe

expertise was necessary to back their judgments and protect themselves from criticism.

I probably don't need to explain what happened when Captain S. Simcha Goldman claimed that an Air Force regulation on proper wear of the uniform violated his constitutional right to free exercise of religion under the First Amendment. In *Goldman v. Weinberger*,[29] a 1986 Supreme Court decision, Justice Rehnquist completed his unprecedented trilogy of cases on civil-military relations that began with *Parker v. Levy* and *Rostker v. Goldberg* by minimizing constitutional values of religious freedom and religious diversity within the military. Rehnquist's opinion held that the government need not explain with any specificity why it was necessary to restrict the wearing of religious symbols while in uniform, just as his earlier opinions held that the government need not explain with any specificity why it was necessary to punish servicemembers for speech critical of the Vietnam War, or why it was necessary to exclude women from responsibility for national service.

In 1981, Captain Goldman was serving as a clinical psychologist in the mental health clinic at March Air Force Base in Riverside, California. He was completing a term of military service he owed to the government in exchange for receiving financial aid under an armed forces scholarship program, and he hoped to continue serving in the military beyond his initial obligation. In a classic example of being in the wrong place at the wrong time, however, Goldman's legal problems began when he was called to testify in an unrelated court-martial as a witness for the defense. He appeared in court wearing his customary yarmulke, which he wore as a badge of devotion to his religious faith both on and off duty, and in and out of uniform. In addition to being a military officer, Goldman was an Orthodox Jew and an ordained rabbi.

The Air Force had never had a problem with Goldman's yarmulke before the court-martial. Goldman spent most of his time in uniform working inside the base hospital, and when he was outdoors his yarmulke was hidden from view by the standard service cap. The prosecutor at the court-martial nonetheless filed a complaint with the hospital commander and reported Goldman for violating Air Force regulations on uniform dress, which generally forbid wearing hats of any kind while indoors. One can speculate on the prosecutor's motive, but if Goldman's yarmulke affected the court-martial, the prosecutor would have complained to the military judge. If the prosecutor wanted to see Goldman punished, however, he needed to complain to Goldman's superior.

The hospital commander ordered Goldman to stop wearing a yarmulke while in uniform, but Goldman was steadfast in his refusal to comply even after he was formally reprimanded, threatened with court-martial, and recommended for discharge. He brought suit against the secretary of defense, arguing that the First Amendment required the Air Force to grant a religious exception to its usual rules for wearing the uniform unless it could show that an exception would undermine military discipline and morale. Goldman conceded that the constitutional freedom to freely exercise his religion while serving in the military was not absolute and that his religious observance might have to give way under compelling circumstances. He saw no reason, however, why the wearing of a yarmulke under his particular circumstances would create a problem for military discipline, and he thought the Air Force had failed to demonstrate one.

Goldman v. Weinberger was not an easy case for Captain Goldman to win. Unlike *Rostker v. Goldberg*, in which Rehnquist pretended to defer to military expertise while ignoring the military's recommendation, here the Air Force argued it had a military reason for denying Goldman's request to wear a yarmulke. In essence, the Air Force argued that uniforms were supposed to be uniform, and deviations from the standard rules for wearing them, even for religious reasons, would detract from a sense of shared military purpose. While a yarmulke might seem unobtrusive and modest in the scheme of possible variations servicemembers might choose as an expression of their religious beliefs, the Air Force may have had valid concerns about future cases seeking religious exceptions. Where would it end? Perhaps servicemembers would ask for exceptions to standard rules for haircuts or facial hair, or they would want to wear religious symbols more "distracting" or "extreme" than a yarmulke. Perhaps the Air Force did not want to be in the business of favoring one religion over another, and a rule that prohibited all visible religious symbols was a neutral way of avoiding any controversy.

The Supreme Court could have decided the case in exactly the same way it decided other cases involving legal restrictions on the exercise of religious beliefs. Under existing precedent, it could have taken into account the special context of military service in deciding whether any limitation on religious freedom was narrowly targeted to achieve a purpose of compelling importance—the maintenance of good order and discipline—and was no broader than necessary to accomplish that goal.[30] All the Court needed to do was ask the Air Force to explain why, in its experience and expertise, an across-the-board denial of religious exceptions to rules about uniforms was necessary to maintain military discipline and morale. Having to explain *why* a certain policy is necessary is certainly more of a burden than being able to rest on bare, unsupported assertions of necessity. However, given the importance of the religious freedoms protected by the First Amendment and, in comparison, the less weighty concern of what members of the Air Force are wearing on their heads, it would seem that Goldman deserved at least that much consideration from the Air Force and from the Court.

For Justice Rehnquist, this was too much to ask. Instead of engaging Goldman's arguments on the merits, Rehnquist hid behind all the superficial slogans of judicial deference in military affairs he had been using since the end of the Vietnam War to keep the Constitution distant from the military and from its members. Once the military has stated its belief that exceptions for religious observance are inconsistent with military discipline, any further discussion of the Constitution was unnecessary. There was no need to pause and consider the nature of military discipline and whether it might be strong enough to bear the weight of religious diversity in this instance. Goldman had argued, with the support of experts, that granting such exceptions would actually strengthen morale "by making the Air Force a more humane place." Rehnquist's opinion abruptly concluded, however, that this was not a discussion that either the Air Force or the Court was obliged to have. If the Air Force believed it was right, then it *was* right.

Goldman lost more than the constitutional argument. Rehnquist painted him as selfish for wanting to combine service to country and the personal obligations of religious devotion. He dismissed Goldman's claims to religious freedom as the mere "desires and interests of the individual" and as insignificant "personal preferences" that must automatically give way to general assertions about "the needs of the service." Rehnquist compared Goldman's request for a religious exception to the sort of "debate" or "protest" that the military need not "tolerate." He seemed oblivious to the fact that the Air Force's ruling on the wearing of yarmulkes meant that Orthodox Jews such as Captain Goldman would not be able to serve in the military at all.

In all constitutional cases, whether decided under rational basis review, strict scrutiny, or something in between, it is important for courts to enforce customary rules that require the government to explain itself. The central purpose of constitutional standards of review is to force government justifications out into the open so courts—and citizens—can determine whether the government is abiding by the expectations and limitations of the Constitution. When the government's justifications and reasoning are on the table for everyone to see, litigants, courts, and members of the public can challenge their accuracy, if necessary, and weigh their persuasiveness.

By human nature, mischief follows when the Supreme Court departs from its usual method of constitutional analysis and instead excuses the government from the responsibility to prove it had valid reasons for its choices, particularly in circumstances that are already constitutionally suspicious. If the government no longer has to offer credible and supportable explanations in response to a constitutional challenge, two things are bound to happen. First, if the government knows it cannot be challenged for anything it asserts in a legal proceeding, it will be tempted to hide or misrepresent relevant facts that are embarrassing or fail to support the "right" answer. Second, judges and courts will be tempted to fill any gaps in the explanation with their own assumptions or beliefs, however inaccurate or misinformed they might be.

This is one of the fundamental analytical flaws of the Rehnquist trilogy of *Parker v. Levy*, *Rostker v. Goldberg*, and *Goldman v. Weinberger*. In all three cases, government institutions—Congress or the military itself—were able to shape and adjust the facts in a way that would lead to a particular result, without fear that anyone might say, for example, "Wait a minute . . . the argument you make today isn't supported by the available evidence or by any specific military knowledge or experience. It's just your opinion. And your argument in this case is inconsistent with what you've said or done on other occasions. Why is this situation different?"

Some of what Rehnquist wrote in *Goldman v. Weinberger* was comically uninformed; some of it was outrageous as a matter of law. Again he insisted, contrary to what students learn in their first year of law school, that courts had no role in civilian control of the military because the Constitution does not specifically mention the military in the Article 3 phrase "*all cases . . .* arising under this Constitution." Again he improvised his own idiosyncratic versions of military values and military necessity, rather than pushing the military to articulate and defend its professional expertise. It was enough that the Air Force offered the bare assertion that its regulations on uniform wear were absolutely necessary to good order and discipline—exactly as they were written, with no possible exceptions.

There was a certain humor in Rehnquist's assumption that the length of the Air Force's regulation on how to wear the uniform properly (190 pages at that time) demonstrated its concern for uniformity of appearance. What the regulation's length really showed was the dizzying array of uniform options the Air Force authorized despite its assertions about the importance of uniformity.[31] It's difficult to take the Air Force seriously on the issue of hats and military discipline when other authorized options for headgear include the wheel-shaped service cap, the foldable flight cap, the baseball cap, the winter cap, and the watch cap, not to mention other distinctive hats worn by flight crew members, security personnel, special operations personnel, and instructors.

Rehnquist also accepted at face value the Air Force's assertion that its rules for uniforms were intended to discourage the expression of "personal preferences and identities" and encourage "a sense of hierarchical unity by tending to eliminate outward individual distinctions except for those of rank." The statement has a superficial appeal, but the reality is that all the military services encourage their members to wear "outward individual distinctions" in the form of ribbons, badges, and other insignia that serve to distinguish one servicemember from another in terms of training, experience, merit, and valor. These distinctions are so informative that a servicemember can "read ribbons" on the uniform of a total stranger and understand at a glance where that person has served, the nature of his or her job duties and qualifications, and how well those duties have been performed. The uniform makes its wearer a walking resume, and so it was disingenuous for the military to defend the *Goldman* case on the basis that it is important to eliminate individual distinctions. The Air Force picks and chooses among many possible individual distinctions, erasing some and welcoming others.

Congress later reversed the result of *Goldman v. Weinberger* by passing a law allowing servicemembers to wear "an item of religious apparel," including a head covering, provided it was "neat and conservative" and would not "interfere with the performance of the member's military duties."[32] It wasn't that hard. The "neat and conservative" standard Congress settled on was easily borrowed from already existing Air Force rules on the wear of jewelry in uniform, demonstrating there was nothing inherently harmful in discussing how to harmonize the needs of the military with the protection of constitutional freedoms. Rehnquist, however, was determined to prevent courts from taking any part in that discussion, even though courts would have more expertise on the constitutional side of the question than either the military or Congress. He thought it was "quite beside the point" whether religious exceptions to uniform wear were a good idea or not, because the military "was under no constitutional mandate to abandon their considered professional judgment."[33] Think about the enormity of that statement. According to Justice Rehnquist, the military does not need to consider the Constitution when making a professional judgment.

In *Goldman v. Weinberger*, a few of the justices began to wake up to the reality that Rehnquist's trilogy of opinions on civil-military relations had fundamentally changed the constitutional balance of civilian control of the military. Two of the dissenters had it exactly right when they described the new reality of the military's relationship to law and the Constitution: "If a branch of the military declares one of its rules sufficiently important to outweigh a service person's constitutional rights, it seems that the Court will accept that conclusion, no matter how absurd or unsupported it may be." Justice Sandra Day O'Connor wrote her own separate dissent to express how disappointed she was that the Court had discarded its traditional constitutional principles, which she believed were "sufficiently flexible to take into account the special importance of defending our Nation without abandoning completely the freedoms that make it worth defending." It was as if they had just noticed how far the Rehnquist transformation had gone in separating the military from the Constitution, but by then it was far too late.

Chapter 5

Constitutional Bargains and Military Ethics

I've been asked to explain how a few obscure pronouncements from the Supreme Court could possibly affect the military's character or its distinctive culture. People laugh and say, "Come on. Show me a nineteen-year-old who knows anything about what Supreme Court justices say in cases involving the military. It doesn't make sense to think court opinions could possibly affect who chooses to join the military or change how the military sees its relationship to civilian society." I think they're right that the typical young person contemplating military service knows little, and may care even less, about how our highest court decides military cases or how it treats servicemembers who raise constitutional grievances. I would also agree that most members of the military—even the most senior officers—do not read opinions of the Supreme Court so they can better understand civilian control of the military, the scope of military authority, or their responsibility for military ethics and leadership. The link that ties the work of the Supreme Court to the character of our military, unfortunately, is not nearly so direct. If it was, it would be easier to see the problem.

The signs of weakening civil-military relations and decaying civilian control can appear in ways that fail to make much of an impression. Consider, for example, this letter to the editor published in the *Gainesville Sun*, the local newspaper in the hometown of my employer, the University of Florida, on March 28, 2004:

> I am in the Army ROTC program at the University of Florida and would like to say that myself and many other cadets within the program support our president and his re-election. Many of us are working to re-elect our president in hopes to serve under him as officers in the military upon graduating. President Bush's leadership is outstanding and myself and other cadets will follow him in whatever he may do.

I was dismayed to see this letter, to say the least. One of the most important lessons ROTC cadets should be learning in their training to become officers is that the military has a professional obligation to remain politically neutral and nonpartisan. Servicemembers cannot trade on their military status or on the uniform they wear in an effort to influence elections or benefit partisan candidates or causes. If this ROTC cadet had been serving on active duty, his letter would have violated a regulation that prohibits servicemembers from soliciting votes for political candidates. Servicemembers are allowed to express political opinions, but only as individuals and not as representatives of the military.[1]

The cadet's letter to the editor was much more than personal political opinion. He believed his endorsement had special value specifically because he was a ROTC cadet, someone who knew more—or at least thought he knew more—than the average citizen about the commander in chief's qualifications. Worse yet, in emphasizing how eagerly his fellow cadets would follow President George W. Bush's orders, he suggested they might be somewhat less enthusiastic in following orders given by the Democratic Party challenger, Senator John Kerry, if he became the commander in chief. This is exactly the kind of civil-military mischief that military regulations about political activities by servicemembers were designed to prevent. Even though he was still in training and not yet an officer, he should have respected this professional military ethic.

What was even more disappointing than the letter to the editor was finding that the active-duty military officers in charge of this ROTC detachment had little interest in educating cadets on the military ethics of political neutrality or in correcting the mistaken impression this letter gave the public. I contacted these officers privately to ask that the cadet retract the letter and explain to *Gainesville Sun* readers that it was inappropriate for servicemembers to suggest certain political candidates carried the military's endorsement. I discovered the officers were much more upset at the idea of a law professor meddling in their ROTC program than they were at the news that one of their cadets had behaved unprofessionally. In the end, we had to agree to disagree. They were clearly angry that I had questioned the behavior of one of their students, and no one ever corrected or retracted the cadet's letter to the editor. As far as I know, the cadet was never educated on this critically important point of professional military ethics.

As a result, the public was left with a dangerous misunderstanding about the military's role in civilian politics. I suspect very few readers realized that ROTC cadets ignore an important civil-military tradition, and cross a significant ethical line, when they try to award the military's endorsement to a particular political candidate or party. One of the clearest signs of decline in healthy civil-military relations, however, is when the civilian world is so distant and removed from military experience and military culture that it no longer has the ability—and, too often, not even the inclination or interest—to play its proper role in our constitutional system for civilian control of the military.

By the mid-1990s, a handful of experts on military affairs were beginning to notice that something could be very wrong in the relationship between the military and civilian society. They had an intuitive sense the military might be drifting off course in a way that threatened some of the most basic assumptions about military professionalism and strong civilian control. Most fundamentally, they worried that a growing distance between civilian and military worlds—the "civil-military gap," as it came to be called—could be changing the nature of the military in ways that were not healthy for either the military or for the civilian society it served. Strikingly, the people who sensed the change had professional ties to the military as veterans, as academics in military fields, or as specialized journalists on military and defense matters. They were not people normally quick to criticize the military, yet they all saw the same problem from their different professional perspectives. They spoke out of deep respect for the military and a genuine uneasiness about the state of our civil-military relations.

It was no coincidence that experts began to notice a shift in civil-military relations about twenty years after the end of the draft, or roughly one generation in terms of a military career. By the mid-1990s, the military was no longer as broadly representative of civilian society as it used to be when the draft circulated a more diverse range of young people through the experience of military service. It was also no coincidence that experts began to notice something was different about twenty years after the Supreme Court started ridiculing the idea that constitutional ideals such as free speech, equal protection, and religious freedom had meaning and value in military settings. The Court's post-Vietnam decisions had set the military apart as a special "Constitution-free" zone, one that was distant and disconnected from civilian society and its legal norms. If this legal transformation was going to cause a shift in military culture or shape the self-selective process of enlistment we depend upon to build an all-volunteer military, the time was right in the mid-1990s to begin to see its effects.

Academic research into the civil-military gap began with a spark from an unlikely source. Scholars were drawn to the topic largely through the work of a journalist, Tom Ricks, who at the time was a senior Pentagon reporter for the *Wall Street Journal*. In 1995, Ricks followed a platoon of Marine Corps recruits from the start of basic training at Parris Island, South Carolina, through the end of their first year of military service. His book about the experience would transform the way political scientists and sociologists studied the military. *Making the Corps*[2] took the politically incorrect position that the military was changing in ways that threatened the stability of civil-military relations. Ricks believed the military was becoming more politically partisan—"Republicanized," as he called it—at the same time it was developing a dangerous sense of moral superiority in its relationship to civilian society. He wrote that servicemembers "seem to look down on American society" and had a "new contempt" for civilians that was so deep it led Ricks to wonder seriously whether civilians and their perceived shortcomings might one day become the military's new enemy.[3]

This was very strong stuff, indeed. Some military officers and civilian military researchers listened, however, because Ricks had the conservative credentials of his distinguished military reporting and his affiliation with the *Wall Street Journal*.[4] They also listened because they had seen the same disturbing trend themselves. One retired admiral, for example, the senior commander of naval forces during the first Gulf War and later the vice chief of naval operations, made the observation that "the armed forces are no longer representative of the people they serve. More and more, enlisted as well as officers are beginning to feel that they are special, better than the society they serve. This is not healthy in an armed force serving a democracy."[5]

Experts who had spent a career either serving in the military or studying the military, or both, expressed concern about its ugly turn toward intense political partisanship. They were disturbed at the rise of fierce loyalty to the Republican Party within the military community, and they mourned the loss of the traditional, "old school" military in which aloofness from politics was a marker of military professionalism.[6] One influential article, aptly entitled "Out of Control: The Crisis in Civil-Military Relations," did not pull any punches:

> [T]he professional military became politicized, abandoning its century-and-a-half tradition of non-partisanship. It began thinking, voting, and even espousing Republicanism with a capital R. . . . In the wake of Vietnam, the officer corps began to attract a larger percentage of people from the most traditional or conservative parts of the country. The switch from the draft to all-volunteer forces further diminished whatever ideological diversity had existed in the officer corps. The military became even more traditional in its values: Republican, conservative, and increasingly conscious of itself as a separate entity in American society.[7]

Some of the worst partisanship was directed at President Bill Clinton in retaliation for his unsuccessful attempt to open military service to gay citizens; other servicemembers targeted Clinton for abuse because they thought he had dodged the draft or was insufficiently respectful of the military. Of course, it ought to go without saying (but, sadly, it doesn't) that even if these servicemembers believed they had good reasons for behaving disrespectfully toward their commander in chief, they still had a professional obligation to keep their insolence to themselves. It was difficult to understand how we ever got to the point where generals and admirals had to remind members of the military that ridiculing, jeering, or mocking the president of the United States was not in their job description. Their behavior was a breach of their professional obligation of subordination to civilian control and, if that was not enough to get their attention, it was also a potential criminal violation of the Uniform Code of Military Justice.[8]

Sometimes the generals themselves were the instigators of insubordination, as when the Air Force's two-star Harold N. Campbell referred to the president as "skirt chasing," "draft dodging," and "dope smoking" in remarks made at a military event. Sometimes senior members of Congress egged the military on, as when North Carolina Senator Jesse Helms encouraged soldiers—jokingly, I'm sure—to consider committing a violent act against their commander in chief. In advance of the president's 1994 visit to North Carolina military bases, Senator Helms said: "Mr. Clinton better watch out if he comes down here. He'd better have a bodyguard."[9] I think most people today forget how out of control the situation was.

The problem was far greater than open disrespect of the commander in chief, although that was surely more than enough of a problem in itself. Scholars were seeing a broader contempt and disrespect from members of the military directed against the "wrong" political party (the Democrats), against branches of government controlled by that party, or even against federal laws associated with or defended by that party. "Out of Control" described a particular instance in which Senator Strom Thurmond was being honored with an award from the Association of the United States Army. When a speaker at the event noted that Thurmond had changed his party affiliation from Democratic to Republican in 1964, the uniformed audience burst into applause. This was an astoundingly unprofessional display in terms of the military's ethic of political neutrality, and the only thing that prevents it from being a racist display as well is a charitable judgment that these senior servicemembers were unaware of what led Thurmond to change political parties. Thurmond switched parties out of resistance to a developing consensus that civil rights should be afforded to everyone regardless of race, a movement that led to enactment of the Civil Rights Act of 1964.[10]

Interestingly, one senior defense official was quick to embrace the new and controversial idea of a civil-military gap, but he believed such a gap could only be a good thing. William Cohen, secretary of defense during President Clinton's administration, once lectured the Yale Law School community on the appropriateness, even the necessity, of a civil-military gap drawn along lines of moral superiority. He couldn't understand why it would be a problem if "this group of highly educated, highly motivated, highly disciplined [military] individuals might be looking down their noses with contempt upon contemporary society whose standards were not quite as high or rigid or moral."[11] If, as he believed, members of the military did have higher moral standards than the civilians they served, why shouldn't they feel a little contempt? Secretary Cohen failed to recognize, however, how intoxicating and dangerous a government license of moral superiority can be in the modern political climate, particularly when the license is granted to the military.

Making the Corps was a critically important book because it created a space for speaking freely about aspects of modern military culture that, until then, had been taboo and untouchable. Researchers began to consider three separate but interrelated issues. The first question was whether the military was becoming less representative of civilian society, especially in ways that could be more constitutionally significant than the typical demographics of race and sex. The second question was whether the military was abandoning, or perhaps had already abandoned, its traditional professional and constitutional ethic of political neutrality. The third and final question was whether an increasing distance between military and civilian worlds had made the military resentful or contemptuous of civilian society and more likely to view itself as morally superior or "better" than the rest of America. Ricks saw the essential connection that could tie these three questions together. Although civilian society certainly had its problems, he warned that it was a different matter "to propose that it is the role of the military— especially an all-volunteer, professional military oriented to a conservative Republicanism—to fix those problems."[12]

The provocative conclusions of *Making the Corps* were reinforced in research published by Duke University political scientist Ole Holsti.[13] Professor Holsti's research documented dramatic changes in the political partisanship of military officers, a trend consistent with Ricks's more intuitive observations about the all-volunteer military. Between 1976 and 1996, essentially the first generation to follow the end of the Vietnam draft, the proportion of military officers who identified themselves as Republicans doubled, from one-third to two-thirds. The reason there were so many more Republican military officers in 1996, however, was not because there were that many fewer Democratic military officers. Instead, in the space of two decades, there had been a sharp decrease—by half—in the proportion of military officers describing their political allegiance as "independent" or "other or none." The most important trend, in terms of military professionalism, was not simply a shift in allegiance from one political party to another—it was a shift from political neutrality to political partisanship.

Professor Holsti's findings were troubling because they showed the military was moving away from its traditional professional ethic of political neutrality and toward a new expectation of political partisanship, one that cut largely in favor of the Republican Party. His findings showed a significant cultural and political development within the all-volunteer military that was much more extreme than any comparable civilian trends during the same period. More ominously, his findings revealed a new disrespect within the military for what used to be a settled understanding of its proper apolitical role.

Samuel Huntington, the author of one of the classic twentieth-century works on civil-military relations, *The Soldier and the State*, believed the United States had strong civilian control of its armed forces because the military had internalized an ethic of political neutrality as part of its professional identity. Huntington drew a strict professional line separating military duty and civilian politics: "Politics is beyond the scope of military competence, and the participation of military officers in politics undermines their professionalism, curtailing their professional competence, dividing the profession against itself, and substituting extraneous values for professional values. The military officer must remain neutral politically."[14] Another notable book on civil-military relations also written during the early Cold War years, *The Professional Soldier*, made the same point: "According to the definitions of military honor, the professional soldier is 'above politics' in domestic affairs," and therefore "generals and admirals do not attach themselves to political parties or overtly display partisanship."[15] This was nothing new, even fifty years ago. Political neutrality has long been an entirely uncontroversial, unremarkable component of the professional military ethic.

Throughout our nation's history, Congress has also played an important role in preventing an unhealthy mix of military service and politics. A number of federal statutes are specifically designed to enforce the constitutional assumption of a politically neutral military. For example, military personnel cannot be stationed at voting locations.[16] They cannot use force, threat, intimidation, or even well-intentioned advice in an effort to prevent qualified persons from exercising their right to vote, and they cannot use their military authority to influence how, or whether, other servicemembers vote.[17] The last thing we want as a democracy is to create the impression that the people who carry the guns also control the elections. Civilians must also respect the same principles. For example, they cannot ask or poll members of the military about how they intend to vote or how they did vote,[18] although I wonder how many hundreds of times this law was violated in November 2000, when everyone wanted to know whether late-arriving absentee ballots from overseas voters could tip the outcome of the presidential election.

The United States Supreme Court—at least the Court prior to the Rehnquist revolution in civil-military relations—had the same understanding about the place of politics in military affairs and the place of the military in political affairs. The Court has pointedly emphasized that a healthy, constitutional relationship between the military and civilian society, including strong civilian control of the military, depends vitally on the military's scrupulous observance of political neutrality. In 1976, just after the end of the draft and the beginning of the new all-volunteer force, *Greer v. Spock*[19] held that the military had a constitutional responsibility to avoid "both the reality and the appearance of acting as a handmaiden for partisan political causes or candidates," and that this obligation was "wholly consistent with the American constitutional tradition of a politically neutral military establishment under civilian control." Under these principles, the Court gave the commander of Fort Dix Army Reservation in New Jersey the authority, despite the First Amendment's protections for free speech, to bar a presidential candidate from handing out campaign literature or holding a political event on post.

In a separate opinion filed in the same case, Chief Justice Warren Burger noted that the military's political neutrality is "a 200-year tradition of keeping the military separate from political affairs, a tradition that in my view is a constitutional corollary to the express provision for civilian control of the military." The chief justice ended his commentary with a few words of caution to remind us that the tradition of nonpartisanship within the military profession has not always been a perfect one, and that we must be alert to the very human possibility of ethical and constitutional weakness:

> History demonstrates, I think, that the real threat to the independence and neutrality of the military—and the need to maintain as nearly as possible a true "wall" of separation—comes not from the kind of literature that would fall within the prohibition [barring distribution of literature on post without prior approval], but from the risk that a military commander might attempt to "deliver" his men's votes for a major-party candidate. . . . It is only a little more than a century ago that some officers of the Armed Forces, then in combat, sought to exercise undue influence for President Lincoln or for his opponent, General McClellan, in the election of 1864.

A third justice in *Greer v. Spock*, Lewis Powell, wrote yet another opinion to drive home the same concern about inappropriate political influence between civilian and military worlds. He was also worried about the potential for improper political influence *within* military society, where the power of rank might be used to sway opinions or votes. What is most fascinating about this third opinion, however, is that it reveals just how much civil-military politics have changed in the last thirty-five years. Justice Powell's description is now so far off the mark it could make you laugh, if it wasn't such a serious issue. He wrote the following in 1976:

> The exclusion of political rallies and face-to-face campaigning from a military base furthers both the appearance and the reality of political neutrality on the part of the military. Such an exclusion, for example, makes it less likely that candidates will fashion partisan appeals addressed to members of the Armed Services rather than to the public at large, whereas compelling bases to be open to campaigning would invite such appeals. Traditionally, candidates for

office have observed scrupulously the principle of a politically neutral military and have not sought to identify or canvass a "military vote." . . .

Even if no direct appeals to the military audience were made, the mere fact that one party or candidate consistently draws large crowds on military bases while another attracts only spotty attendance could and probably would be interpreted by the news media and the civilian public as indicating that the military supports one as opposed to the other. Questions also could arise as to whether pressures, direct or indirect, to support one candidate or rally more generously than another were being exerted by commanders over enlisted personnel.

This picture is a stunning one because it is so different from the way things work now that we have an all-volunteer military. Today, we regularly speculate about which candidate or party will benefit the most from "the military vote." Incumbent politicians eagerly use the military as a patriotic backdrop to their activities, very much hoping that voters will assume their proposals carry the military's support. They completely disregard the Court's earlier caution about political appeals to the military—if they ever understood why it was a problem for military professionalism to begin with—and they openly jockey for position as "the military's candidate." No one blinks.

Politicians encourage the military to choose political sides even when they really ought to know better. Senator John McCain, the 2008 Republican presidential nominee and a career naval officer, enlisted seven uniformed servicemembers to stand by his side at a September 2007 campaign event in New Hampshire, an early primary state that was critically important to the party's nomination. The rally had an explicit military theme—the "No Surrender Tour"—and the soldiers identified themselves by rank and their wartime service before endorsing McCain and his views on how best to conduct the war in Iraq. Violations of the military's ethic of political neutrality don't get much worse than this, yet the Army took no disciplinary action against the soldiers or their superiors.[20] Neither did anyone on the civilian side ask Senator McCain why he had encouraged such a clear ethical lapse by these servicemembers, or had at least looked the other way.

Another instance that stands out for its sheer audaciousness and visual impact was President George W. Bush's speech to the Army's 101st Airborne Division in March 2004, the one-year anniversary of the Iraq invasion. The soldiers whooped and hollered for the cameras like they were at a political rally, interrupting the president with enthusiastic, boisterous applause on more than forty occasions.[21] The president's campaign aides were reported to say that this visit to Fort Campbell, eight months before the 2004 presidential election, was part of a concerted effort to portray him to the voters as a steady commander in chief.[22] Such a plainly partisan use of the military should have at least raised some eyebrows, if not complaints, but it passed entirely without notice. We have apparently reached the point where partisan use of the military is more the norm than the exception.

Worse yet, these instances reveal how easily the political pressure that civilians place on the military can migrate inside the military profession itself. The more that civilians attempt to politicize the military, the greater the risk that servicemembers themselves will feel a professional expectation to conform their views accordingly. A West Point professor told Tom Ricks that cadets were somehow learning that open allegiance to the Republican Party was "part of the implicit definition of being a member of the officer corps." An internal Navy survey found a similar trend toward political conservatism at the Naval Academy. Midshipmen who were not that different politically from their civilian peers twenty years ago were now sharply more conservative. That's a significant degree of change at both West Point and Annapolis given that the same twenty years have brought more women and racial minorities into the federal military academies, groups one might expect to lean more toward liberal or progressive viewpoints and temper the force of conservative trends.[23] Perhaps cadets and midshipmen sense, or perhaps they have been told, what side of the military bread has the butter on it.

Ten years after Ricks made his observations, the problem apparently persists at the academies. A new secretary of defense, Robert Gates, was the graduation speaker for newly commissioned officers at the Naval Academy and the Air Force Academy in the summer of 2007, and he felt the need to remind graduates of their professional obligation to treat members of Congress with respect regardless of political party. For this point to be a subject of the secretary's attention on graduation day is very revealing, but as with most discussions of civil-military relations, it received little attention. People don't realize that political partisanship within the military undermines professional military ethics because they don't understand enough about the military or the relationship it should have to civilian authority. Gates also slipped in a short constitutional lesson for those who might need one:

> The Congress is a co-equal branch of government that under the Constitution raises armies and provides for navies. Members of both parties now serving in Congress have long been strong supporters of the Department of Defense, and of our men and women in uniform. As officers, you will have a responsibility to communicate to those below you that the American military must be nonpolitical and recognize the obligation we owe the Congress to be honest and true in our reporting to them.[24]

The corrosive effects of political partisanship can and do cascade through the military like a line of dominoes. Two recent examples illustrate the problem. In 2007, members of Congress visiting Iraq as part of their constitutional responsibility to make informed decisions when funding the war effort accidentally discovered that military personnel were vetting them in advance for their political support of the president and his views on the war. Senior officials and rank-and-file servicemembers alike carried sheets of paper that identified congressional visitors as presidential supporters or critics, apparently so military escorts would know how hospitable or forthcoming with information they should be. Representative Ellen Tauscher of California described the politically partisan biographies as "being slimed in the Green Zone."[25]

The 2008 presidential election once again raised the temperature of political partisanship within the military, and in a predictable direction. The Army had to issue a memo to soldiers in its medical command instructing them to stop using military computer networks to circulate chain e-mails falsely charging that Barack Obama was a Muslim and had attended radical religious schools.[26] The memo warned against violations of Army regulations prohibiting unauthorized use of government communications equipment and on-duty political activity. It says a great deal about the state of the military's professional ethic of political neutrality that the thousands of servicemembers sending or receiving the messages did not realize there was any problem with using military equipment to influence an election.

The chairman of the Joint Chiefs of Staff, Admiral Michael G. Mullen, took a very unusual course in trying to impress upon members of the military the critical importance of abiding by their professional and constitutional ethic of political neutrality during the 2008 election season. He wrote an open letter directed to all servicemembers that was published in the journal of the National Defense University, *Joint Force Quarterly*, entitled "From the Chairman: Military Must Stay Apolitical." Such a strong statement of one of the military's most basic professional obligations should not be necessary, but sadly it was. The admiral felt the need to remind members of the military that their responsibility was to all Americans, not only those with a compatible brand of politics:

> I am not suggesting that military professionals abandon all personal opinion about modern social or political issues. . . . What I am suggesting—indeed, what the Nation expects—is that military personnel will, in the execution of the mission assigned to them, put aside their partisan leanings. Political opinions have no place in cockpit or camp or conference room. We do not wear our politics on our sleeves. . . . We defend all Americans, everywhere, regardless of their age, race, gender, creed, and, yes, political affiliation.[27]

Another consequence of pervasive political partisanship in the military, one that very few think about, is its effect on propensity to enlist. Young people become more or less likely to join the military, depending on whether they see themselves as ideologically compatible with the military's political image. Trends of self-selection like this can only increase the likelihood of a military that is less representative of civilian society, more politically partisan than the ideals of military professionalism would normally allow and, finally, more contemptuous and disapproving of civilian society than is healthy in a democratic society. These are all the same trends that military experts sensed were developing in the 1990s. In the decade to follow, empirical research in military sociology and political science would begin to provide some explanations.

The Triangle Institute for Security Studies, a consortium of university experts in defense and military affairs, conducted a large research study designed to test the anecdotal arguments for and against the existence of a civil-military gap. Its Project on the Gap between the Military and Civilian Society was based on information obtained from a large and diverse survey of Americans: elite military officers with top promotion potential, influential civilian leaders of the "Who's Who" variety, and also an assortment of regular people drawn from civilian society as a whole.[28] Survey respondents gave their opinions on a variety of topics that might reveal a gap of politics, ideology, or culture between civilian and military societies, including issues such as national defense, foreign policy, civil-military relations, political partisanship, constitutional values, social and economic policy, the media, morality, and religion. In other words, the Gap Project asked not whether the military looks like America, but whether it *thinks* like America.

Researchers wanted to know whether thirty-five years of reliance on self-selected volunteers had produced a military that was no longer ideologically representative of civilian society. The military takes credit, some deserved and some undeserved, for developing and strengthening diversity on the basis of race and sex. At the same time, however, it may have lost much of what is really the most important kind of diversity for purposes of civil-military relations: the political, ideological, and cultural diversity that preserves the bond between civilian society and the military and also protects and strengthens civilian control of the military under the Constitution.

The results of the Gap Project survey confirmed many of the concerns that Ricks raised in his groundbreaking work, *Making the Corps*. Several key findings stood out from the mass of survey data. First, there were some areas of significant difference and distance that separated the military and civilian respondents and showed a distinctive cultural gap. For example, the military viewed itself as starkly more conservative than civilian society in general. By itself, this would not be terribly important, because it is entirely reasonable for different professions to embrace different cultural expectations or values based on the nature of their work or their special responsibilities. The military has a very distinctive mission in comparison to civilian America, and one would expect to see that special purpose reflected in the general beliefs or characteristics of people serving in the military.

The civil-military gap, however, becomes an important concern when the nature of the divide between civilian and military worlds cuts against the grain of military professionalism or constitutional tradition. The Gap Project found that a prominent part of the civil-military divide was the military's fierce political and ideological connection to the Republican Party, despite the professional military ethic that discourages displays of political partisanship. Another troubling finding was that military respondents (although not civilian respondents) tended to view the gap separating military and civilian cultures as not just a point of difference but as an indication of moral worth and superiority. The results strongly affirmed the sense of vague unease in some military experts that the military had come to view itself not as different from America, but as better than America.

An increase in political partisanship within the military is typically one of the first and most noticeable signs of civil-military deterioration because it runs so directly against the military's core ethic of political neutrality. Using the new data set from the Gap Project, Professor Ole Holsti confirmed all the same trends he found in his earlier research.[29] Among "up-and-coming" elite military officers, self-identified Republicans out-numbered Democrats by a factor of eight to one (64 percent to 8 percent), with only 28 percent declaring an affiliation of "independent" or "other or none." Twenty years earlier, at the beginning of the all-volunteer force, 55 percent—twice as many—of a similar sample identified themselves as independent. Holsti's most amazing finding was that active-duty military officers claimed a partisan political affiliation more frequently than any other group in the survey except for civilian leaders who were military veterans. Members of the general public (both veteran and nonveteran) and nonveteran civilian leaders were more likely to be politically neutral than military officers *who have an ethical and constitutional duty* to be politically neutral. It's an absolutely stunning result. The only people in the survey with a professional obligation to *avoid* partisan political entanglements turned out to be more politically partisan than almost everyone else.

Holsti believed the Gap Project data might have actually understated the size of the partisan divide between military and civilian worlds, based on the many e-mails he received from members of the military commenting on the study and the consequences of a civil-military gap. For example, one officer shared this reaction:

> I am sorry to say that you would not believe the fierce Republican partisanship of what seems to me to be the preponderance of my fellow officers, especially when confronted with President Clinton's ongoing crisis. What troubles me most about my fellow officers is the general contempt they hold for civilian society.

The all-volunteer military's shift to stronger political partisanship has been accelerated and magnified by other political and demographic trends. First, the active-duty military today is dramatically smaller—one-third smaller—than it was in the 1980s, and a reduction in size tends to concentrate the impact of self-selection as fewer new recruits step in to replace a larger number of separating and retiring personnel. Second, the ideological homogeneity or uniformity of the all-volunteer force has been enhanced by a significant "legacy" factor. Children of servicemembers are now much more likely to serve in the military than peers without that family experience, to such a degree that a former secretary of the Navy, John Lehman, expressed concern about developing a permanent "military caste" in our society.[30] Third, a particularly powerful trend affecting the military's political identification has been the rise of the Republican Party in the South since the beginning of the civil rights era. A disproportionately high number of new recruits, measured as a percentage of the population, come from the South (and a disproportionately low number from the Midwest and the Northeast), and so the shift in the region's political allegiance inevitably spills over into an all-volunteer military that draws more heavily from that part of the country.[31] Fourth, and finally, the military's national presence has also been skewed "southern" by congressional decisions to close military installations for cost-saving purposes. A disproportionately high number of bases and posts have been closed in the Northeast and the West, places where the land tends to be more expensive, the civilian neighbors tend to live closer to the noise and disruption of military activity, and the population tends to be more politically liberal.[32]

Holsti also found that ideological perspectives were closely paired with allegiance to political parties. Only 4 percent of the military elite identified themselves to any degree left of moderate. A disproportionately high number—two-thirds—of the military respondents reported they were either somewhat or very conservative, although their answers to specific questions suggested what they meant by "conservative" was a very narrow form of social conservatism rather than a more general economic or "small government" conservatism. Questions about defense and foreign policy did not distinguish servicemembers from civilians to any great degree, which seems surprising, given the very different stakes the two groups had in these areas. In contrast, the civil-military gap was most profound with respect to social values.

The civil-military gap across the ideological spectrum tended to be greatest when the questions prompted respondents to judge whether the military was morally superior to the rest of America. Military respondents were twice as likely as their civilian peers to agree that "through leading by example, the military could help American society become more moral," and they were three times as likely to agree that "civilian society would be better off if it adopted more of the military's values and customs." Broad moral judgments were disproportionately attractive to the military. For example, elite officers thought it was very important to preserve categorical distinctions between "moral" and "immoral" behavior, and they were less than one-third as likely as their civilian peers to agree with the statement "the world is changing and we should adjust our view of what is moral and immoral behavior to fit these changes."

This finding that the size of the civil-military gap grows when the focus is on broad themes of social conservatism and moral values is an illuminating one. Our society is most divided about the meaning of the Constitution when it touches social and moral issues, such as the equality of persons under law or the role of religious belief in secular government. Whenever the government uses the military as a platform for taking a position on controversial constitutional issues, establishing rules for the military that might otherwise violate the Constitution in a civilian context, those rules inevitably involve notions of public morality and favor the preferences of social conservatives. A substantial civil-military gap in ideology that focuses narrowly on social conservatism is troubling because it suggests an ideology primarily based on resistance to constitutional values or principles.

One only has to think back as far as the Rehnquist trilogy of civil-military cases to see the principle in action. In *Parker v. Levy* (antiwar protest), *Rostker v. Goldberg* (equal rights and obligations of citizenship for women), and *Goldman v. Weinberger* (free exercise of religion by those outside majority faiths), differences between military and civilian perspectives on social values and moral judgment—or at least differences in how the Court portrayed them—were in the forefront. In all three, the bottom line was the Court's ruling that military society could serve as a safe harbor from the usual constitutional expectations that would apply elsewhere in America. The military could be used to validate and reinforce socially conservative viewpoints on the scope and meaning of constitutional rights in the areas of free speech, equal rights, and religious freedom, even if these purposes were only distantly related, if at all, to military effectiveness.

In August 2007, the Army held a formal event to announce a new center for professional military study, the Army Center of Excellence for the Professional Military Ethic at the United States Military Academy at West Point. The center would be part of an initiative aimed at "bolstering the moral and ethical foundations of military service." The vice chief of staff of the Army, a four-star general, spoke to an audience of cadets, faculty, and graduates about the importance of professional military ethics, the code that "guides leaders to choose the harder right over the easier wrong."[33]

This new Army Center of Excellence was a great idea. West Point, the Army's premier institute for leadership training, was the right place for an educational center that brought together Armywide wisdom on military ethics. What was a problem, however, was General Richard Cody's explanation of why young officers should care about their ethical and moral development. He told these officers, the cream of the Army's present and future crop of leaders, that it was their responsibility to provide moral guidance not only to the men and women they would lead in military service but also to the rest of America. He said: "You are the moral compass and strength of this nation. You are the promise that no matter what the disaster, no matter the conflict, no matter the war . . . this institution will not bend, this Army will not bow and this nation will never break."

The Army is "the moral compass" of the nation? With all due respect to the military, this is not part of a professional soldier's duty, or at least it was not thought to be before the advent of the modern all-volunteer military. A sense of moral superiority, however, has become an important part of how the military views itself and its role in relation to civilian America. Two political scientists working with the Gap Project data described the phenomenon using the phrase "moral crisis," which they defined as "a negative view of society's moral health and a belief that the military is morally superior."[34] Military service, they found, was strongly associated with a belief that America is in that moral crisis. Few of the elite military respondents had anything good to say about civilian America, and they were much more likely than civilian peers to believe the military had a responsibility to do something about it. The authors concluded this perception of moral superiority was a symptom of a dangerously alienated military.

Not one of the Gap Project researchers considered the possibility that their findings showed how successful the Supreme Court has been in pushing the military away from civilian society and weakening its bond to our shared constitutional values. Justice Rehnquist's legal road map was a perfect fit for what the all-volunteer military had become. The Gap Project revealed that the military viewed itself as sharply different from American society, particularly along certain narrow ideological lines. Those ideological differences tended to be the most extreme in the areas in which Rehnquist encouraged a civil-military gap to grow—those most closely related to constitutional values and constitutional obligations. Under Rehnquist's theory of civil-military relations, the military was so different, so separate, and so remote from civilian society that we should exempt it from those constitutional expectations. If you tell an institution like the military that it is different—and different in a particularly privileged way—you can expect it will gradually but steadily become more different.

Even some of the most respected scholar-soldiers today parrot the Supreme Court's words about the military's moral superiority over civilian society. In an editorial in the *Los Angeles Times*, a lawyer who is also an Army military police officer, an Iraq veteran, and a prolific and thoughtful writer on civil-military relations—someone not normally inclined to overstatement—offered his opinion on the moral status of civilian America (with my emphasis added):

> *Soldiers and civilians also share a different moral code.* . . . Soldiers exist for their team; they will do anything for love of their brothers and sisters in uniform. Civilians, by contrast, live for themselves . . . pursuing their self-interest above all else, seeking enrichment and gratification. To be sure, Americans engage in a great deal of altruism, and this is to be praised too. But the sporadic acts of selfless service performed by civilians cannot compare to the life of service chosen by our military personnel.[35]

If the military lives by a standard that is higher than that of law, then it must also be above the law. This kind of moral comparison between civilian and military life has come to dominate much of our current thinking on issues involving the military. Once we have a matching Supreme Court doctrine—judicial deference to the military—teaching us that decisions involving the military need not be explained under the usual legal standards that apply to other parts of government, the effect is predictable. Institutions that do not have to explain how their conduct complies with the law tend to become annoyed when second-guessed. Institutions that do not have to explain their conduct also tend to become lazier in their decision making, because it is the anticipation of having to justify decisions and offer good reasons for a particular choice that sharpens the mind.

Particularly in today's climate of ostentatious patriotism, few citizens want to step forward and accept their constitutional responsibility to participate in thoughtful civilian control of the military. Undertaking this civic obligation seems to be, unfortunately, a no-win proposition. In the Gap Project survey, just over half of the elite military respondents thought they were not getting enough respect from the American people, a sense of entitlement that seems inconsistent with the idea of selfless service we normally associate with military duty.[36] But when the Supreme Court has been beating the drum for more than thirty-five years now about how civilians are incompetent to understand military issues and are undeserving of any serious role in military affairs, the lesson sticks and it generates pervasive resentment within the military.

The Supreme Court's efforts, particularly those of Justice Rehnquist, created a constitutional vacuum in military affairs that was quickly filled by the influence of political partisanship. This was the inevitable effect of a fundamental shift in how the Court viewed the relationship of the military to civilian government and to civilian society after the Vietnam War. Gradually, every bond that once connected military and civilian America was stripped away: the draft, the shared values of the Constitution, and, most fundamentally, the interest that average citizens used to have in how we as a nation govern and regulate the military. Unfortunately, the bond that eventually replaced these more traditional, historical connections was one that directly violated important principles of military professionalism and ethics.

Chapter 6

Facing the Consequences

From time to time, *USA Today* publishes a column about military life written by an Army captain who serves as a chaplain. On the day after Thanksgiving in 2007, he wrote about having his restaurant tab picked up by a couple at another table when he was dining alone while in uniform.[1] They paid without identifying themselves and asked the waitress to quietly pass on their appreciation for his military service. It was a nice story about anonymously generous people thanking a solitary soldier who may have been away from home, separated from family. Such small gestures of appreciation for servicemembers are probably fairly common in these times.

The chaplain was moved by their kindness, but in a way that unexpectedly exposed some of the raw edges of the civil-military relationship today. After thanking the couple, he used their generosity to make a point about how ungrateful he thought most Americans were for the military service that others provide. Rather than just accepting their graciousness in the spirit in which it was given, the chaplain turned his thoughts instead to all those occasions when someone did not offer to pick up his lunch tab. Offering a grudging, backhanded compliment to America, he said the gesture showed him "there are still a few people left in our society who haven't forgotten how to say 'thank you.'"

Did the chaplain really intend to suggest that the other people in the restaurant had forgotten how to say "thank you" or were unappreciative of his military service? Does he really stew and steam with resentment each time he dines in uniform and someone doesn't pay the bill? One has to wonder whether this might be the case, because he went on to contrast his experience with a biblical tale of ungratefulness in which Jesus cured a group of ten lepers, but only one returned to express his gratitude.[2] The military chaplain asked his readers to ponder the lepers who went on with their lives without acknowledging the great gift they had received: "Did the other nine not appreciate what Jesus did for them?" Apparently he saw some meaningful parallel between civilian diners who fail to pay for servicemembers' meals and biblical lepers who fail to thank Jesus for healing them. That's a great deal of resentment to carry, especially for a chaplain and an officer who was probably better off financially than most of the people he thought should be treating him to lunch.

Traces of resentment can bubble up from the military community in a variety of contexts. Most civilians seem to assume the resentment is warranted, because very rarely will someone respond with puzzlement or curiosity. If people say anything, it is likely to be some general statement of sympathy or apology, even when it is unclear what the specific grievance might be. We accept as an article of faith that some civilians have treated military people unfairly, especially civilians who are left-of-center in their politics. The specifics of that article of faith, or how it came to be, seem less important than everyone's common understanding that it is true.

Another small burst of military resentment emerged during congressional hearings into the horribly neglectful treatment of wounded servicemembers at Walter Reed Army Medical Center in Washington, D.C. The *Washington Post* won a Pulitzer Prize for public service in journalism for its investigation and reporting of the conditions under which servicemembers received outpatient care. Its coverage revealed that some wounded servicemembers were living in military housing that was squalid and unsafe, and they were left largely on their own to navigate an inefficient and complicated system for care and rehabilitation.[3] The uniformed commander of Walter Reed, the uniformed surgeon general of the Army, and the civilian secretary of the Army were fired in quick succession, and senior officials acknowledged that the disaster of Walter Reed was a failure of leadership.[4] The military had failed to pay attention to the quality of outpatient care, it had failed to recognize there was a serious problem, and it had failed to provide the resources necessary to care adequately for the large number of wounded servicemembers returning from Iraq and Afghanistan.

Despite the acknowledgment of Army leaders that they had failed in their obligations to the wounded, a former Army officer—also a West Point graduate and a wounded veteran of the war in Iraq—told a presidential commission that he believed part of the problem at Walter Reed was the animosity some civilian employees had for members of the military. This Army officer was convinced that sometimes soldiers were neglected not because of any institutional failure in the military's medical system, but because some civilians working at Walter Reed did not support the troops and their mission. He testified: "On several occasions, I and others I have spoken to felt that we were being judged as if we chose our nation's foreign policy, and as a result, received little if any assistance."[5]

Given the incredible magnitude of governmental failure found in the military medical system by presidential and Defense Department commissions,[6] it was curious to hear an experienced military officer blame the problem on civilian animosity for wounded veterans. Where does this perception of civilian ungratefulness and hostility toward military people come from? What leads a veteran to assume that when a solder fails to receive timely and proper care, the failure must be motivated by hostility for the soldier or for the administration that championed the war, and not by breakdowns in the leadership, training, or staffing of the military medical system? Military resentment directed at the imaginary political slights of civilians could be an enormously counterproductive response that interferes with real military reform.

The resentment that infects the civil-military relationship is difficult to eradicate because it is continually fed and nurtured, from both inside and outside the military. It can begin quite early. For example, one Army lieutenant colonel has become a viral Internet sensation for his speeches at military graduation ceremonies for young soldiers who have just completed their initial infantry training.[7] His words have inspired a rabid following, oddly, *because* of the huge wedge they drive between military and civilian America. People love the speeches because they contrast what is right with the military against what is wrong with everything else in America, unaware that military graduation ceremonies have to be among the most professionally inappropriate occasions for encouraging military people to resent civilian society. Whatever these young people are taught about military culture at this early point in their careers is likely to have great and lasting impact.

It was not enough for this lieutenant colonel to encourage a sense of well-earned pride in the graduates' service and in their completion of difficult, challenging training. Instead, he exhorted his audience to believe they were "better than the average young man." Civilians did not appreciate their sacrifice. They did not have the military's "moral clarity," and so they were unworthy of the military's respect. College students—"kids running around on some university campuses protesting, breaking things and whining"— were just one of the many groups of civilians he thought should be treated with scorn and disgust:

> Your head will not be filled with the empty theory of those who, in actuality, know very little because they lack the intestinal fortitude to commit to anything that requires risk. I'm speaking of the snide arrogant sort who spend the day blaming America for every wrong in the world before going home to sleep at night under that blanket of freedom provided by better men, men like you. . . .
>
> Don't let the pessimistic television talking heads, high browed newspaper writers, Hollywood idiots, or any other faction of the "Blame America First" crowd get you down! I'm speaking of the latte-biscotti crowd. They are simple background chatter men . . . and will always exist on the periphery of any endeavor that requires selfless service or loyalty. They are not worthy of your concern.

This commissioned officer was speaking on a public stage and in an official capacity as a representative of the United States Army. If one wonders why so many members of the military expressed deep resentment of civilian society in the Gap Project surveys, perhaps part of the answer begins with military education and training like this. If one is looking for evidence of the disturbing disconnect in civil-military relations today, it can be found in the belief that this speech represents the height, and not the depth, of military professionalism. Twice in his speech, the lieutenant colonel mocked civilians as selfishly relying on the "blanket of freedom" the military provides, perhaps channeling Jack Nicholson in his role as the Marine commander Colonel Nathan Jessep ("You can't handle the truth!") in the 1992 movie *A Few Good Men*, who said, "I have neither the time nor the inclination to explain myself to a man who rises and sleeps under the blanket of the very freedom that I provide and then questions the manner in which I provide it."

The fictional Colonel Jessep seemed comfortable with the doctrine of judicial deference to the military. He believed that military lawyers outside the combat arms could not possibly understand his reasons for ordering an informal disciplinary measure that led to the death of one of his marines. If military lawyers could not understand, you can imagine what he would have thought of civilian judges questioning his judgment. He believed that good order and discipline in a military context—as he, of course, would define it—rested on a higher moral plane than the call of any law. More than anything, he deeply resented being asked to explain his decisions. He had "neither the time nor the inclination" to explain whether or why he gave the order, and he was outraged at a system that called him to account for his choices under the law. The best way to show appreciation for his years of military service would be to keep quiet and let him do his job. Asking questions disrespected his service.

The doctrine of military deference in real life plays out exactly like the colonel's tirade. It teaches Americans to believe they cannot understand the military or the nature of military discipline, that the military is guided by moral principles of a higher order than principles of law, and that Americans only demonstrate their ungratefulness and disrespect for the military service of others when they ask for explanation. Given the doctrine of judicial deference and how it operates in practice, we should expect some resentment on the military side when average citizens dare to engage in the everyday discussions that ought to be part of the democratic process of civilian control of the military under the Constitution.

One cannot overestimate how much young people who are new to the military lap up this language of contempt and resentment and make it their own. Tom Ricks, the author of *Making the Corps*, was especially struck by how much new enlisted Marines came away from basic training filled with contempt for their civilian peers. One newly minted Marine told Ricks that when he returned home after basic training, "You felt like smacking around some people." In this disturbing chapter, entitled "Back in the World," Ricks said it seemed almost every Marine in the unit experienced "a moment of private loathing for public America." Civilians were, in a frequently used word, "nasty." Bruce Fleming, a long-time professor at the Naval Academy at Annapolis, thought most Americans were unaware just how much his college-age midshipmen looked down on the rest of America. Professor Fleming said: "I wish I had a dollar for every time I've heard the phrase 'civilian scum' here at Annapolis, a taxpayer-supported institution."[8]

Is it really necessary to drive such a wedge between civilian and military America in order to build an effective fighting force? Does this sound like the military of our grandparents and great-grandparents? Did they need to be taught disdain and contempt for fellow Americans before they were able to defend them in war? Why would we as a society ever consciously choose to reinforce this kind of alienation and distance across the civil-military line? Resentment persists so tenaciously because it serves a purpose, but not the military purpose you might suspect. It persists because it serves an ideological purpose that is attractive to civilians. Unfortunately, it is very difficult for the military not to get caught up in the game when civilians use the military for reasons that exceed normal constitutional boundaries. When a sense of resentment is manufactured and nurtured under the assumption that the military is better than America, is more moral than America, and is guided by higher principles than the Constitution or the law of America, who wouldn't want to be on the winning side of that comparison?

Of all the things military personnel experts considered in deciding whether to dispense with the draft and move to an all-volunteer force, one of them was probably not whether servicemembers would be more resentful of civilian society if they were no longer conscripted involuntarily into service. It's a counterintuitive notion. Most people would probably assume that civil-military problems arising from feelings of resentment, disaffection, or alienation would be characteristic of a draft military, not a volunteer force. Why would resentment creep in when presumably every member of the military makes a deliberate choice to join and no one is forced to serve? At the moment of transition from a draft to an all-volunteer military, defense experts likely thought their efforts would ease these concerns, not make them worse.

Something else the Department of Defense and Congress failed to consider in the early 1970s, however, was what a valuable civilian commodity a distant, alienated military—or at least the perception of one—would become. In order to understand why the post-Vietnam military has become so resentful of civilian society and civilian influence, it is helpful to understand who is in the best position to exploit the resentment for reasons that have little to do with military effectiveness. The exercise is similar to the familiar advice to "follow the money." If you can determine which civilians are most likely to benefit ideologically or politically from the creation of a military society that sees itself as quite distant and different from America, you are much closer to understanding why the change came about.

The most important thing Americans do not understand about the military today is how much it has changed in the last generation, and the second most important thing is how much this transformation has been shaped by civilian influence, not military influence. The nature of the military in this new century cannot be explained entirely by the easy reasoning of "well, that's how militaries are," as if there is some static and enduring measure of what militaries are supposed to be like. The choices of civilians determine the kind of military we have much more than the choices of military leaders. Every day we take some action, or fail to act, in ways that affect the quality and professionalism of our armed forces.

There is an escalating arms race between hero worship for those who serve and resentment for those who do not. There seems to be no limit to the level of open, even ostentatious, adoration of people serving our nation in uniform.[9] Any program or event related to military service inevitably features the word "hero" in a prominent place; anyone who enlists in the military immediately joins the ranks of heroes, well before any opportunity to act heroically. The pressure to maintain artificially high levels of esteem and admiration for the troops is enormous, and the slightest slip from uncritical reverence brings a harsh backlash of resentment both from servicemembers and civilians. Even in a time of the highest respect for all things military, the size of the resentment waiting to be unleashed grows greater. It is a truly bizarre dynamic in which greater and greater resentment can be triggered by lesser and lesser slights.

Civilians jockey with one another to be viewed as the most zealous supporter of the military among other similarly supportive citizens. One of the easiest ways to signal one's patriotic allegiance to the military, unfortunately, is to question the commitment of others, even when there is no reason to believe they support the military any less or any differently. For example, when the governor of Kansas, Kathleen Sebelius, gave the Democratic response to President Bush's 2008 State of the Union address, she said, "Here in the heartland, we honor and respect military service. We appreciate the enormous sacrifices made by soldiers and their families."[10] What is that supposed to mean? It certainly suggests she thinks other Americans, apparently those living somewhere other than the heartland, don't honor or respect military service as much as they should.

It has become practically impossible to maintain a level of public admiration for the military that is high enough to tamp down regular eruptions of grievance against civilians, civilian government, or civilian law. A small sample of this dynamic can be viewed at *Blackfive.net*, *Military.com*, or *Mudvillegazette.com*, high-traffic blogs on military subjects that capture a sense of our deteriorating civil-military relationship. The postings and comments frequently express resentment, contempt, and bitterness for one of these favored targets: our constitutional structure of government and law; any civilians, including elected officials, who dare to inquire about decisions involving the military; and, lastly, all the imagined slights against members of the military that lurk around every corner.

But, you might ask, even if public support for the military is at times a bit over-the-top, isn't that a natural correction—an apology of sorts—for the terribly disrespectful treatment of Vietnam veterans just a generation ago? Is there something wrong with trying to make amends with a new generation of servicemembers and ensure we will not make the same mistake of blaming the individual soldier if we disagree with our government's policies? Shouldn't we make certain that political dissent related to war never again spills over into disrespect for the military? Everyone remembers—or believes they remember—how atrociously Vietnam veterans were treated when they returned to the United States from their overseas service.[11] Those who opposed the war had such low regard for members of the military they tried to shame them in public, and sometimes they even spit on them. Our collective memory of those spit-upon soldiers is often resurrected as a reminder of how important it is to honor and respect members of the military who are serving today. As one young soldier was quoted, "It's nice that people care. At least it's not like Vietnam and people don't just spit on us."[12]

The problem with this line of reasoning—even if our adoration of the troops may be a little excessive in a civilian democracy, it makes up for our disrespectful treatment of the troops a generation ago—is that the premise is entirely wrong. The conventional wisdom that has antiwar protestors spitting on Vietnam veterans works the same way as the conventional wisdom that has elite universities banning ROTC from their campuses. There is no contemporaneous evidence that Americans who opposed the war expressed those beliefs by spitting on or otherwise assaulting returning Vietnam veterans. This is not to say, of course, that an antiwar protester has never once hurled spit at a returning soldier. This is a big country, and therefore just about anything has likely happened at some time, in some place, to some person. The idea, however, that spitting on or mistreating Vietnam veterans was in any way typical or representative of anything in that era is completely false.

The common notion that many Americans of the 1960s and 1970s could not distinguish between the servicemember and an unpopular war, and as a result engaged in petty acts of disrespect against individuals in uniform, is certainly the way we have come to remember the Vietnam War. It is by far the most powerful Vietnam War meme—a cultural unit of information passed from one person to another, like a biological gene—because it can be deployed instantly to silence difficult but necessary conversations about the military. For that reason alone the conventional wisdom is important, because it explains much about our civil-military dynamic today. It is also important, however, to understand why that accepted memory is untrue, and who benefits most from keeping it alive.

The myth of the spat-upon Vietnam veteran is a difficult one to challenge. Most people are not old enough to have meaningful personal experience with the Vietnam era, and most people have no particular reason to discount the stories that are repeated and confirmed endlessly. One intrepid soul, Professor Jerry Lembcke, both a Vietnam veteran and an academic researcher from Holy Cross University, stepped into the fray and published a 1998 book detailing his comprehensive study of reports about spat-upon Vietnam veterans.[13] Every time he discusses his findings in a public forum, a hail of angry responses follows, but his explanations and conclusions are compelling and unsettling. I'll note only a few of his observations here, because his book does a much better job of describing how we have come to the point where an urban myth drives much of the debate about civil-military relations. His research should lead even the skeptical reader to stop and think about whether some of the easy assumptions we carry about the Vietnam-era military ought be examined again—or perhaps for the first time.

Lembcke's central point is that he found no contemporaneous accounts—newspaper and magazine articles, photographs, police reports, or investigations—supporting the often-told and eerily similar stories of the solitary soldier, just returning from Vietnam, who is spat upon in an airport terminal by a war-protesting hippie. These stories only began to appear in bunches a decade after the events were supposed to have taken place and, interestingly, shortly after the Sylvester Stallone *Rambo* movies introduced a fictionalized, spat-upon Vietnam veteran into American popular culture. Critics have turned up a handful of published reports from the war era that mention servicemembers and spitting in some combination, but not war opponents spitting on returning Vietnam veterans.[14] Professor Lembcke's work stands up well in the face of a tremendous amount of emotional outrage that arises whenever the stories are questioned as urban myth.

The existence or nonexistence of news accounts describing the iconic spitting may not even be the most persuasive way of debunking the myth. Much more powerful are the contemporaneous words and actions of Vietnam veterans themselves. Lembcke notes that polls of Vietnam veterans taken in 1971 showed that 94 percent reported receiving a "friendly" reception from civilians their own age.[15] Something doesn't match up. Why do we assume that Vietnam veterans were treated like dirt by antiwar civilians when the veterans themselves, at the time they completed their service, said that other young people who had not served in the military treated them in a friendly manner? How does one begin to reconcile that inconsistency?

The Spitting Image offers a potential explanation. Lembcke agreed that veterans were treated poorly by some fellow citizens, but generally not by the antiwar protesters or the hippies. He concluded, strangely enough, that older military veterans were the most likely to shun them. Men who had served in World War II and the Korean War, the men who made up the core of veterans' organizations like the American Legion and the Veterans of Foreign Wars, were not at first welcoming of new veterans from the Vietnam conflict. While they strongly supported the war, they believed this new generation of servicemembers was unworthy of the brotherhood. Somehow, their disrespect and disdain came to be remembered as acts of scorn by liberal opponents of the war:

> There were actual acts of hostility toward GIs and veterans and, depending on how we interpret these acts, they help clarify the historical record or they become grist for the myth. The fact that most of the documentable hostility emanated from pro-war groups and individuals is a detail that is often lost. Members of such groups as the Veterans of Foreign Wars and the American Legion shunned Vietnam veterans because of the long hair, love beads, and peace symbols that many wore.[16]

If this conclusion still seems unlikely, consider the significance of the official founding principle adopted by the Vietnam Veterans of America (VVA), a military veterans' group still active today. Frustrated with being shunned by older veterans and realizing their needs were not being met by the traditional veterans' organizations, in 1978 the VVA chose as its founding principle the following vow: "Never again will one generation of veterans abandon another."[17] Note that VVA did not speak of abandonment by those who opposed the war, by those of a liberal political persuasion, or by civilians in general. Its founding principle reflected a belief that Vietnam veterans had been shunned and left behind by other soldiers. This would be a very odd founding principle to adopt if the real problem for Vietnam veterans was antiwar protesters spitting on them when they returned home.

Lembcke's contribution was to document and preserve the historical reality we have all so quickly managed to forget. His work gave strong support to the conclusion that Vietnam veterans were much more likely to be disrespected by conservatives who supported the war but not the soldier, which is the ironic flip side to today's defense of supporting the soldier but not the war. A senior defense department official (and Vietnam veteran) recently recalled the VVA motto as he emphasized the importance of protecting today's veterans. "You may take from that a certain sense of grievance," he said, "but that's not the important part. The important part is this: that [Vietnam] generation is determined to take care of this generation." The direction of the blame is unmistakable, and it's not toward people who opposed the Vietnam War.[18]

Another news story, aptly enough about servicemembers and airports, helps to explain how military urban myths like this take hold. In September 2007, an incident at Oakland International Airport in northern California led to a flood of complaints that civilians were once again disrespecting soldiers, blaming them for an unpopular war. A charter flight of Marines returning from overseas was held outside the passenger terminals for over three hours while airport authorities fumbled to figure out how security rules applied to a group carrying a large number of weapons. Airport authorities may not have handled the task well, but an investigation by the Department of Transportation inspector general later found the delay was not caused by any disdain for the troops.[19]

Congressman John Mica from Florida, however, stoked the controversy with a statement that "this [the airport incident] is like spitting in the face of the brave men and women who risk their lives to protect our freedoms." In a climate of civil-military tension and distrust, there is but a fraction of an inch between a story about *feeling* like you've been spit on and a story about *actually* being spit on. Perhaps many of the after-the-fact spitting reports over the years can be explained by the same rhetorical leap Representative Mica was so irresponsibly quick to make, especially when they are made in response to eager questions like "Were you spit on too?" instead of a less suggestive inquiry about how one was treated. I would bet that years from now, when people recall the Oakland incident, the retelling will include some real spitting. We are so quick to believe the myth that it only has to be reinforced every now and then, even rhetorically, to remain firmly in its psychic place. No one wants to question the myth, because no one wants to appear disrespectful of the troops.

Washington Post writer William Arkin felt some of the backlash in early 2007 when he commented about a television news report featuring soldiers in Iraq who were incensed at civilians who disagreed with the government's decision to wage war.[20] For the soldiers, it was simple: the only way you can support us is to support the war, and if you don't support the war, don't bother claiming you support the soldier, because you don't. Arkin, himself a military veteran of the all-volunteer era, rightly observed that Americans owed members of the military their support, but they did not owe them agreement with government policy. Americans had no obligation to abandon their right and responsibility to engage in political dissent. Arkin hoped their military superiors would set the younger soldiers straight on this important point of military professionalism.

The electronic roof then fell in. Arkin received online comments from hundreds of enraged readers who took his civil-military critique as a personal attack on individual servicemembers. People were beside themselves at the idea of a newspaper writer questioning the viewpoints of people serving our country in uniform. Arkin tried for a time to respond and explain his position, but the crush of electronic criticism was so unrelenting the *Washington Post* soon advised Arkin to move on to other topics. The entire affair was a perfect illustration of how whipped-up resentment, either from the military or from others on its behalf, can shut down debate about the civil-military relationship and the meaning of military service in America. Civilians with less tolerance for mean-spirited and unconstructive criticism are unlikely to bring up military subjects at all, except to reflexively assure everyone they really do support the troops.

Most people don't have the stomach for wading into civil-military discussions if there is any prospect for criticism or disagreement. The law school at Indiana University in Indianapolis experienced the phenomenon first hand in a controversy related to a junior law faculty member. This professor went public with his allegations that tenured members of the faculty were sabotaging his chances for promotion because they objected to his conservative political viewpoints and his background as a decorated Army officer.[21] As you can imagine, he was portrayed as the target of political correctness run amok. Like the urban myth of universities that banished ROTC from their campuses, it was yet another example of the contempt that universities hold for all things military.

Only when a retired Army officer contacted the *Indianapolis Star* with his suspicion that the professor had fabricated his military background did the story begin to unravel.[22] Fabrications about military service happen, not infrequently.[23] However, in this case the fabrication was so ludicrous and so impossible it is difficult to understand why this law professor's record passed muster at any stage. He actually expected people to believe that while he was serving as an Army infantry officer from 1990 to 2001 and rising to the rank of major, he found time to complete a Ph.D. in International Relations, attend three years of law school, enroll at Harvard and earn a second degree in law, serve as an advisor to the chairman of the Joint Chiefs of Staff and, for good measure, earn a Silver Star for gallantry in action. That's not possible. In reality, the professor was a reserve second lieutenant with no active military service.

The only way to explain why this false inflation of military credentials went as far as it did without objection is that civilians are extremely disinclined to question a servicemember's bona fides, even when the assertions are implausible on their face. It may also be possible that no one at the law school understood enough about military service to realize the professor's record could not be accurate, but this explanation is less convincing. There had to be suspicion, but no one wanted to be the one to raise it. It's generally not worth it, because the din that follows often drowns out any rational discussion of the issue. No one wants to put themselves in the position of disrespecting the troops unless they are certain beyond doubt, and civilians very rarely feel certain beyond doubt in matters involving the military.

The *Washington Post* published an interesting first-person account of military service written by an Army first lieutenant with three years in uniform, one of them in Iraq.[24] What made the story newsworthy was the author's sense of tremendous wonder at becoming a competent military officer. He described himself as an educated, bookish sort, a law student who began to consider joining the military a few months after the September 11 attacks. What gave him great pause about the idea, however, was his perception that people who joined the military were not like regular people. The traditionally American concept of the "citizen-soldier" was not the way he thought about the military; to him, servicemembers had to be physical specimens of almost superhuman abilities. He continued to doubt himself for years before he finally enlisted—after all, he had never used weapons, climbed mountains, captained a sports team, or finished an Ironman triathlon. How could he possibly serve in the military?

This lieutenant survived the training, and he was apparently very successful as a junior military leader. What is telling about his perspective, however, was his serious concern that regular people—especially regular people who were educated and economically comfortable—might not be able to "hack it" in the military. He seemed truly amazed that military service was within the capability of someone who did not resemble a pumped-up action hero in a video game. In the end, he said he learned something important about the military, that "by and large the people in it are just people." Only "lazy prejudice" had led him to wrongly assume that "some Americans are at once too good, and not good enough, for the military."

Anyone who serves in the military competently and honorably should take enormous pride in that achievement. The military asks a great deal of its members, often under circumstances in which the margin for error is extremely small. I can understand why some young people would be attracted to military service for the opportunity to meet challenges not easily available in the civilian world. But it cannot be helpful to military recruiting in an all-volunteer era for qualified Americans to believe they are incapable of military service. It cannot be helpful to informed civil-military debate for Americans to assume that the world of the military is so distant, so different, and so difficult that regular people are not suited for the job.

Whenever a military draft helps to fill the ranks, the standard assumption is very different. Military service becomes an expected and unexceptional obligation (and for some, a privilege) of living in this country, shared by all who are considered full participants in our great democratic experiment. (Not so fast, you women, at least not yet.) When national service is the norm, we no longer think of military service as the special province of a select and unusually qualified few. The military today has not even begun to grasp the possibility that our efforts, conscious and unconscious, to portray military people as larger-than-life, uniformly heroic, and always better than America are actually counterproductive in terms of military recruiting. Every time, for example, the Army trots out its unsubstantiated assertion that seven out of ten young Americans are unqualified to serve in the military,[25] it adds to the perception that the military is something to worship from a distance, but not to join.

The Supreme Court has devoted much effort in the years following the Vietnam War to erasing the egalitarian assumption that we all owe something to our national defense. One of the most effective ways to accomplish this goal is to emphasize how different Americans become when they join the military, or perhaps how different they already must be because they have chosen to join the military. The bedrock civil-military cases of *Parker v. Levy*, *Rostker v. Goldberg*, and *Goldman v. Weinberger* were all based on the assumption that the military was not really a part of America. Rather, the military was a society *apart from* America, so idiosyncratic in character that it was difficult for civilians to understand it, let alone live by its higher standards.

It wasn't always that way. Thirty-five years ago, an Air Force navigator, Captain Albert Glines, earned his fifteen minutes of Supreme Court fame when he was discharged from active duty for circulating a petition without his commander's approval.[26] His petition asked the secretary of defense and a few congressmen to reconsider the Air Force's hair grooming regulations—restrictions on hair length, Afros, sideburns, mustaches, and the like. He was not suggesting the military throw out standards requiring a neat and conservative appearance, but he did believe rules requiring servicemembers to look so starkly different from their civilian peers was an unnecessary source of frustration that caused more harm than good in terms of discipline. He felt so strongly about it that he shaved his head in protest, which to the Air Force was yet another breach of good order and discipline.

Only in retrospect does the case tell us something interesting about the civil-military gap that was just beginning to develop, and it had nothing to do with the Court's eventual ruling against the navigator. At the time, a service-member could actually be disciplined for shaving his head because extreme hairstyles were discouraged. Regulation military haircuts were very similar to conservative business styles in the civilian world. Some servicemembers even devoted an inordinate amount of effort to tiny evasions of haircut reg-ulations, not because they were ashamed to be serving in the military, but because they didn't see the need to look so different from civilians. Looking neat, conservative, and uniform was one thing; looking odd was another.

A military haircut today, on the other hand, is specifically designed to identify someone as a member of the military, pointedly separate and apart from civilian peers. (I'm referring to routine haircuts long after the tradi-tional shearing of men at the start of basic training.) Extremely shaved styles that would be unusual for a young civilian professional—a burr cut, a clean shave of the entire head, or a side and back shave with a oval tuft of hair left on top—are chosen because they have become a cultural marker that a per-son is no longer a civilian. Interestingly, the civilians that military people most resemble when they adopt these extreme hairstyles are the "skinheads" who wish, for their own reasons, to distance themselves from civilian norms of appearance.

But aren't haircuts a matter of military necessity? Shouldn't we take that into account when weighing the utility of any particular style of haircut? If we did take military necessity into account, however, we might consider taking our norms of military grooming in another direction. When Ameri-can sources revealed that Prince Harry, third in line to the British throne, was serving as a forward air controller in a combat unit in Afghanistan, media coverage showed a group of young British military men with long, bushy hair. The prince's colleagues seemed to think longer hair was a small gesture of friendliness and solidarity to Afghans and their hair-friendly cul-ture.[27] It was a nonthreatening way to send a militarily useful message that said, in essence, "We are not that different from you, and you can trust us." The American military, serving alongside the British, has largely taken the opposite approach.[28]

Our modern cultural expectations for a military haircut are even very different from how the military itself defines a military haircut. According to Army Regulation 670-1, *Wear and Appearance of Army Uniforms and Insig-nia*, men's hair must only be "neatly groomed" and "tapered," not "ragged, unkempt, or extreme." Hair cannot be so long that it falls over the ears or eyebrows or touches the collar when combed. By this standard, a military haircut includes a wide array of neat and conservative hairstyles commonly seen in any professional setting in the civilian world. Military regulations have never required soldiers to choose extreme hairstyles—and in fact have generally discouraged them, particularly for women—but for some reason there is this strong pull toward maintaining a culture of difference from the civilian world, one that is more pronounced today than at any other time in American history. Incidentally, the Army would eventually bow to this cultural divide in 2002 and officially amend its grooming regulations to authorize the wildly popular "skinhead" shaved styles as an approved option.[29] That horse, however, was already long out of the barn.

Similar trends are in motion with military uniforms. In recent years, the Army's defining image has been the Army Combat Uniform (ACU), a digitally camouflaged, many-pocketed, shirt-over-the-trousers field uniform with tones of gray, tan, and green. For the Army, this utility uniform has become the symbol of our engagement in a desert war, worn by soldiers of all ranks (from privates to generals), in all locations (whether abroad or at home), and when performing all duties (whether deployed in the field or not). This current state of uniformed affairs, however, is neither normal nor traditional. The usual military rule is that when servicemembers interact with the civilian world, they do so wearing a uniform that is consistent with the standard of civilian dress for the occasion. For example, when attending professional conferences, testifying before Congress, giving briefings to the press, or speaking before business or university audiences, a servicemember should normally wear a standard military uniform with creased trousers, jacket, and necktie. Back in the day, a member of the military would no more attend a professional event in a field uniform than a surgeon would speak at a medical convention wearing green scrubs.[30]

Today, on the other hand, Army lawyers give guest lectures in law school classrooms wearing the field ACU. Army members of all ranks wear the ACU desert outfit for all manner of professional duties in civilian environments, everything from military doctors speaking at medical conferences, to senior officers giving public speeches, to noncommissioned officers on recruiting duty, and to formal events for awards and oaths of citizenship. Military medical personnel at Walter Reed dress in rumpled ACUs as though they are on duty in Iraq and not at one of the premier medical facilities in the United States.

The senior commander of forces in the Middle East in 2006, Army General John Abizaid, once gave a joking explanation of why he wore an ACU to speak at an academic event held at the John F. Kennedy School of Government at Harvard University. Referring to the congressional testimony he gave earlier that week, he said, "I usually wear my green uniform. But there was so much blood on it, I had to come in this uniform."[31] The audience's response was reported as "polite laughter," but they should have been appalled. In two short sentences, the general had managed to make light of the military's tradition of respectful dress at civil-military events, to mock Congress's constitutionally mandated responsibility for oversight of the war, and to diminish those servicemembers who have actually bled on their uniforms. It was a trifecta of disrespect for civil-military tradition and military professionalism.

As with extreme haircuts, the problem with extreme uniforms is that they contribute to an artificially exaggerated "warrior" culture that unduly distances the military from civilian society. It would be one thing if this deliberate push for distance, difference, and separation contributed to military effectiveness, but it has little justification based on military needs. The more important point is to convey the message, "I serve in the military, therefore I am not at all like you, and you are not at all like me. There is a divide between us you have not earned the right to cross. I need not explain myself to you, and it is disrespectful for you to expect me to do so."

All the services have embraced the "warrior" as a substitute for the traditional identities of "soldier," "marine," "airman," and "sailor," blurring the distinction between professional military forces and untethered collections of rogue fighters.[32] The warrior tag has become an all-purpose term capable of covering all that is good and all that is bad in the use of violence. It serves as an unintentional leveling mechanism that tends to diminish the professional soldier and elevate the unaffiliated fighter. For example, during the first military commission to try a suspected terrorist, the chief military prosecutor referred to the defendant—one might say he went out of his way to honor the defendant—as an "al-Qaeda warrior." This supposed "warrior," however, was actually quite far from what most people think of as a warrior. He was just a driver for Osama bin Laden.[33]

It is unclear what military purpose it serves to dramatize anyone and everyone connected to terrorism, pro or con, as a privileged member of some warrior caste. Nonetheless, the "warrior" reference is near universal today, in circumstances ranging from the misguidedly serious to the sadly unfortunate to the ridiculous. Today, soldiers cannot be just soldiers, they have to be "Warriors," enhanced with a capital "W." It is no longer enough to be trained as a leader or as a noncommissioned officer; one must now be a "Warrior Leader."[34] Members of the Army Reserve are no longer the traditional "citizen-soldier"; in an odd reversal of priority, they are now "Warrior-Citizens."[35] Soldiers recuperating from their injuries are no longer patients, military patients, or even injured soldiers; they are "Wounded Warriors."[36]

Sometimes, however, the usage is just comical and self-indulgent. When a Marine Corps public affairs officer was temporarily away from his e-mail, he left an automated reply for his correspondents that announced, "Warriors, I will be out of the office until Monday."[37] The one football team that should understand the difference between football and war managed to confuse the two by dressing up its players in football facsimiles of the ever-present ACUs. For its 2008 intercollegiate game with Navy, Army took the field wearing Nike-designed "Enforcer" uniforms with digitally camouflaged helmets and pants, each cadet plastered like a highway billboard with the venerable "Duty, Honor, Country" across the shoulders and the Army-centric motto "Boots on the Ground" down a pant leg.[38]

Even the Air Force and the Navy, services much less oriented to ground combat, have adopted some of the artificial trappings of a faux "warrior" culture intended to be more "military" and more distant from civilian life than traditional military culture. The Air Force developed a new "Airman's Creed" for its members to recite that begins, ominously, "I am an American Airman. I am a warrior."[39] Both the Air Force and the Navy have adopted camouflaged field uniforms styled in the manner of the ACU,[40] although it remains unclear why people who typically work against an expanse of industrial gray need to blend into the background, or whether in any event shades of digitized blue will achieve the desired effect. It is also unclear why the services would give personnel who work around aircraft a huge number of pockets, because it just encourages them to carry small items that can get sucked into a jet engine. None of this matters, however, if the changes were made to emphasize difference, distance, and superficial militarism, not to achieve any military advantage.

It is important to distinguish military advantage from civilian convenience or preference. For example, a RAND study concluded that fighting the "war on terror" primarily as a military operation was a counterproductive way of approaching the problem. Based on an examination of the reasons that terrorist groups have failed over the last forty years, the study strongly recommended we shift our focus to nonmilitary means of meeting the threat of terrorism, such as policing and intelligence. These RAND experts believed the phrase "war on terror" has itself caused us to misdirect our efforts against terrorism:

> The phrase raises public expectations—both in the United States and elsewhere—that there is a battlefield solution to the problem of terrorism. It also encourages others abroad to respond by conducting a jihad (or holy war) against the United States and elevates them to the status of holy warriors. Terrorists should be perceived and described as criminals, not holy warriors.[41]

Not only do we characterize everyone as a warrior—soldiers, marines, sailors, airmen, and suspected terrorists alike—but we even play the "holy war" card ourselves. One active-duty three-star general, Lt. Gen. William G. Boykin, took things to another level by characterizing our military efforts as a holy war that evangelical Christians must wage against Muslims. He delivered public speeches in uniform taunting Muslim beliefs and vowing that Christianity would prevail, apparently delivered at the end of a weapon by the United States military. Boykin preached: "I knew my God was bigger than his. I knew my God was a real God and his was an idol."[42]

Even in a time of war, it is unnecessary and dangerous to transform the American military into a separate and distinct warrior caste. People have noticed, even if Americans generally have not. British Brigadier Nigel Aylwin-Foster was a senior officer of one-star rank who served with General David Petraeus as part of the coalition effort in Iraq. In 2005, he wrote an article so uncommonly candid that our own Army chief of staff sent it to every one of his general officers.[43] Much of the article, published in the United States Army's professional journal, *Military Review*, focused on our reluctance to shift away from "big war" methods involving kinetic military operations— kicking doors in and destroying the enemy—toward "small war" principles of counterinsurgency and winning a "hearts and minds" campaign. Work on this problem was already under way, and by the end of 2006, General Petraeus would distribute his major revision of Army Field Manual 3-24, *Counterinsurgency*, a 280-page compendium of Army doctrine on nation building and stability operations.

Aylwin-Foster's additional observations on the culture of the American military received less attention than his recommendations on counterinsurgency, but they were amazingly dead-on for someone without much experience with our all-volunteer military. He had great respect for the Army, but he noticed we had a very different style of civil-military relations, one that tended to work at cross-purposes to success in Iraq. While recognizing that military forces would always be distinct from their civilian roots, given the nature of the job, he believed the United States took things to an extreme. He thought members of our military went out of their way to be so "military" they sometimes seemed almost cartoonish:

> The U.S. Army's habits and customs, whilst in some respects very obviously products of American society, are also strikingly distinct, much more so than most militaries, to the extent that some individuals almost seem like military caricatures, so great is their intent on banishing all traces of the civilian within. U.S. Army soldiers are not citizen-soldiers: they are unquestionably American in origin, but equally unquestionably divorced from their roots.

All this might be an abstract point of cultural interest but for Aylwin-Foster's belief that this stance of difference and distance was making things worse in Iraq. In eerie parallel to the Gap Project research—although I can't imagine he would have had reason to read it—Aylwin-Foster wrote that the American military was impeded by a "sense of moral righteousness combined with an emotivity that was rarely far from the surface, and in extremis manifested as deep indignation or outrage that could serve to distort collective military judgment." This sense of moral superiority left the Americans "culturally ill-disposed" to nation building and stability operations, to the extent that their insensitivity "arguably amounted to institutional racism." The problem emerged in an uncountable number of small ways. Soldiers routinely swore at civilian Iraqis and referred to them by the intentionally insulting term "haji," this war's version of the Vietnam-era term "gook." Soldiers were immaturely obsessed with cultural difference related to gender and ridiculed traditional Arab clothing as "man dresses." Aylwin-Foster summed it up this way: "I never saw such a good bunch of people inadvertently piss off so many people."[44]

Although the Gap Project attempted to identify and quantify the military's alienation and sense of moral superiority in relation to civilian society, it did not consider whether this distance from and disdain for civilians could have a direct effect on military operations. Moral superiority, unfortunately, is a mind-set that is difficult to turn on and off depending on the circumstances. Even those who see no problem if servicemembers view themselves as better than fellow Americans should be able to agree there is a problem when this perspective infects the relationship we have with civilian populations during war. Aylwin-Foster believed the American military's emphasis on "warrior" culture was interfering with the important lesson that "on many occasions in unconventional situations they have to be soldiers, not warriors."

It soon became apparent that Aylwin-Foster was only scratching the surface of the problem, as serious as he believed it to be. The military's new culture of difference, distance, and disregard for civilian influence had already infected its legal operations for the detention and prosecution of suspected terrorists, causing irreparable harm to the war effort and to national security. The next chapter connects the dots that lead from a constitutionally estranged military to the failure of our system of military tribunals and commissions—and to the infamous acts of torture and abuse of prisoners committed by members of the military.

Chapter 7

A Dangerous Disregard for Law

How did we ever get to the point where we take pride in defining the military as what America is not, rather than what America is? How did we become so comfortable with the idea that the more different the military is from America, and the more the military drifts from the American commitment to the rule of law, somehow the better? A measure of how far the military has traveled—and not in a good direction—comes from an offhand statement by a military public affairs officer commenting on the first military commission convened at Guantánamo. The officer was asked why reporters were not allowed to see all the evidence and witnesses offered by military prosecutors in the trial of Salim Hamdan, a driver for Osama bin Laden. After all, the questioner added, reporters could always see evidence and witnesses at trials in America. The public affairs officer answered the question with absolutely brutal, unapologetic candor. She said: "This is not America."[1]

Although her comment drew very little attention in the press, it was a devastating commentary on the state of the military and of civil-military relations in the United States. Consider that the system of military commissions is a legal entity run almost completely by the military. The judge is military; the jurors are military; the prosecutors are military; many of the defense lawyers are military. The trial takes place on military property, inside military facilities. Press coverage and information are managed and controlled entirely by the military. Yet this public affairs officer was able to look out over this sea of military uniforms and say, without a bit of shame or embarrassment, "This is not America."

Now, you might say, that's not what she meant. Perhaps she only intended to say that Guantánamo Bay, Cuba, is outside the geographical jurisdiction of the United States, and so observers should not expect the trials to be conducted like trials held within the United States. The only problem with this interpretation was that the Supreme Court had already rejected it. As early as 2004, in *Rasul v. Bush*, and as recently as June 12, 2008, in *Boumediene v. Bush*—just a few weeks before the officer spoke—the Court made absolutely clear that Guantánamo was part of America as far as the Constitution was concerned, and everyone would have to behave accordingly.[2] *Boumediene* forced the Court to repeat what it considered to be a perfectly common-sense point: "As we did in *Rasul*, however, we take notice of the obvious and uncontested fact that the United States, by virtue of its complete jurisdiction and control over the base, maintains de facto sovereignty over this territory."

In short, the Court ruled that the United States government could not play games with the definition of national sovereignty in order to shirk its legal obligations. If the government treated the Guantánamo naval facility as its own territory for every other official purpose, it could not pretend otherwise when convenient and argue that the base really belonged to Cuba—and was therefore beyond the reach of our Constitution. With American power comes American responsibility, and so the government cannot, as the Court put it, "switch the Constitution on or off at will." The Constitution gives the elected branches the power to acquire or dispose of territory such as Guantánamo, but not the power to decide whether the Constitution should apply there. This is a constitutional question, not a political one open to majority vote.

It seems unlikely this public affairs officer, a major, was unaware of or did not understand the Court's rulings on the legal status of Guantánamo. What is left as an explanation for her remark, however, is a conclusion far more damning than simple ignorance. I believe when she said, "This is not America," her statement came from the unspoken, unconscious assumption, one we have bred into the military for more than thirty-five years now, that the military is not part of America when it comes to law and to the responsibilities of law. Beginning with *Parker v. Levy* in 1973 and continuing through *Rostker v. Goldberg* in 1981 and *Goldman v. Weinberger* in 1986, the Supreme Court has been sending a clear and consistent message to the military and to the political branches of government. This message is that the military does not have the same connection or bond to the Constitution that other functions of government have, and therefore the military does not have the same obligations under law.

Interestingly, perhaps ironically, the Supreme Court has only recently begun to resist the assumption that civilians can use the military, with little restraint, to achieve unconstitutional purposes, but the pushback has come in cases involving the detention and prosecution of persons suspected of supporting terrorist activities. In cases involving people who serve in the military or who might wish to join the military, however, the divide between the military and the Constitution is still as wide as it has ever been.

Given the Supreme Court's clear signal since the end of the Vietnam War that the military should be treated as a distant outpost on the legal frontier, separate and apart from civilians and civilian legal expectations, it should be no surprise to anyone that the military was one of the first options that came to mind when administration officials began casting about for ideas on how to avoid constitutional requirements in detaining and prosecuting suspected terrorists. Their first assumption seemed to be that if government sees a need to operate outside the law and outside the Constitution, it should use the military to do the job because the military will receive by far the most generous berth by courts.

In the old commercial for Life cereal, the kids who didn't want to taste a strange cereal containing suspiciously healthy ingredients said, "Let's get Mikey," their compliant little brother. They wanted him to try the cereal first, because why take chances when you can push the risk off on someone else who is not in any position to complain? In the Bush administration, executive officials who didn't want to be hampered by constitutional or legal requirements did the same thing. They said, "Let's get the military to do it," and they created a system of military tribunals and commissions for suspected terrorists—courts of sorts, but not regular courts used for anyone else—that would operate from inside the military and be shielded from civilian inconvenience.

When the Supreme Court struck down the administration's first plan for prosecuting suspected terrorists by military commission because it violated the UCMJ and the Geneva Conventions,[3] Congress attempted to shore up the process by creating its own version, presumably new and improved, in the Military Commissions Act passed later in 2006. Once again, the strategy was "Let's get the military to do it," under the assumption that if the president acting alone could not pass this task to the military, then certainly the president and Congress acting together could use the military to avoid the unpalatable prospect of complying with domestic and international law. Clearly the two elected branches intended to cut the third branch, the courts, largely out of the picture. What neither the president nor Congress took time to consider, however, was whether giving the military the responsibility to pass legal judgment on suspected terrorists could cause harm to the military as a profession. The military was certainly convenient enough to use, but neither the president nor members of Congress thought seriously about the consequences of putting the military at the center of a system designed to avoid the law, not respect the law.

Few people seemed to understand how much military professionalism depends upon respect for the civilian rule of law. Law is the last tie that bonds civilian and military worlds, and if that tie is lost, there is nothing left to hold them together. A system that teaches members of the military to disrespect or disregard law in the presumed service of either military necessity or national security is a disaster for military professionalism and military ethics. For all our professed respect and admiration for the military, we have paid little attention to this gradually unfolding problem.

The war we have declared on terror has generated an elaborate legal system for persons suspected of supporting or engaging in terrorist activities, organized into two separate legal tracks. First, there is a legal process for justifying the indefinite detention, without trial, of persons who are suspected of being enemy combatants. This detention process is akin to holding someone as a prisoner of war until the end of hostilities, except without most of the protections traditionally afforded by law to prisoners of war and without any reasonable expectation that a war on terror will ever officially end. Second, there is a separate legal process for prosecuting detainees for specific war crimes and imposing sentences of punishment, including the possibility of the death penalty. Most of the legal procedures for both detention and prosecution are sheltered safely inside our armed forces, with very limited supervision and review by civilian courts.

Specialized courts that dispense military justice are certainly not new. The Constitution allows our own servicemembers to be tried by court-martial rather than by civilian courts, under the assumption that good order and discipline will be better served if military commanders control the process and people with military experience pass judgment on conduct in military settings. The recently established terrorist tribunals and commissions, however, cannot be justified by the usual reasons offered for bypassing the civilian justice system. Unlike courts-martial, the special legal system we apply to detainees held in military custody typically has very little to do with the military at all, other than the obvious fact that military people run the system. The military operates terrorist tribunals not because our government thought people with military experience would be more qualified to decide these cases, because most of the cases have no particular connection to military operations or military expertise. The military was handed this job because the government believed it could use the military to help shield detainee-related legal procedures, decisions, and outcomes from intrusive meddling by civilian courts.

Many people assume these military legal proceedings are designed for suspected terrorists captured on the field of battle in the course of a military conflict. Under those circumstances, it would be sensible for people with experience on the battlefield—members of the military—to review evidence related to how suspected terrorists were captured and what they were doing at the time in order to determine whether they were properly detained. The facts, however, fail to support this assumption at all.

An analysis of the Department of Defense's own data from more than five hundred combatant status review tribunals found that in only 4 percent of the cases did the military allege the detainee had ever been on *any* battlefield. In only one case out of more than five hundred tribunals studied did the military allege that American forces had made a battlefield capture.[4] In the overwhelming majority of cases, our military took persons into custody because someone sold them to the United States for a financial bounty. If these cases typically have little to do with reviewing military operations or evaluating military judgment—if there is nothing particularly "military" or "combatant" about the cases other than the fact that the people who run the panels are members of the military—then the basic premise for giving them the benefit of the doubt begins to fall away. If military tribunals conducted as part of a nontraditional "war on terror" are not particularly "military" in nature, then we ought to consider what we are teaching the military when we insist that only servicemembers are qualified to conduct them.

Combatant status review tribunals—CSRTs—are the military tribunals that determine whether detainees have been properly labeled as enemy combatants, meaning they can be held indefinitely in military custody.[5] Under the rules, a junior military officer called the "Recorder" assembles evidence in support of detention and presents it to a panel of three more senior military officers. The detainee is free to testify in front of the panel and may offer any reasonably available evidence he has, although chances are very small that any helpful witnesses or information will be "reasonably available" to someone confined at Guantánamo. The panel members then vote on whether the evidence shows the detainee is "more likely than not" an enemy combatant.

The system was designed to give every benefit of the doubt to the military and the United States government. For example, the military panel is told to assume any evidence offered by the government is accurate and truthful unless the detainee is able to prove otherwise. The government-friendly rules are understandable, at least to some degree, given the potential stakes of mistakenly releasing a dangerous individual and the practical difficulty of producing conclusive evidence of either innocence or guilt. The definition of "enemy combatant" also casts a wide net beyond those who actually engage in combatant activities, also including anyone who "supports" the Taliban, al Qaeda, or any other "associated" hostile forces. The system has some intentional flexibility in order to cover persons whose connection to terror may be very indirect, but with that flexibility comes the risk that a detainee may be incorrectly classified as an enemy combatant based on how loosely one defines what it means to "support" some organization, or on how one decides whether one group is sufficiently "associated" with another.

Although detainees were not allowed to have a lawyer or other advocate help them during a CSRT, lawyers challenged the entire CSRT process as a violation of the constitutional right of habeas corpus,[6] which is the right that anyone has, not only American citizens, to challenge the circumstances of their detention by the United States government and argue their case before a neutral decision maker. Habeas corpus is not a "get out of jail free" card, but it does require the government to explain why a person is being held. These lawyers were not getting traction on their legal claims until an Army lieutenant colonel working on the prosecutorial side of the system revealed his insider's perspective on how CSRTs were operating in practice.

In June 2007, Lieutenant Colonel Stephen Abraham, an Army intelligence officer and a lawyer, prepared an unclassified affidavit describing his service with the military office responsible for the CSRT process, the Office for the Administrative Review of the Detention of Enemy Combatants.[7] He was an agency liaison who worked with various government offices to gather and validate the information offered to justify detention, and he was one of the few people involved in the task of building an evidentiary record against detainees who had the experience and training to understand both the intelligence and legal issues involved. Abraham believed the junior officer "Recorders" were typically unable to assess the value of the evidence they presented. In his words, "The information used to prepare the files to be used by the Recorders frequently consisted of finished intelligence products of a generalized nature—often outdated, often 'generic,' rarely specifically relating to the individual subjects of the CSRTs or to the circumstances related to those individuals."

Abraham described a process in which information was routinely pre-screened, prepackaged, edited, and manipulated to reach a predetermined conclusion. Although Abraham's job was to obtain or review information related to the cases of individual detainees and, more specifically, to certify for CSRT members there was no "exculpatory information" available that might suggest the military had mistakenly detained someone, apparently very few people thought this duty should be taken seriously. Everyone seemed to assume Abraham would fabricate or "pencil whip" his approvals, a term used in military circles for the act of falsely certifying a safety check or inspection in writing, knowing it never took place.

From Abraham's perspective, the process for combatant status review was a sham, designed to package information—whether relevant or irrelevant, specific or general, current or outdated, accurate or inaccurate, complete or incomplete—in a way that would support the expected result. At no stage of the process did the military members of CSRT panels have a fair chance to consider whether the decision to designate an individual as an "enemy combatant" was correct. When on one occasion Abraham and two other officers declined to label a detainee an enemy combatant because there was no "objectively credible evidence" to support such a finding, senior officers ordered them to go back and try again, presumably until they came back with the right answer. Abraham said the focus was always on "what went wrong" in these cases, not on what actually went right when the military discovered a mistaken detention.[8]

A few months later, another military lawyer who had served on forty-nine CSRT panels filed a similar affidavit confirming all the same problems that Abraham raised. The second lawyer, who was not identified by name in the legal record, also said his JAG colleagues believed many of the military officers serving on CSRT panels could not tell the difference between actual evidence of a fact and having someone tell you their opinion or conclusion about the same thing.[9] His observation may or may not have been correct, but I suspect part of the problem was that the officers did not think the distinction was important, given the results-oriented purpose of the CSRT process.

It turned out that these affidavits from frustrated JAG officers working within the CSRT process were describing the problem in relatively mild, understated terms. The very first time a federal court had the chance to examine a CSRT ruling and check whether it had been conducted properly under Department of Defense rules,[10] the judges were openly incredulous at what was being passed off as a credible legal process. Although most of the opinion was written in the traditional politeness of legal language, the impolite message of the case was that truth and integrity still mattered, even in a system designed to be forgiving of practical difficulties in gathering evidence.

In *Parhat v. Gates*,[11] the detainee had the most remote of connections, at best, with any groups engaged in hostilities against the United States. Huzaifa Parhat was a Chinese citizen and a Turkic Uighur, a member of an ethnic group of Muslims from a northwestern Chinese province seeking independence from the Chinese government.[12] The United States labeled Parhat an enemy combatant because he had traveled across the border to a Uighur camp in Afghanistan in June 2001. One of the camp organizers was also believed to be a leader in a Chinese separatist group called the East Turkistan Islamic Movement (ETIM), and the United States alleged that ETIM was associated with al Qaeda. Parhat insisted his disagreement was only with the government of China, never with the United States, and there was no evidence he or his fellow Uighurs had any connection whatsoever to al Qaeda. The court agreed:

> The documents [provided to the CSRT] make assertions . . . about activities undertaken by ETIM, and about that organization's relationship to al Qaida and the Taliban. The documents repeatedly describe those activities and relationships as having "reportedly" occurred, as being "said to" or "reported to" have happened, and as things that "may" be true or are "suspected of" having taken place. But in virtually every instance, the documents do not say who "reported" or "said" or "suspected" those things.

Comically, the government argued the information had to be accurate because several of the assertions were repeated in at least three different intelligence documents, disregarding the fact that identical language appearing in each document suggested the information had been copied from one to the next. The court ridiculed the government's position, even comparing it to a humorous poem, Lewis Carroll's *The Hunting of the Snark*, which includes the line, "I have said it thrice: What I tell you three times is true." Neither was the court persuaded when the government said the evidence must be reliable because the government would never say something unless it was true. The lesson of *Parhat v. Gates* for the military and its civilian superiors was as simple as this: in the world of law, *you cannot just make stuff up* and expect courts will go along with it. A perfectly fair question, however, is whether courts have the expertise to accurately overrule decisions made by military officers and decide who is making stuff up and who is not. One military lawyer who has argued we should reduce the influence of law in military operations—a viewpoint not held by most members of the JAG Corps—cited *Parhat v. Gates* as yet another example of courts intruding in matters best reserved for the military.[13]

Criticism that courts are overstepping their bounds might carry some weight if the decisions had anything to do with military operations, but generally they do not. Members of CSRT panels are most often asked to assess political relationships and decipher the motivations various groups might have to cooperate with the United States or with each other, but these are not questions military training helps them answer. The affidavit submitted by the unnamed JAG officer even used the Chinese Uighurs as an example of a political situation generating inconsistent CSRT results. The panel members, all midlevel and senior officers, had no particular expertise about Uighurs or their political interests or allegiances. There was no reason to ask the officers to decide questions like this, other than the fervent hope of some civilians that they would, like proverbial good soldiers, disregard any messy problems of evidence, proof, and truth and arrive at a predetermined conclusion.

One of the most convenient and dangerous assumptions underlying military exceptions to the usual rule of law is the idea that if the military is involved in some activity, then anything the military does must automatically be a matter of military necessity. In too many instances, the government asks its citizens to accept, without explanation, that the only way to protect the military's interests is to suspend the operation of law. Taking the next step in this all-too-common chain of logic, it becomes much too easy to flip an argument in favor of following the law into something more sinister—if you support the rule of law, it must mean you do not support the military.

So whatever happened to Huzaifa Parhat? Once the government's efforts to paper over his case were exposed by the court, the military's civilian superiors in the executive branch retreated. The United States conceded that Parhat and the other Uighurs being held at Guantánamo are not, and never were, enemy combatants, and the district court ordered their release after seven years in custody, adding, with some understatement, "I think the moment has arrived for the court to shine the light of constitutionality on the reasons for detention."[14] Nonetheless, the government appealed the order to release and a federal appeals court reversed, ruling that although the United States had no authority to hold them as enemy combatants, neither did courts have any authority to release them. A few Uighurs have been freed and transferred to island countries, but others remain in custody at Guantánamo.[15]

Not one word was written by anyone, however, about the military's role in the fiasco. No one asked why the president had put the military in the awkward position of having to deliver a political result outside its professional expertise and counter to the available facts. No one asked why the military had cooperated in such a legal charade so willingly, except for the objections of a few military lawyers. No one asked what had happened to the political independence and the traditional professional ethic of the military, which normally would have served as a solid check on civilian temptation to misuse the military for purposes outside its proper constitutional role. Most of all, no one apologized to the military or vowed it would not happen again.

Think about what a system like the CSRT process teaches members of the military. Others have questioned what impact our actions in the metaphorical "war on terror" may have on the individuals detained, on others who may be radicalized into enemies by the perception that detainees are treated unfairly, or on the respect and standing the United States will have around the world. We must also consider the impact of these special systems of law on the military itself and on the future of military professionalism. This is the problem, unfortunately, that receives very little attention.

We chip away at the military's professional ethic when we cavalierly use the military to avoid the temporary inconvenience of a commitment to law. Imagine what it does to the military's sense of professionalism to be taught it is part of the military's job to launder facts and law to achieve a political success for the administration or the Congress holding office at the time. Imagine what it does to the military's sense of professionalism to be taught that truth is not important. Imagine being taught that "law" and "justice" mean something very different in the hands of servicemembers, when these are the same people who take a solemn oath to support and defend the Constitution of the United States.

It was inevitable that political partisanship would soon infect the military's separate legal system for detainees. When civilians suggest that military performance will be measured by political loyalty, they place tremendous stress on professional military ethics. The symptoms of this stress are now most visible in the broken process for military commissions, which are the Guantánamo trials for prosecution of specific war crimes. More than a few military prosecutors resigned or refused to bring cases—*prosecutors*, not defense lawyers—because they believed the military commissions process was a sham and their participation would be a violation of both military and legal ethics. One of the prosecutors, Army Lieutenant Colonel Darrel Vandeveld, said he used to be one of "the true believers," someone who had "zero doubts" about the rightness of the system. He resigned when he realized the system had only "sullied the American military and the Constitution."[16] These consequences were sadly inevitable, yet our distance from the military and our lack of serious engagement with the health of our civil-military relations prevented us from seeing the problem.

The Supreme Court's treatment of civil-military issues since the end of the Vietnam War demonstrates that claims based on military necessity or military expertise can sometimes be misused as reasons for bending or disregarding the usual rule of law. Over time, the effect has been to set up the needs of the military as a counterpoint to law, as if each one necessarily diminished the other. The lesson learned from these cases, even if not directly stated, is that when the military succeeds, it succeeds despite law, not because of law. In the eyes of the Supreme Court, law has been the antithesis of military might, and the Court's job has become one of protecting the military from law, not preserving its traditional relationship to law. This way of thinking about the military and law tends to seep across government institutions and also trickles down throughout civilian society. This lesson becomes so engrained we sometimes forget to check whether actual military necessity, experience, or expertise is at issue, or whether civilians are only waving the military flag in an effort to shield themselves from scrutiny. At our very worst civil-military moments, civilians insist they are acting in the best interests of the military at the same time they are disregarding, censoring, or misrepresenting real military judgment.

Army field manuals did not have much of a public profile before they became the unexpected centerpiece in a debate over whether the United States should employ tactics of torture and abuse in interrogating persons detained in the "war on terror." In the Detainee Treatment Act of 2005 (DTA), Congress enacted uniform standards for the interrogation of persons held in military custody, although these "new" standards were really nothing new. Expectations that were once considered unambiguous had become confused and inconsistent amid reports of misconduct at Abu Ghraib, and so Congress tried to restore order by referring back to an already-existing gold standard of professional behavior in the military, the Army Field Manual. The DTA made it simple: "No person in the custody or under the effective control of the Department of Defense or under detention in a Department of Defense facility shall be subject to any treatment or technique of interrogation not authorized by and listed in the United States Army Field Manual on Intelligence Interrogation."[17]

Army field manuals[18] are literally what they are called: they are Army "how-to" books designed for use by actual soldiers when performing their jobs in the field. These manuals are not written for generals or for politicians. They are primarily for the benefit of soldiers to help them learn tasks and perform duties "the Army way," consistent with traditional Army values and based on the hard lessons learned from both military successes and military mistakes. For the most part, they are not classified or kept under military wraps. Army field manuals are available for anyone to read at a variety of web sites, from both governmental and private sources.

On September 11, 2001, anyone looking for the collected Army wisdom on methods for conducting interrogations would have consulted Field Manual (FM) 34-52, entitled *Intelligence Interrogation*.[19] The military values, principles, and techniques contained in FM 34-52 are stated in simple terms, and not only because its drafters intended to make them clear to the youngest and least experienced within the Army. Oftentimes important facets of military thinking can be explained in disarmingly plain language because they are so fundamental, so settled, and so uncompromising in nature. How many civilians would have known, for example, that the core of military regulation prohibiting abusive and unprofessional behavior during interrogation of captured enemies could be as simple as the Golden Rule— treating others as you would want to be treated? FM 34-52 required military interrogators to stop and ask themselves this question in times of uncertainty: if the enemy treated an American servicemember the same way, would you consider it a violation of international or United States law? If the answer was yes, then the manual prohibited the conduct. One JAG officer even concluded his training sessions on lawful treatment of prisoners with this admonition: "I know you won't remember everything I told you today, but just remember what your mom told you: Do unto others as you would have others do unto you."[20]

The Army Field Manual taught the art of military interrogation within explicit boundaries of law. It emphasized repeatedly that military interrogators had to comply with the Geneva Conventions and the Uniform Code of Military Justice, and at one point the manual even highlighted pertinent language from the Geneva Conventions by surrounding it with an attention-getting "black box" border, like the ominous health warnings on a pack of cigarettes or a potentially dangerous prescription drug. FM 34-52 was unmistakably clear about the Army's position on the importance of following the rule of law when performing military duty:

The [Geneva Conventions] and US policy expressly prohibit acts of violence or intimidation, including physical or mental torture, threats, insults, or exposure to inhumane treatment as a means of or aid to interrogation. Such illegal acts are not authorized and will not be condoned by the US Army. Acts in violation of these prohibitions are criminal acts punishable under the UCMJ.

In the event soldiers might have been unclear on the principle, FM 34-52 went on to specifically prohibit a long list of activities that an unprofessional interrogator might be tempted to use, such as electric shock; forced standing, sitting, or kneeling in uncomfortable positions for prolonged periods; food or sleep deprivation; beating; mock execution; or threats of torture to others. The manual emphasized that interrogators must learn to distinguish torture and abuse from proper techniques that rely on nonviolent or noncoercive ruses. One chapter, entitled "The Interrogation Process," explained in extensive but easy-to-understand detail how an interrogator could most effectively develop rapport with a subject and design questions for eliciting useful information. The use of fear was mentioned only briefly, along with a warning that it was rarely effective and may foreclose any productive interrogation in the future. In contrast to standard television fare, the manual directed that the subject should never be made to fear the interrogator; instead, the key point is that the subject may have reason to fear consequences from others, such as punishment for the commission of war crimes. "A good interrogator will implant in the source's mind that the interrogator himself is not the object to be feared, but is a possible way out of the trap."

By now, readers may be wondering how this can possibly be official Army doctrine. Isn't the "war on terror" so different from other armed conflicts that the military no longer has the luxury of relying on cooperation from subjects during interrogation? Aren't interrogators supposed to be tough and "take the gloves off" when necessary to extract information? This concern, however, seems to be a poor reason for discarding decades of military expertise, because FM 34-52 was expressly designed for interrogation during all types of conflicts, including a nuclear conflict, which is surely the quintessential "ticking time bomb" scenario. If FM 34-52 was the knowledgeable military answer when nuclear weapons were involved, then it should work well enough with terrorists not suspected of controlling armed nuclear weapons.

Intelligence Interrogation took care to explain not only the proper techniques of interrogation, but also the reasons *why* torture, coercion, and abuse have no place in professional military interrogations. First, this conduct is against the law. ("Acts in violation of these prohibitions are criminal acts punishable under the UCMJ.") Second, it hurts the war effort. ("Revelation of use of torture by US personnel will bring discredit upon the US and its armed forces while undermining domestic and international support for the war effort.") Third, it puts our own servicemembers at risk. ("It also may place US and allied personnel in enemy hands at a greater risk of abuse by their captors.") Fourth, and most simply, it just doesn't work. ("Use of torture and other illegal methods is a poor technique that yields unreliable results, may damage subsequent collection efforts, and can induce the source to say what he thinks the interrogator wants to hear.")

This is precisely why the senior lawyers in each military department were so disturbed to find, in early 2003, that civilian leadership in the Departments of Justice and Defense intended to erase the military's long-standing tradition of adherence to law in the art of interrogation and ignore the military's professional experience that torture and abusive conduct were ineffective and harmful to the war effort. Each of the services strongly objected—in terms as sharp as senior officers are ever likely to use in writing when disagreeing with civilian leadership—to twisted legal interpretations advising that most physical and mental abuse couldn't be defined as torture under the law; that even if it was torture, servicemembers could raise a legal defense of necessity; and that lastly, even if it was torture, and even if servicemembers had no defense, the laws prohibiting torture (including the military's own UCMJ) could not be enforced if the president believed torture was necessary for reasons of national security.

These senior lawyers, all generals or admirals, wrote memos to their civilian superiors documenting their objections and standing on the same justifications set out in FM 34-52.[21] The Air Force memo captured the sense of all the services when it explained just how much of a radical shift it would be for the military to disregard the rule of law and abandon its professional history:

> Finally, the use of the more extreme interrogation techniques simply is not how the U.S. armed forces have operated in recent history. We have taken the legal and moral "high-road" in the conduct of our military operations regardless of how others may operate. Our forces are trained in this legal and moral mindset beginning the day they enter active duty. . . . We need to consider the overall impact of approving extreme interrogation techniques as giving official approval and legal sanction to the application of interrogation techniques that U.S. forces have consistently been trained are unlawful.

The Marine Corps memo noted, with what seemed to be barely concealed disgust, that civilian lawyers in the Department of Justice seemed to have little regard for the military and the effect of reversing several generations of training: "The common thread among our recommendations is concern for servicemembers. [The Department of Justice's Office of Legal Counsel] does not represent the services; thus, understandably, concern for servicemembers is not reflected in their opinion." I assume the Marine Corps conclusion was laced with mild sarcasm, because the president's lawyers do have an obligation to consider military interests when crafting advice for the executive branch, even when they are not specifically assigned to represent the uniformed services. Otherwise, it wouldn't be very good legal advice.

One has to wonder how it was so easy to convince the military that its traditional bond with the rule of law was now suddenly obsolete and it should disregard its own professional teaching that "torture is the technique of choice of the lazy, stupid, and pseudo-tough."[22] With the exception of senior military lawyers and a handful of military operational experts who tried to warn that coercive interrogation techniques were useless and dangerous,[23] the military managed to turn on a dime and disregard generations of hard-won experience in the art of interrogation. At a 2007 reunion of World War II military interrogators now in their eighties and nineties, several criticized the contemporary military's abandonment of traditional techniques and principles. One veteran who played chess with Adolph Hitler's deputy, Rudolph Hess, said, "We got more information out of a German general with a game of chess or Ping-Pong than they do today, with their torture."[24]

In February 2007, Jane Mayer wrote an article in the *New Yorker* about the television show *24* and its effect on West Point cadets, entitled "Whatever It Takes." *24* is the immensely popular series in which Jack Bauer, an agent in a fictional antiterrorism unit, routinely uses torture to extract time-sensitive information from "bad guys" and save American lives. Mayer told the story of how General Patrick Finnegan, dean of academics and formerly the chair of the Department of Law at West Point, traveled to Hollywood to plead with the producers and writers of *24* to stop portraying torture as the all-purpose answer to terrorism that always works. Finnegan explained that it was becoming increasingly difficult for him to convince his students—cadets who would soon be leading soldiers in Iraq and Afghanistan—that Jack Bauer's conduct did not reflect the state of the law or of military professionalism.

The difficulty Finnegan was having in teaching law, ethics, and professionalism to future military officers should have been foreseeable, because we have at least one member of the Supreme Court who seems to believe Jack Bauer's conduct does reflect the state of the law. At a Canadian law conference in summer 2007 on the subject of, ironically, the "Administration of Justice and National Security in Democracies," Justice Scalia cited Jack Bauer for the proposition that federal agents need some legal flexibility in times of crisis: "Jack Bauer saved Los Angeles. . . . He saved hundreds of thousands of lives."[25]

For some time now the military has been at a fragile tipping point with respect to its bond with law, and the "torture memos" may have sent it over the edge. It's too easy an excuse to say, "Well, the military was told the Geneva Conventions no longer applied to the treatment of prisoners deemed 'unlawful enemy combatants,' and what the military does best is follow the orders of civilians." That's not the way the military works, or at least not the way it's supposed to work. Even if the military accepted the accuracy of civilian legal memos assuring readers that servicemembers could not be held accountable under laws prohibiting torture and abuse—a tall assumption, given that the military's own lawyers insisted the memos were clearly wrong in authorizing illegal conduct—no one directly ordered the military to disregard its own professional experience and take actions that were counterproductive to the war effort and inconsistent with military effectiveness. It seems difficult to understand why the military was so quick to get on board with increasingly abusive, even sadistic, treatment of prisoners that violated every professional military understanding. It wasn't just Abu Ghraib. According to the unanimously bipartisan report of the Senate Armed Services Committee in December 2008, it was a systemic problem throughout the military detention system:

> The abuse of detainees in U.S. custody cannot simply be attributed to the actions of 'a few bad apples' acting on their own. The fact is that senior officials in the United States government solicited information on how to use aggressive techniques, redefined the law to create the appearance of their legality, and authorized their use against detainees. Those efforts damaged our ability to collect accurate intelligence that could save lives, strengthened the hand of our enemies, and compromised our moral authority.[26]

And the military was more than a passive recipient of bad information. It was an active participant in undermining its own professional ethic. According to congressional findings, "interrogation policies and plans approved by senior military and civilian officials conveyed the message that physical pressures and degradation were appropriate treatment for detainees in U.S. military custody. What followed was an erosion in standards dictating that detainees be treated humanely." The military went along without much objection—except from the senior JAG Corps lawyers—even though, in the opinion of some senior military officers, the program was putting American servicemembers at risk. The armed services committee report quoted the congressional testimony of former Navy General Counsel Alberto Mora that "there are serving U.S. flag-rank officers who maintain that the first and second identifiable causes of U.S. combat deaths in Iraq—as judged by their effectiveness in recruiting insurgent fighters into combat—are, respectively, the symbols of Abu Ghraib and Guantánamo."

I suspect the entire military tragedy of detainee abuse would have unfolded quite differently if the military had not been so thoroughly indoctrinated by civilian leaders during the past few decades that the rule of law is inconsistent with military effectiveness and that constitutional values are at odds with military values. It has become so natural for the military to assume it has a standing exception to compliance with law that almost no one blinks when the military is presented with yet another exception. It has become so natural for the military to assume law is an impediment to military success that almost no one objects when civilians conclude the military's hard-earned professional expertise in interrogations is suddenly wrong. The military tragedy of detainee abuse may have also marked the moment when gradual erosion of the military's professional ethic of political neutrality had finally showed its hand. I suspect the military may have been a more candid and forceful advisor with respect to its professional expertise had it not been influenced by an unspoken obligation of political allegiance to civilian policy preferences.

This fundamental distortion of the military's relationship to civilian authority, civilian society, and the Constitution has the potential to affect military policy and military operations in countless ways. The consequences can be specific and immediate, as they were with respect to detainee operations, but they can also be more diffuse and difficult to recognize, unfolding over time. Many of the nagging social and personnel issues that have bedeviled the military for years fall in this category. Both Congress and the military have failed to understand that they cannot hold civilians at a distance from the military and at the same time convince enough of them to enlist. Neither can they dismiss the importance of constitutional values within the military and at the same time expect servicemembers to treat one another with respect.

Chapter 8

Recruiting for a Constitutionally Fragile Military

In early 2003, not long before the beginning of the war in Iraq, Representative Charles Rangel of New York sponsored a congressional bill called the Universal National Service Act, which would "provide for the common defense by requiring that all young persons in the United States, including women, perform a period of military service or a period of civilian service in furtherance of the national defense and homeland security."[1] Under the act, everyone between the ages of eighteen and twenty-six—citizens and noncitizens alike—would serve their country for two years in either a military or a civilian role, with deferments available only for extreme hardship or disability. Rangel's theme was one of shared sacrifice among Americans: "Those who would lead us into war have the obligation to support an all-out mobilization of Americans for the war effort, including mandatory national service that asks something of us all."[2]

Although most would have ended up serving in civilian roles because the size of the pool exceeded military needs, all the attention focused on the part of the proposal that would have brought back the military draft after thirty years of an all-volunteer force. Rangel recognized that the special needs of the military would have to take first place in any proposal for national service. For example, under his bill the military would have "first dibs" on the best candidates, and the rest would complete their national service obligation in civilian roles. The military would not have been forced to take anyone it believed was unqualified for military service.

Secretary of Defense Donald Rumsfeld was asked at a press conference what he thought of Congressman Rangel's proposal for mandatory national service, including a reactivation of the military draft. It was an important question. A national service requirement would be a substantial change in the way Americans had come to view what they owed their country as citizens, and the subject raises some discomfort about how fairly we share the obligation of military service. But it wasn't as if the idea of returning to a draft had come out of the blue. Questions had been raised about the possible need for military conscription in combating terrorism and protecting national security since shortly after September 11, 2001, and they deserved serious discussion.[3]

Secretary Rumsfeld's response to the reporter's question, however, was bewildering. Clearly, Rumsfeld disagreed with the proposal, because he flatly dismissed it: "We're not going to re-implement a draft. There is no need for it at all." But it was apparently so important to bury the idea of national service as ludicrous or loony that he began to invent reasons that were flatly false, or at best misleading:

> If you think back to when we had the draft, people were brought in; they were paid some fraction of what they could make in the civilian manpower market because they were without choices. Big categories were exempted—people that were in college, people that were teaching, people that were married. It varied from time to time, but there were all kinds of exemptions. And what was left was sucked into the intake, trained for a period of months, and then went out, adding no value, no advantage, really, to the United States armed services over any sustained period of time, because the churning that took place, it took enormous amount of effort in terms of training, and then they were gone.[4]

First, Rumsfeld had to know that almost all of the Vietnam-era exemptions and deferments—especially the controversial college deferment—were no longer available. If Congress reactivated the draft today, college students would be allowed to defer military induction only until the end of a semester they had already started or, for seniors, until the end of the academic year.[5] The extended college deferment that Rumsfeld mentioned, the one that postponed any obligation for military service until a student finished his entire undergraduate education, hasn't been available under selective service law since 1971, before the Vietnam draft ended.[6] Something else must have been going on for Rumsfeld to point irrationally to an unfair draft deferment for college students—one that doesn't even exist anymore— as a reason why we shouldn't discuss a return to the military draft today.

Rumsfeld also stretched the truth when he argued that the reason the all-volunteer force was so strong was because all its members had chosen to serve. He said, "We have people serving today—God bless 'em—because they volunteered. They wanted to be doing what it is they're doing." Rumsfeld left out the small detail that he had authorized "stop-loss" orders *that same day* to prevent approximately fourteen thousand Marines from leaving the military even though they had completed the term of active service required by their enlistment contract or had qualified for retirement.[7] At that moment, servicemembers who were involuntarily retained might have felt a little less like the "volunteers" Rumsfeld was so proudly portraying them to be. Something else must have been going on for Rumsfeld to rail against the idea of compulsory military service even though he was already making substantial use of stop-loss authority, which is milder than a draft but still a compulsory way of meeting military personnel needs.

But what got Rumsfeld in a world of trouble was his casual insult of millions of veterans who have been drafted into this nation's military service over the last half-century and served their country with honor. Veterans' organizations were devastated by Rumsfeld's comment that the service of draftees added "no value, no advantage, really" to the military.[8] Particularly in the case of young men who had been killed or wounded, it seemed coldly insensitive to use phrases like "sucked into the intake" to describe their military service. It was unclear why Rumsfeld assumed that most draftees did not serve in good faith, despite our historical experience to the contrary. A 2002 report from the Army Research Institute noted that, in a draft era, draftees actually have lower rates of desertion than soldiers who volunteer, and the reason was that draftees tended on average to be of higher quality.[9] A book praised as a "definitive account of the draft" reported that draftees during the Vietnam era were better behaved and superior in education, intelligence, and maturity in comparison to volunteers.[10] The Vietnam draft didn't lower the quality of the military; it actually kept it from getting worse. Something else must have been going on for Rumsfeld to be so dismissive of young men who have answered their country's call and served to the best of their abilities.

Rumsfeld did eventually apologize. He explained that he only meant to say a volunteer military had a smaller rate of turnover in personnel, or "churn," than a draft military.[11] In deciding whether Rumsfeld's explanation was genuine, however, one should consider that a study of Army recruiting and retention from 1995 to 2001 found that 20 percent of those who signed Army enlistment contracts never showed up for active duty and, of those who did report for duty, 36 percent failed to complete even three years of service.[12] To say the least, there is still a tremendous amount of "churn" even in an all-volunteer military. Defense Department statistics show that between 1974 and 1996, the average length of an enlisted person's service increased by only a year and a half, from 6 to 7.5 years.[13] It can be tempting to belittle a military that features shorter initial tours of duty for draftees as unprofessional and ineffective, but the overall difference in experience doesn't seem large enough to justify Rumsfeld's curt dismissal of draftees as being too transient to have any value to the military. At best, Rumsfeld's statements comparing draft and volunteer forces were exaggerated and misleading. One of the nation's most respected military researchers thought Rangel's proposal would actually make the military stronger by bringing in larger numbers of high-quality people for duties that were important to the mission yet appropriate for short-term service.[14]

It seemed the defense secretary's first priority was to ensure Rangel's proposal was never taken seriously as a subject for discussion. The Department of Defense quickly generated a report—it was out even before the apology—discrediting the idea of mandatory national service.[15] The report picked up on an earlier newspaper editorial in which Rangel noted that military service "is no longer a common experience" and "a disproportionate number of the poor and members of minority groups make up the enlisted ranks of the military, while the most privileged Americans are underrepresented or absent."[16] These points were undoubtedly true and have since been pressed by promilitary advocates in books such as *AWOL: The Unexcused Absence of America's Upper Classes from Military Service—and How It Hurts Our Country.*[17]

The authors of the DOD report, however, engaged in a bit of clever misdirection, avoiding the hard questions about shared responsibility for service and instead suggesting that Rangel, a black congressman, was just "playing the race card" and was not serious about military readiness. With language that could easily be interpreted as a personal (and racial) slap at Rangel, the report noted that a 1970 commission on the all-volunteer military had already "addressed a concern raised in some quarters about a volunteer force becoming 'too black.'"[18] But Rangel's point was very different. As he explained to the *Wall Street Journal*, "patriotic duty is not a question of race or class. All Americans who share in the bounty of this great country are duty-bound to share the sacrifice of her defense."[19] Still, the report managed to recast the controversy as a bitter, divisive complaint about the inequalities of race and class, not a unifying call based on citizenship, service, and responsibility.

An exceptional series of events had followed from a simple proposal for mandatory national service, military or civilian, for young Americans. The secretary of defense in a Republican presidential administration was forced to apologize for his inadvertently demeaning comments about military veterans. Liberals called for a return to the military draft; conservatives were so hostile to the idea that they objected indiscriminately and frantically. The world had apparently turned upside down. This fleeting skirmish, however, was just a small symptom of a larger civil-military divide. There must have been a reason Rumsfeld was so viscerally opposed to a national service program—opposed even to any discussion of it—and his reason likely had little to do with an informed belief it would weaken the military's effectiveness. When civilian defense officials respond to a national service proposal with misrepresentation and bluster, and when senior military officers say they are "horrified" by the idea of shared sacrifice, something else is going on.[20]

As we saw with justices of the Supreme Court, there is something about the military that causes perfectly intelligent people to make arguments they'd be much less likely to offer in another context. A University of Chicago economist, for example, dismissed the idea of returning to the draft because he thought mandatory national service puts the "wrong" people in the military: "people who are either uninterested in a military life, not well equipped for one, or who put a very high value on doing something else."[21] Market forces, he believed, were the best way of allocating people to the right tasks. I wonder, however, whether he would float the same theory for other forms of public service traditionally considered obligations of citizenship, such as jury duty, for example. Would he argue that the best way to put the "right" people on juries, and the best way to find people "well equipped" to render accurate verdicts, is to eliminate all mandatory calls for jury duty and instead fill juries with people who were motivated to serve for pay? In some cases, a desire to perform an important civic obligation would correspond with a desire to be paid well, but in the majority of cases it probably would not. I suppose it depends on whether we care if a representative range of American society carries the responsibility and privilege of serving on juries, or of serving in the military. Does that representativeness have value?

You might be curious to find out what happened to Rangel's Universal National Service Act. Republicans pushed it to a vote, and all House members voted against it but two.[22] Even Rangel himself voted against it. A reasonable and important question had been raised about the obligation of citizenship and the responsibility for national service, and almost every member of Congress ran terrified from the possibility they might be seen as a critic of the present all-volunteer force.

Research on the civil-military gap suggests an explanation for these irrational reactions to proposals to bring back the draft. The Gap Project found a divide between civilian and military worlds that was most prominent along lines of political ideology and partisanship. Once the military defines itself in terms of socially conservative ideology, assertions of moral superiority, political allegiance, and resistance to constitutional values, forces of self-selection affecting who chooses to join the military will increasingly entrench those differences. A military that sells itself as an institution necessarily distant and different from the society that surrounds it—conveniently consistent with the Supreme Court's view of the military and its connection to law—has a strong interest in preserving that distance and difference. A draft that imposes an obligation for military service broadly and fairly across American society, however, would by definition shrink the civil-military gap and produce a military that was much more representative of civilian society on a number of grounds, including ideological and political allegiance. This may be the change that contemporary opponents of the draft fear the most. One thing the military has never considered, however, is whether encouraging the civil-military gap is losing the military many more recruits than it gains.

Military recruiting and military conscription are almost impossible subjects for serious discussion today. Any suggestion that the all-volunteer force might have a serious problem with the quality of its personnel is inevitably taken as an insult against those who have chosen to wear the uniform. The arguments in favor of the current way of doing things are often blunt and simplistic, with all the nuance of a big club. If someone questions, for example, why the military's recruitment of high-school dropouts is sharply increasing, someone will respond, "You're assuming everyone who joins the military lacks intelligence. I know enlisted men and women who excelled at academics, who even have college degrees." If someone questions why the military is accepting more people who require waivers for criminal records, drug abuse, or health problems, someone will respond, "You're assuming people join the military because they are losers and have no other choice. That's insulting to people who enlist out of a selfless desire to serve their country. Our servicemembers represent the best of what America has to offer."

This chapter does not make sweeping generalizations, because they would be inaccurate in many, or even most, individual instances. The military is a huge organization, and no knowledgeable person would ever contend that members of the military are all the same on any measure. Some are of high quality, some are of low quality, and reasonable people could even disagree about how to measure quality in military recruiting. The critical questions, however, are always at the margins. In order to fill the military personnel slots we have—not to mention the additional ones we might need—are we forced to accept too many volunteers who lack the aptitude, maturity, moral strength, or physical fitness required for military service? Does the all-volunteer force market itself in a way that draws disproportionately from an unnecessarily narrow slice of young Americans, while ignoring or discouraging a broader base of potential recruits? Is the government wrong when it insists that attracting a broader base of recruits would only lead to weaker recruits? Is the government wrong when it insists a military dependent in part on an obligation for national service—a draft—cannot possibly be as strong as an all-volunteer military? In my opinion, the answers to these questions are all "yes," but I would be satisfied if readers were at least persuaded these questions are very difficult and none have answers as obvious as we are led to believe.

Myths abound on the subject of military recruiting for all the same reasons myths abound on the subject of military service in general. The gap of experience and culture between military and civilian worlds that has developed since the end of the draft makes many of us less knowledgeable about military recruiting and the reasons why young people might, or might not, have a propensity to enlist. The informal rules that govern conversations about the military also tend to limit candid exchanges of information. People who haven't served in the military are often discouraged from taking part in the debate about who serves and who should serve. Maybe some people shy away from the topic because they don't want to call attention to their failure to volunteer but realize, at some level, that others must have had to go in their place. Finally, who wants to criticize the results of military recruiting in a political climate in which criticism means you don't support or respect the troops? But when exaggerated, misleading, or false statements about military recruiting and retention are repeated often enough, and insistently enough, eventually they begin to resonate as truth even if the facts themselves are contrary. Anyone trying to dislodge the myths—or at least put them back in the realm of debatable points—is rolling that boulder up a very long hill.

In talking about military recruiting and the composition of the all-volunteer force, it would be helpful to respect a few guidelines for productive discussion and constructive criticism. We should promise not to take observations that the military cannot meet its personnel requirements without taking some volunteers it should not accept, or that the military has become unrepresentative of civilian society in some way, and read them as accusations directed at all members of the military. One can conclude the quality of the all-volunteer military is not as high as it should be at the margins without intending to paint everyone in the military with the same criticism.

The most important misunderstanding about military recruiting today is probably the one endorsed most heavily by the government and by the military itself. Americans are encouraged to believe that because our self-selected, all-volunteer military is already higher in quality, on average, than civilian society, any significant change in how we raise military forces—perhaps a draft, or different incentives to broaden the pool of volunteers—could only weaken the military. This ideological campaign went into full swing as the length of the conflict in Iraq strained the military's capabilities and people began to call for a broader base of recruits for military service. The point is usually not a subtle one. For example, one DOD report defending the all-volunteer force labeled its charts comparing the achievement and aptitude of civilian and military youth with the presumptuous slogan "Military Better Than America."[23]

This argument has developed into a standard talking point for military recruiters, who are now taking the position that only 25 percent of young Americans are physically and morally qualified for military service.[24] This talking point resonates as true because it is consistent with our newly ingrained cultural belief that the military is fundamentally better than civilian society—a theme first cultivated by the Supreme Court in an effort to explain why constitutional values were less important in a military environment. As a bonus, it even provides a ready excuse for why military recruiting can be so difficult. If the military can accept only the cream of the American crop, a select group with competing options for their talents, it makes sense that recruiting duty would be a challenge. It all seems plausible, except the military has never revealed precisely how it calculated that only 25 percent of youth are eligible and, as far as I can determine, the number is without factual basis.[25] Even if the number was correct, which anyone who works on a large college campus filled with tens of thousands of apparently qualified students would find dubious, the claim would still be misleading because the military routinely waives compliance with most of the "requirements" that presumably underlie its statistical calculation.

The military deploys statistics in unusual ways in a determined effort to convince policymakers and the American public that all is well—or well enough—with military recruiting and no fundamental change in our approach is necessary. At most, maybe the military needs to try harder, but it doesn't need to try differently. Perhaps the military's most frequent statistical claim of this kind compares the rate of high-school graduation between military enlistees and Americans in general. According to this argument, the military is smarter than America because a higher percentage of enlistees have graduated from high school than in the general population. The comparison is flawed, however, for two reasons. First, the military tends to average its graduation data across all the services, which obscures how difficult it is for the Army—the service under the greatest personnel strain due to the ground war in Iraq—to fill its slots with graduates. In fiscal year 2007, according to a study of DOD data conducted by the National Priorities Project, only 70 percent of new Army recruits had a high-school diploma, a number not that far off from the percentage of Americans overall who have earned a diploma.[26]

The second reason the comparison is flawed is because it isn't even the right comparison. The military inflates its success by comparing its recruits to the population as a whole, which unfortunately includes a significant minority of young people lacking the skills or abilities to train in many lines of work because of functional illiteracy or physical or mental disability. Almost any profession, including the military, ought to be able to beat the general population's average, because the average includes people on the bottom rungs who would have trouble succeeding anywhere. The more pertinent question is how the quality of military recruits compares to the quality of young people beginning similar professional or technical training in the civilian world, but this is a comparison the military does not make. What we do know is the military generally considers a high-school diploma a minimum qualification for enlistment, yet almost a third of recent Army recruits did not meet that standard.

Military recruiting has been an especially difficult challenge since the mid-1990s, years before our current military conflicts began and made the task even more difficult.[27] The propensity of our young people to enlist in the military is not high enough to guarantee a sufficient number of qualified volunteers will walk through a recruiter's door, let alone high enough that the military would be in a position to choose the best qualified individuals from a larger pool of the minimally qualified. Consider how different this process is from the typically competitive situation of applying for a civilian job or for admission to college. Everyone understands some qualified people will inevitably be rejected in favor of other applicants who happen to be more highly qualified. The all-volunteer military, however, is very far away from the recruiting nirvana of being able to pick and choose among qualified candidates. Any qualified candidate will be accepted for military service—with the proviso that qualified candidates automatically become unqualified if they are gay—and the only question is how much the military will be forced to reduce or waive those qualifications to ensure an adequate number of enlistments.

Military recruiters have been working under tremendous pressure to keep up with quotas for enlistees, and the task is so unrelenting some recruiters say it is more stressful than combat service. The pressure for results has led to a significant number of incidents in which recruiters have misrepresented the qualifications of enlistees, helped them cheat on tests for drug use or intellectual aptitude, or ignored disqualifying conditions. In May 2005, the Army took the unusual step of ordering a total "stand-down" of its recruiting operation, meaning that all recruiting activities servicewide were suspended for a day so personnel could use the time to refocus on the rules and ethics of recruiting. In February 2009, the Army ordered yet another stand-down to examine the reasons for a cluster of suicides by Houston-area recruiters.[28]

When military recruiting is extremely difficult, the military can respond in one of two ways. It can either expand the base from which it finds recruits or, alternatively, it can dig deeper where it already has been looking. Over the last decade, a number of indicators suggest the military has been holding tight to the second approach, turning over fewer rocks with more passion rather than figuring out ways to increase the number of rocks. The military has opposed any consideration of resurrecting a national service obligation as an answer to shortfalls in military recruiting. It has resisted proposals that would make brief stints of voluntary military service more compatible with plans for college or civilian employment. It has consistently argued that a bigger candidate pool could only lead to lower quality enlistees, not higher quality. The military has a tenaciously long, but oddly selective, memory of the Vietnam draft era.[29] It tends to associate the draft era with quality issues in the armed forces, but it falls victim to the fallacy of confusing causation and correlation. The draft was actually the mechanism keeping the quality of the draft-era military from getting worse. Ironically, the military may have crafted a volunteer force that is more unrepresentative of civilian society and more tilted toward the non-college-bound than the unsatisfactory draft-assisted force it replaced.[30]

Defense and military researchers have observed that the military tends to write off a majority of the available pool of young adults—those who see themselves as college-bound coming out of high school—as not worth the effort to recruit. These experts have questioned why we rely so much on the very thin slice of the demographic that will have enough aptitude and drive to earn a high-school diploma yet have no immediate plans for college or civilian vocational training.[31] The key to broadening the pool and making military service a more common experience, they thought, was to create incentives that would make the military more attractive to college-bound youth, especially since the percentage of college-bound youth is only increasing. As perceptive as these observations are, however, they miss what may be a more powerful deterrent to enlistment.

It is difficult to understand why the government and the military would be so opposed to making military service more attractive to a broader range of Americans. Their resistance often seems forced and dependent on the assumption that people interested in joining the military for a shorter term of active service—two years or less—would not be very helpful to our national defense. Some very knowledgeable people disagree with that assumption and believe that short-termers are extremely well suited for the kind of work our current military deployments require. More importantly, a shorter term of service attracts smarter, more mature youth who might consider national service if the obligation was more compatible with civilian educational and career plans. Higher-quality recruits would be easier to train, more adaptable in the complex circumstances of modern counterinsurgent warfare, more likely to have critical skills in technology, and more likely to be single and without children, relieving some of the burden on the military's extensive social services.

Congress made a small gesture toward making brief stints of military service more compatible with college plans when it created the National Call to Service program in 2003, but the end product demonstrated how difficult it is for government to think creatively about military service. The original idea was to encourage a new sense of national service with shorter terms of enlistment that would appeal to larger numbers of young Americans. By the time Congress was finished, however, it had watered down the concept so much that the final legislation created terms of service just a few months shorter than the contracts already being offered by some of the services, and the price of those few short months was ineligibility for the full G.I. Bill educational benefits provided to other members of the military. It was a program designed to appeal to almost no one.[32]

I suspect the major sticking point is an unspoken distrust of Americans who would approach military service from something other than a "lifer" perspective, with "lifer" defined as someone with a distinctive cultural affinity for the modern, all-volunteer, ideological version of military life. This is a strange dynamic, because the military personnel system has always been designed for a substantial level of turnover and a constant infusion of youth. If you imagine the military as a pyramid based on rank, with lower-ranking members forming the wide base at the bottom, only 15 percent of the base will serve for twenty years.[33] It would seem counterproductive for the military to market itself as a special lifestyle and cultural destination for young people who see themselves as "career military" types, because the vast majority will never stay for a career. Yet this is exactly what the military is doing.

In the past, military reserve forces might have offered a cultural bridge between the civilian world and the active military. They had a presence in both worlds and should have been in the best position to represent the historical ideal of the citizen-soldier and connect local communities to the national military effort. At the beginning of the all-volunteer era, in fact, the Department of Defense realigned part-time forces with the specific intent of making them an indispensible part of any mobilization—the "Total Force" concept.[34] This closer connection, however, made it much less likely that reserve forces could have any significant moderating effect on the civil-military gap. When the reserves are routinely called to augment all mobilizations, short-term and long-term, by definition they will develop a character consistent with their active-duty counterparts. In *Perpich v. Department of Defense*,[35] the Supreme Court affirmed this understanding by ruling that the National Guard's federal connection trumps its local connection when federal authorities and state governors disagree.

Reliance on cultural affinity as a recruiting tool is a natural consequence of the wide cultural and ideological divide between civilian and military worlds identified in the Gap Project research. If the military really is that separate and apart from the rest of American society, it makes sense that those culturally suited to live in that separate community would receive the warmest welcome and be the most likely to apply. This is a large part of how the military sells itself in the all-volunteer era, but it seems unaware that its methods send a strong message to the majority of young people that the military is not the place for them. This also helps to explain why the military is increasingly becoming a legacy organization in which people are far more likely to enlist if they follow other family members into military service. A family tradition of service is commendable, but the tradition becomes a problem when it concentrates responsibility for military service within a narrow slice of America.

A shrinking recruiting base forces the military—in particular the Army—in a predictable direction. If the military resists recruiting and personnel management proposals that would make military service more attractive to the college-bound, it is writing off more than half its potential pool. If within the remaining minority it sends the message that joining the military is a cultural, ideological, or political decision as much as it is a patriotic or vocational decision, the military has reduced its field even more. It simply cannot be good in terms of recruiting success for the military to sell itself as a separate community that is distinctly socially conservative, politically Republican, and disrespectful of constitutional rights. The military is setting itself up to fail.

While the propensity of young men to enlist in the military has been decreasing since the first Gulf War, the propensity of young black men to enlist has fallen even more sharply. Interestingly, while the propensity of white males to enlist is responsive to changes in the civilian economy, the propensity of black males is not.[36] Senior military officials tend to brush off declining enlistments from the black community as a function of political opposition to the conflicts in Iraq and Afghanistan, but the civil-military gap and the military's close identification with a socially conservative brand of partisan Republicanism may be another part of the explanation. It would be unreasonable to expect minority communities that rely on enforcement of constitutional values to remain loyal to an institution increasingly identified with constitutional resistance. The military, however, seems unaware of the possibility that its endorsement of a cultural and constitutional gap between civilian and military America may also be shrinking the pool of people with an interest in military service.

When the military makes choices that decrease propensity to enlist in large segments of the population, the only option left is to dig deeper within the group that remains and relax the definition of who will be considered qualified for military service. Almost every marker of recruiting quality confirms this is the direction the military has taken. In recent years, Congress and the military services have changed or waived the rules of recruiting as necessary to reach quotas for new personnel, and the results at the margins are not encouraging. The military touts its recruiting as an unqualified success whenever it hits its target numbers, but then deflects any criticism of how it got there as uninformed or unpatriotic.

The trend receiving the most attention, more than the declining rate of high school graduates in the military, is the increasing number of recruits that require "moral waivers" for criminal records. Federal law directs that felons are ineligible for military service, although exceptions may be granted "in meritorious cases." In fiscal years 2006 and 2007, the Army and the Marine Corps enlisted felons in more than thirteen hundred presumably "meritorious" cases, including persons with convictions for aggravated assault, burglary, robbery, and in a few cases, for making terrorist threats. During the same time period, the two services also granted almost twenty thousand waivers for serious misdemeanor offenses.[37] Worse yet, the problem is probably understated. Defense researchers note that background checks on military applicants are incomplete, particularly for juvenile criminal records, and the military relies in part on the honor system—self-reporting by recruits—to discover criminal histories.[38]

The irony of so many moral waivers in an institution that prides itself on moral superiority is huge, yet senior military officers are bracingly unapologetic. A three-star general from the Army's Training and Doctrine Command said that Americans ought to be grateful the military is offering a way for these people to serve their country. He minimized the problem of enlisting young people with criminal records—these serious offenses were nothing more than "a slight stain on their shirts"—and rejected any thought of returning to the draft, even though, he conceded, "the pickings are pretty lean."[39] Just like former secretary Rumsfeld, he was convinced a military draft could only lead to enlistments of lower quality, even though he was surely aware that current draft authority is much more sweeping and inclusive than Vietnam-era draft authority. One has to wonder whether the military consciously understands that it is trading away quality as the price of maintaining the civil-military divide.

Other data confirms the military is meeting recruiting goals by accepting more people with criminal histories. In 2007, the FBI issued a report, *Gang-Related Activity in the U.S. Armed Forces Increasing*, warning the military it has a growing problem with the enlistment of gang members. It found that a rising level of gang-related activity in the military introduced risks to both domestic and international security:

> While allowing gang members to serve in the military may temporarily increase recruiting numbers, U.S. communities may ultimately have to contend with disruption and violence resulting from military-trained gang members on the streets of U.S. cities. Furthermore, most gang members have been pre-indoctrinated into the gang lifestyle and maintain an allegiance to their gang. This could ultimately jeopardize the safety of other military members and impede gang-affiliated soldiers' ability to act in the best interest of their country.[40]

The FBI report included photos taken in Iraq of gang-related graffiti spray-painted on public thoroughfares and military equipment and of soldiers proudly flashing gang signs to one another. Congress later passed a measure directing the secretary of defense to "prescribe regulations to prohibit the active participation by members of the Armed Forces in a criminal street gang."[41] You might think it should go without saying that participation in criminal street gangs diminishes good order and discipline in a military environment, but apparently Congress believed the military needed a reminder, and probably with good cause. An Army recruiting regulation, for example, encourages recruiters to look the other way when applicants are members of extremist organizations or gangs. Recruiters are told to put aside "personal bias" about groups linked to criminal or extremist activity, and membership "may not be grounds for disqualification." The regulation directs recruiters to consider these applicants under a more forgiving "whole person" standard.[42]

The markers of a shrinking base and declining quality at the margins of military recruiting are everywhere. Congress responded to the problem by increasing the maximum age for enlistment in the active military to forty, and then to forty-two. The Army established its own prep schools for high-school dropouts in an effort to mentor them through a General Educational Development (GED) certification. It relaxed its weight and fitness standards to permit enlistment by some overweight or obese individuals, and it is considering a residential program where new recruits could try to trim down before starting their military training. It adjusted its rules so it could enlist people who have tattoos on the backs of their necks and on their hands—the most visible kind that even some tattoo artists will decline to ink because they can make it difficult to find a job in the civilian world.[43]

Perhaps the most startling indicator was the recent announcement by the Army that it is beginning a pilot program to open military service to noncitizens who are present in the United States on temporary visas. These enlistments would be in addition to the noncitizen permanent residents ("green card" holders) who are already eligible for military service.[44] The program will start slowly and build up gradually, but the Army predicted that in the future it might find one out of every six recruits it needs in this pool. The valuable "carrot," of course, would be an offer of quick citizenship that is unavailable to most applicants under current immigration law. This announcement came and went with little reaction, but it is impossible to understate the severity of the problem we have if the military believes it must rely on the service of noncitizens to this degree.

If you've heard it once, you've heard it a hundred times. People must enlist in the military for love of country, because they certainly don't do it for the pay. In a *Newsweek* magazine essay, a former sailor and future Navy doctor repeated the tale perfectly:

> I knew one sailor, for instance, who could have supported his wife and baby more easily by flipping burgers at McDonald's. He joined the Navy because he cherished his country's freedom and wanted to give his time and energy in return.[45]

I can only assume this Navy man has never worked in the fast-food busi-ness, because he doesn't know what he is talking about. One of the persistent myths about military service is that it doesn't pay well in comparison to civilian occupations. The Government Accountability Office found the mili-tary has developed a "culture of dissatisfaction" on matters of compensation, with almost 80 percent of servicemembers assuming they would be paid better in a civilian job even though reality is just the opposite. Military cash compensation alone, *without benefits*, already places servicemembers, on average, at the 70th percentile of like-educated civilians.[46] It makes no sense why the military would allow this myth to survive, because it must depress interest in enlistment. Perhaps it is a function of the military's willingness to believe, despite all evidence to the contrary, that civilian America disrespects the military and therefore pays accordingly. Most Americans accept this myth because they don't know any better, and the idea of selfless and unfairly compensated service fits well with our cultural understanding that the mili-tary is morally superior to the rest of us. We would be much closer to the truth, however, if we said the military manages to barely keep pace with its personnel needs only because it outcompensates almost everyone else, par-ticularly at the recruiting end of the rank structure.

Military compensation is easy to misunderstand and easy to misrepresent because it is broken up into numerous and complex subcomponents of salary, allowances, and substantial "in-kind" benefits. The military cash pay-ment referred to as "basic pay" best approximates what civilians would call a salary or wage, but basic pay is only the first component of an unusual com-pensation system providing housing, utilities, and a broad array of other benefits *in addition to* basic pay. The most important components of military pay and benefits include basic pay, which is the same for all personnel of the same rank and time in service; housing and utilities, either provided in-kind or by a nontaxable cash allowance, indexed to match regional housing costs and protected against inflation by cost-of-living increases; medical benefits for the servicemember and his or her family; and meals in-kind for the ser-vicemember, or a nontaxable cash allowance to pay for them. In the military, there is no such thing as living in a high-cost housing area, because the mili-tary will either provide housing or an allowance to make up the difference.

For example, a typical junior enlisted person—twenty years old, two years of service, married with one child—would be paid $1,753.50 per month ($21,042.00 per year) in basic pay.[47] A fair comparison to the civilian world would ask how many young high-school graduates with a family (and with-out college) have $1,753.50 left over from their paycheck at the end of the month *after* paying for housing, utilities, medical insurance and health care, and part of the food bill, assuming a job with medical benefits was even avail-able. The answer must be close to zero. In today's service-oriented economy, a high-school graduate without college cannot reasonably expect to earn anything close to the level of compensation and comprehensive social welfare support that the military provides. Indeed, one of the constituencies that is likely self-selecting into the all-volunteer force in disproportionate numbers are people with children whose need for family income and support exceeds the ability or willingness of the civilian economy to pay for it, a recruiting trend that plays havoc with military readiness when these parents are ordered to deploy.[48]

The military has cornered the market in the current economy for entry-level jobs in which young people can earn a living wage, support a family, and obtain medical care, but it is still not enough to generate a sufficient number of volunteers. Rather than expanding its base by reaching out to the college-bound, or by accommodating a more representative range of cultural, political, and ideological beliefs, the military instead turns to recruiting methods that attract people to national service for all the wrong reasons. When necessary, it offers cash enlistment bonuses that put enormous sums of money—as much as $40,000—in front of teenagers. It shifts from methods that are merely inappropriate or unwise to those that border on the immoral when it tempts people to join the military without full deliberation by offering an additional $20,000 "quick-ship" bonus if they agree to enlist within days. It builds state-of-the-art video arcades in shopping malls to serve as military recruiting stations, even though military service is too serious a proposition to be confused with the mindless amusement of electronic games in which no one dies and no one ever has to exercise real moral judgment. No matter how high-tech military equipment becomes, the "look at the shiny keys" attraction of video games can never replicate the gravity of the duty recruits will be asked to perform.[49]

The military's resistance to relying on a broader range of the population for its recruiting needs, and its insistence on maintaining a wide civil-military gap under the guise of preserving military effectiveness, tends to drive everything about how the military keeps enough bodies in uniform. We rely on increased rates of reenlistment and retention to cover up shortfalls in recruiting and accession,[50] which just exacerbates the military's lack of representativeness in relation to civilian society. The sense of the military seems to be that "if we can just get them in the door, and if we can somehow convince them to stay, then we can worry less about recruiting." This is a nontraditional and counterproductive way, unfortunately, of thinking about military personnel needs. A military in which everyone is a career soldier is not necessarily a good thing, even though it seems to have some superficial appeal.

The military is showing all the signs of an institution that is overusing the people it has in an effort to avoid having to find more people. Its reliance on longer retention to cover up weak recruiting is causing an increased rate of injuries that could all be classified as the result of repetitive stress from multiple deployments, including concussive brain injuries from explosions, posttraumatic stress disorder, major depression, substance abuse, divorce, domestic violence, and suicide.[51] In early 2009, the Army was losing more soldiers to suicide than it was to combat, and suicide rates were continuing to increase beyond a level that was already the highest in three decades. A horrible, unintended consequence of the government's efforts to be financially generous with families who lose a servicemember to war—most receive an immediate cash payment of half a million dollars—may be to give servicemembers under stress yet another temptation to consider suicide.

In an "old school" military in which the burden is shared by a much larger number of people who rotate through a limited period of military service, the risk and severity of repetitive-stress injuries like these would be greatly reduced. Today, in contrast, we pretend that we can meet vastly increased mission requirements with the same number of servicemembers, all the while hoping we do not cross an unpredictable line and cause irreparable damage to the military. We mask overwhelming personnel shortages by hiring civilian contractors for war-zone duties once performed by members of the military, more than doubling our personnel footprint in Iraq but introducing risks to our security when we cannot control them as effectively as we can control soldiers. Instead of "packing our own trash" the way we used to—having a military large enough to provide its own support services—we hire foreign nationals from around the world to perform menial tasks for the military in war zones, which creates the distinctively unhelpful impression, especially when we force them to work under guard, of an American system of slavery abroad.[52]

Our government no longer operates under the assumption that the military needs a much larger force than what is necessary to meet the immediate task at hand. Excess capacity would allow for the strength that comes not just from extended "down time" at home, but also from the latitude to pull more soldiers from duty for physical or psychic injury, for training, for professional advancement, or for the safety of others. If the military had excess capacity, it would not need an informal policy in which soldiers who commit domestic violence at home, but who are slated to deploy overseas, are allowed to escape punishment because we need them to fill a position. The military would not be tempted to abuse injured recruits in an effort to force them back to duty before they are ready.[53] If we were willing to spread the burden, we could make the right choices more often, but that would require a different perspective on the nature of military service and our obligation as citizens to defend the nation.

One perfect example of the dilemma between a broad base of military experience throughout the population and a more narrow, culture-driven definition of military service played out in the recent debate concerning expansion of the G.I. Bill for military educational benefits. The traditional way of thinking about the G.I. Bill was that servicemembers would receive financial support for attending college after they left the military, in exchange for having taken their share of the burden of national service. These benefits, however, were becoming progressively less valuable over time because of the escalating price of higher education. When Congress took up the matter, the military and a number of self-described military supporters took the position that G.I. Bill benefits should be limited, because if they were better, people would just want to use them—and therefore leave military service at the completion of their term of service. There was a time when the universal reaction would have been, "well, that's the idea," but today, educational benefits earned by military service run against the insular principle that once someone has joined the military, we can't give them an incentive to leave. After a series of heated exchanges about who was or wasn't supporting the troops and the military, Congress eventually passed legislation preserving and enhancing G.I. Bill benefits.[54]

The final version of the law, however, included a cynical provision designed to discourage servicemembers from using the educational benefits they earned. It permits servicemembers to transfer benefits to their spouse or children, but only if they have completed six years of service and agree to serve at least four more years. Those target points weren't chosen randomly. Once members of the military reach ten years of service, it becomes much more likely they will stay and serve for twenty years, the point at which full retirement benefits vest. In and of itself, a policy allowing transfer of educational benefits to family members is not a problem. It is a problem, however, when the system dangles college money for a spouse or child in exchange for a long-term commitment to the military, encouraging veterans to give up their own educational opportunities.

Even those who had the best interests of servicemembers in mind missed a significant irony in all the celebration. Military recruiters highlight the G.I. Bill as one of the principal benefits earned by military service, but then they focus their recruiting attention on a slice of the population that will be less prepared academically, on average, to take advantage of it. Department of Education data shows that veterans have a dismally low rate—3 percent— of completing four-year college programs,[55] but no one has ever stopped to consider whether part of the problem is a lower academic readiness to succeed at college-level work. Even among the college-bound population, more than one-third of students need to take remedial courses before attempting college-level study. Community-college officials see the frustration of many of their students: "They think they graduated from a high school, they should be ready for college."[56] Imagine what the higher-education landscape looks like to a population who is targeted by the military primarily because they are *not* college-bound, let alone to the servicemember who never received a high-school diploma. It is irresponsible, if not cruel, for the military to entice recruits with the promise of future college success at the same time it deliberately expands its reach among those who are much less in a position to benefit.

The debate over military recruiting and retention is a good example of the sham discussions we so often have in the world of military affairs. Sometimes we obscure or stretch the facts to fit what we have already decided must be true, and sometimes we make what sounds like a military argument for reasons that have little to do with the military. Perhaps there is no better example of this phenomenon than the subject of the next chapter, the seemingly endless controversy concerning "Don't Ask, Don't Tell" and the service of gay people in the military.

Chapter 9

It Never Was About the Mission

In May 2005, the secretary of the Army, Francis Harvey, gave an interview to *USA Today* on a broad range of topics related to the difficulties of military recruiting, the heavy burden undertaken by our part-time servicemembers in the National Guard and the Reserve, the stress of repeated deployment, and the slow pace of supplying the military with new equipment. His most abrupt comment was in response to a question about discharging gay soldiers under the "Don't Ask, Don't Tell" policy at the same time the Army was having trouble finding enough qualified people: "Given the recruiting woes, isn't it time to revisit this policy?" Harvey, however, thought the subject wasn't even worth talking about. He responded: "No. Next question! If you look at the past ten years, the numbers (discharged) aren't huge. There is no motivation to make a change in the policy that has existed since the Clinton administration."[1]

Military and defense officials often make the argument that we shouldn't be too concerned about the collateral effects of "Don't Ask, Don't Tell" because not that many servicemembers are discharged under the policy each year—less than a thousand, in round numbers. They assume the impact of a policy banning gay people from military service can be measured by counting the number of people who are formally discharged under the law each year. But this is a very shortsighted way of thinking about how "Don't Ask, Don't Tell" might affect our military, the health of our civil-military relations, and our national security.

"Don't Ask, Don't Tell" may have enduring consequences beyond the discharge of individual servicemembers, and these effects may ripple throughout the military and across the rest of American society. We know the number of gay people discharged under the policy each year must be only a fraction of the number of gay people who decide, unnoticed and uncounted, to leave the military because of the extra burdens the policy asks them to bear.[2] It's difficult to dismiss this effect when the policy itself is designed to allow "under the radar" service. In turn, the number of gay people who choose to serve in the military may be only a fraction of the number who would serve in the absence of "Don't Ask, Don't Tell." This assumption also makes sense because relatively few people will volunteer for service under conditions more difficult than straight servicemembers are asked to accept.

The next logical step is one the military has never considered, but it's potentially the most important. The military worries that ending "Don't Ask, Don't Tell" could give young people a reason *not* to join the military, but it doesn't seriously think about the possibility that holding onto "Don't Ask, Don't Tell" could be depressing enlistment to a far greater degree. It ought to consider whether propensity to enlist is being affected by the increasing percentage of straight youth who don't understand the need for policies requiring discrimination based on sexual orientation. In their lives, for the most part, the issue is irrelevant. Is it possible that a significant number of straight young people—orders of magnitude greater than the hundreds of gay servicemembers discharged each year—are turned off to military service in part because they can't understand the government's obsession with the issue? Both the military and Congress are stubbornly blind to the possibility that for every gay servicemember they discharge, they might be reducing the propensity of a hundred, or a thousand, or even ten thousand other young people to enlist in the military. This effect is invisible and impossible to quantify, but generational changes in attitudes make it inevitable.

To say the government is obsessed with sexual orientation in a military context is not too strong a word. Very intelligent people say some very bizarre things on the subject, including justices of the Supreme Court. During the oral argument of a recent case about donated religious monuments and whether the government could choose to display some, but not others, on public property without violating free-speech rights, for some inexplicable reason the issue of military service by gay citizens jumped to the forefront. Justice John Paul Stevens asked one of the lawyers whether the government could legally remove the names of gay soldiers from the Vietnam Memorial in Washington, D.C. The lawyer representing the United States answered that, yes, it could—"it can choose who to memorialize and who not"—but it wasn't enough to put the issue to rest. Justice Stephen Breyer brought it up again, asking three more times for "the answer to the homosexual hypothetical." The lawyer agreed, again, that the government would be free to deny fallen gay servicemembers their engraved line of honor on the Memorial. Justice Scalia could not let it go, adding his opinion that "the government could disfavor homosexuality [by erasing names on the Memorial] just as it could disfavor abortion, just as it can disfavor a number of other things. . . . The Government can disfavor all of it, can't it?"[3]

What is it that compels perfectly intelligent people to have discussions like this, seemingly unaware of how oblivious and uninformed they sound? Apparently we think it might be necessary for the government to deny the obvious and pretend, for public consumption, that gay people do not serve in the military and do not give their lives in service to their country. Even if we are willing to concede gay people do serve in the military and do sacrifice, we think it might be necessary to dishonor or humiliate them for their service. In a case that had absolutely nothing to do with military service, with gay citizens, or with military service by gay citizens, when the justices needed an example of a situation in which government might need to carve its official disapproval on a public monument, this is what came to mind. It is appalling to hear some of our most senior constitutional officials amusing themselves with hypothetical cruelties against gay people who have lost their lives in military action, but perhaps it is even more appalling that their commentary raised no objection from anyone, as far as I know, until now.

People have a natural desire to make the unexplainable more understandable, to make the nonsensical more sensible, and to make the irrational more rational. We are uncomfortable with ideas that seem illogical or foolish for no good reason, and so our minds automatically set out on a course to improve them. This is what we unconsciously do with the government policy that bans gay people from serving in the military. Few other laws are as misunderstood as "Don't Ask, Don't Tell," and I think the reason we misconstrue its real meaning and effect is because we desperately want to minimize its fatal silliness. We assume that Congress and the military could not possibly have settled on a solution so distant from reality and common sense.

A brief review of "Don't Ask, Don't Tell" itself is a good place to begin. Most people assume the law is a compromise of sorts, halfway between the previous policy that did not allow military service by gay people at all and the more progressive result once promised by President Clinton that would have allowed openly gay people to join the military and serve without hiding their sexual orientation. "Don't Ask, Don't Tell" was billed as an improvement over the status quo because it would allow gay people to serve provided they were "discreet" and did not "flaunt" themselves or otherwise "push" their sexual orientation on military colleagues. Everyone would be fine as long as gay people kept their private lives to themselves.

Every one of these assumptions is wrong. We tell ourselves the policy must mean gay people can serve in the military if they are discreet, because this is the only interpretation of the policy that makes any sense given that everyone must know (they do know, don't they?) gay people do and always will serve in the military.[4] It's also the only sensible interpretation because Department of Defense regulations consider sexual orientation "a personal and private matter" that is "not a bar to continued service . . . unless manifested by homosexual conduct."[5] But that's not the reality of the policy, not in any practical sense. "Don't Ask, Don't Tell" was never a compromise. It codified into federal law exactly the same policy barring service by gay people that was already in effect before the 1993 debate, and it did so almost word for word.[6] As far as the law was concerned, absolutely nothing changed. The only thing that changed was how it was sold to the American people.

"Don't Ask, Don't Tell" sets out three circumstances in which a servicemember can be discharged or "separated" (the official terminology) from the military. First, the statute prescribes that a member of the armed forces will be separated if "the member has engaged in, attempted to engage in, or solicited another to engage in a homosexual act." This rule doesn't just bar intimate conduct with another servicemember, or in military housing, or when deployed in the field, or under any other circumstances with some close military connection. It bars physical intimacy with anyone of the same sex at any time, in any place, under any circumstances whatsoever, for as long as a person serves in the military. The definition of a prohibited "homosexual act" isn't what you might think either. In addition to what common sense would define as a homosexual act—contact between persons of the same sex "for the purpose of satisfying sexual desires"—a disqualifying act also includes any bodily contact "a reasonable person would understand to *demonstrate a propensity or intent* to engage" in sexual acts. This prohibits holding hands with or kissing someone of the same sex, even in complete privacy, if a hypothetical observer would think it "looks gay." Again, the prohibition on holding hands or kissing applies to any partner, including civilians, at any time, in any place, under any circumstances whatsoever, for as long as a person serves. No circumstance exists that is private or discreet enough to legally comply with "Don't Ask, Don't Tell."

The second disqualification lines up with the second half of the "Don't Ask, Don't Tell" slogan, but it makes about as much sense as the blanket prohibition on all forms of physical affection. Under the law, a servicemember may not make a statement that he or she is homosexual, bisexual, gay, or lesbian, or any other words to that effect. This rule doesn't just bar telling your commander you are gay or revealing your sexual orientation to a newspaper reporter. It means you can never tell another person you are gay, not your close friends in the military, not civilians, not a prospective date, not your family, not your mother—no one, for as long as a person serves. If you do, according to the law, you will be separated from the military. No statement exists that is private or discreet enough to legally comply with "Don't Ask, Don't Tell."

The third disqualification is an interesting historical quirk. It prohibits marrying, or attempting to marry, someone of the same sex, but this provision was written many years before anyone remotely imagined same-sex marriage would be a legal reality. The original idea behind the provision, bizarre as it may seem, was that gay people might present themselves to a marriage authority masquerading as persons of the opposite sex, and it was therefore important to have a mechanism for separating them from the military. It is a sure bet, however, that any same-sex couple entering into a marriage would already have violated the first two provisions of the policy. Today, however, the marriage ban in "Don't Ask, Don't Tell" is a relevant and serious proposition because it discourages gay servicemembers from taking advantage of civilian legal protections for their families, even if they believe they can manage to live secretly and conceal violations based on "acting" and "telling."

It should be clear by now that it is impossible to be gay and also live in compliance with the policy. The experts who drafted and approved the policy must think there are gay people who do not have personal intimacy in their private lives and who will never tell another soul why they aren't interested in partners of the opposite sex, but these hypothetical people generally don't exist. We can assume for all practical purposes that every gay person who serves in the military has violated the policy, and the only question is whether it is possible for them to keep violations of the policy secret. This is very difficult to do, for the same reason it would be very difficult for heterosexual servicemembers to keep their sexual orientation a secret for very long, especially if they had spouses or children. People have private lives apart from their professional military lives, but they generally don't have secret lives. They may share a household with a partner, go to the grocery store together, travel on vacations together, or write letters back and forth when one of them is deployed overseas. If people are paying attention, they understand some of their peers are gay.

Even Senator John McCain, always a strong supporter of "Don't Ask, Don't Tell," understood some of his peers in the Navy were gay. One day during the 2000 presidential campaign, McCain was engrossed in telling war stories and casually mentioned he served with many gay colleagues in the Navy, although they had not specifically talked with him about their sexual orientation. He said, "I think we know by behavior and by attitudes. I think that it's clear to some of us when some people have that lifestyle." He then realized his easy candor—that perceptive, thinking servicemembers are perfectly aware they serve with gay people—was inconsistent with all the assumptions underlying "Don't Ask, Don't Tell." Supporters of the policy insist that unit cohesion and military effectiveness would suffer if straight servicemembers knew some of their colleagues were gay. McCain, of course, had never reported his naval "gaydar" readings up the chain of command or warned anyone the Navy could be at risk. Shortly after the interview, McCain adjusted his story and explained he only became aware of the obvious after he left the Navy.[7]

What is most interesting to me as a law professor is how we use law to protect our tender minds from the irrationality of "Don't Ask, Don't Tell."

The government uses the Supreme Court's post-Vietnam doctrine of judicial deference to the military to hide facts, data, research, information, and any other indicia of reality that might upset our uninformed beliefs and assumptions about the significance of sexual orientation in a military environment. I understand these are harsh words to use about an issue that appears to divide civilian politicians, military professionals, and the American public, but there are few circumstances in which political debate is affected to such a large degree by the government's ability to withhold information and distort our traditional constitutional process.

The constitutionality of "Don't Ask, Don't Tell" has been a persistent question since the law was first enacted, and federal courts have recently entertained two new constitutional challenges to the policy—and issued two very different decisions. One of them was a depressing example of the stilted and artificial conversations we tend to have about the policy, always designed to avoid difficult questions about the constitutional bonds between civilian authority and the military. The second, however, which is still circulating its way through the judicial system, offers a tiny glimpse of what it would look like if we treated "Don't Ask, Don't Tell" as a sincere, genuine attempt to preserve military effectiveness. If we were serious, we would be willing to put all the facts on the table and consider whether, in constitutional terms, the ends of military effectiveness justified the means of "Don't Ask, Don't Tell."

In the first case, *Cook v. Gates*,[8] twelve servicemembers discharged under "Don't Ask, Don't Tell" sued in federal court for reinstatement to military service, arguing the policy violated the Constitution by infringing upon interests in privacy and liberty protected by the due process clause of the Fifth Amendment. This was not a frivolous lawsuit based on imaginary or exaggerated perspectives on constitutional rights. These military veterans were raising fair, important, and difficult questions about how we ought to define constitutional values in a military environment. Although the Supreme Court has never decided the constitutionality of "Don't Ask, Don't Tell," the plaintiffs based their claims on other rulings that serve to protect the rights of individuals to form personally intimate relationships without undue interference from the government.

In 2003, *Lawrence v. Texas*[9] held that the government could not make it a crime for consenting adults to engage in private sexual conduct, even if the conduct at issue—sodomy—raised moral objections from others.[10] According to the majority of justices in *Lawrence*, "adults may choose to enter upon [intimate personal relationships] in the confines of their homes and their own private lives and still retain their dignity as free persons." The Court acknowledged there was "an emerging awareness that liberty gives substantial protection to adult persons in deciding how to conduct their private lives in matters pertaining to sex." The plaintiffs in *Cook v. Gates* believed that "Don't Ask, Don't Tell" was no longer constitutionally valid after *Lawrence*, absent some distinctively *military* reason for allowing straight servicemembers to have private lives that included personal intimacy, but denying similarly private lives to gay servicemembers.

Lawrence added weight to a 1996 Supreme Court decision, *Romer v. Evans*,[11] holding that the state of Colorado could not amend its constitution to forbid the enactment or enforcement of any law, present or future, local or statewide, designed to protect gay people from public discrimination. Colorado wanted to foreclose any possibility that state or local officials might choose to add sexual orientation to the usual list of prohibited discriminations—race, sex, religion, among others—in public services or accommodations. The Supreme Court, however, ruled that Colorado had no legitimate interest in enshrining hostility against gay people in its laws. The federal constitutional right of equal protection under the law meant that government had to have a better reason for discriminating against people as a class than simple animus or dislike for the class, or the sheer desire "to make them unequal to everyone else." Taken together, *Lawrence* and *Romer* meant that moral disapproval, in and of itself, was not enough to justify laws that discriminate. Without a better reason, such laws were irrational and unconstitutional.

Despite what sounds like a generous measure of "live and let live" sentiment from the Court, however, it's a long leap from *Lawrence* and *Romer* to the conclusion that "Don't Ask, Don't Tell" must be unconstitutional as a matter of law. Interpreted narrowly, all *Lawrence* said was that government couldn't imprison people for their private, consensual sexual conduct. Whether the government could deem people ineligible for military service based on their private, consensual sexual conduct is a very different question. Interpreted narrowly, all *Romer* said was that government couldn't deny gay people across-the-board access to all forms of legal protection if the sole reason was to accommodate someone else's personal or religious objections to homosexuality. There has to be some specific and legitimate government interest in classifying certain people as more worthy than others. The military, however, could possibly have such an interest. Congress clearly believed that it did. Under the usual rules for handling constitutional claims, the government would therefore need to justify why it was important to military effectiveness that only straight servicemembers be allowed to conduct their private lives with a measure of constitutional dignity.

The stories of the twelve plaintiffs in *Cook* vividly illustrate some of the wastefulness, arbitrariness, casual cruelty, and lack of dignity inherent in the enforcement of "Don't Ask, Don't Tell."[12] One servicemember was discharged based in part on an allegation he had held hands for a few seconds with another man. Another was found to have "told" in violation of the policy when he sought protection from death threats his military superior made against gay servicemembers. Some revealed their sexual orientation to military colleagues after realizing "Don't Ask, Don't Tell" required an intolerable level of lying and deceit to avoid the suspicion of others. One doctor was forced to tell the Air Force she was gay because it was the only way she could justify a request to delay a new assignment. Her female partner was dying of cancer and needed to remain close to her treating physicians. If she had been heterosexual, the officer's request would have been routinely granted. Because she was not, she was discharged from the service, and the Air Force began legal proceedings to force her to repay the government for the cost of her medical education.

In constitutional cases like this, courts have the responsibility to balance the needs of the government against the liberty of the individual, guided by legal doctrines that invite more or less scrutiny depending on the importance of the interest at stake. Courts do it all the time, and no one takes particular notice. If the case had not involved a military personnel policy, the *Cook* court was prepared to apply an intermediate level of constitutional scrutiny, somewhere between rational basis review (does the law at least rationally relate to some legitimate purpose) and strict scrutiny (do compelling circumstances demand this law, and nothing less). Under this middle-range level of review, the government would simply need to explain why, under the circumstances, it needed to be so intrusive in the private lives of gay individuals, and the court would balance the strength of the government's interest against the degree of its intrusion on individual liberty. The standard does not strongly suggest a result either way, but it does require the government to do more than claim or insist it is right without having to justify its decision to anyone.

Because *Cook v. Gates* was a case about the military, however, the federal appeals court looked for additional guidance in the trilogy of Supreme Court decisions written by Justice Rehnquist that established the doctrine of judicial deference to the military. Once it took that step, it was as if someone had turned the lights off to signal no one was at home. Before the court had considered a single piece of evidence bearing on the need for "Don't Ask, Don't Tell," it first explained why it was so important that such evidence never see the light of day. All the standard slogans of judicial deference were deployed once again: the military's "unique context" required "the highest deference"; courts were incompetent to understand "complex, subtle, and professional decisions" about military personnel policies; and therefore judicial deference was "at its apogee" when congressional action was challenged as unconstitutional. It endorsed Rehnquist's embarrassingly shaky constitutional understanding that Congress's express constitutional power to govern the military meant that courts had little power to ensure Congress complied with the Constitution when exercising that power—an analysis Rehnquist would not have applied in any case not involving the military.

Having set the stage for a result that already seemed predetermined, the court then pointed to the congressional debate on "Don't Ask, Don't Tell" fifteen years earlier as the reason, strangely enough, it could not permit the introduction *today* of facts, data, research, and other information that might reveal there was no longer—if there ever was—an actual military need for the policy. The plaintiffs would not be allowed to show that Congress manipulated the proceedings in 1993 to exclude information—in many instances, information from the military—exposing the weaknesses of "Don't Ask, Don't Tell." They would not be allowed to offer research studies conducted during the fifteen years following the debate that further undercut justifications for the policy. Congress had once made findings and had once enacted a law based on those findings, and as far as the judges were concerned, that was the end of the constitutional story. The principal effect of *Cook* was to freeze a 1993 congressional decision in time and insulate it from any contradicting research or reality for the indefinite future.

The court showered praise on Congress's performance almost thirty years earlier in the *Rostker v. Goldberg*[13] controversy, when Congress disregarded military advice that we should register women for the draft—and disregarded the Constitution—so it could impose its own perspective on the proper place for women in American society. The factual underpinning for *Rostker* was less than accurate at the time it was decided in 1981, and today it would be completely false, given how much the role of women in military service has changed. *Cook* seemed to assume the constitutional rights of military women, like the constitutional rights of gay servicemembers, could also be frozen in time, never to be eligible for protection by courts, because, after all, Congress had once decided the military had little use for more women:

> The [*Rostker*] Court discussed, in detail, the process Congress employed in considering the issue, its consultation with all interested parties, its serious consideration of the issues, including the constitutional implications, and its clear articulation of the basis for its decision. The Court then declared the district court's analysis striking down the law "quite wrong" because the district court undertook "an independent evaluation of evidence rather than adopting an appropriately deferential examination of Congress' evaluation of the evidence."

This bland citation of *Rostker* reveals something quite interesting about the current state of civil-military affairs. In *Rostker*, the Supreme Court went out of its way to chastise a lower federal court for failing to be "appropriately deferential" to Congress, which on last check was still a separate constitutional branch of government. How dare a court, according to *Rostker*, embark on an "independent evaluation" when Congress has already decided that constitutional values of equality and professional military expertise must both be disregarded if they are inconsistent with how the majority of Congress views the legal status of women? Who do courts think they are, being so bold as to interpret the Constitution, enforce a right to equal protection under law, or take an interest in information that might shed light on the best interests of the military and national security?

In *Cook*, the federal appeals court clearly followed in the footsteps of *Rostker* as an enabler of congressional prerogative, whether or not the result was consistent with the Constitution or even consistent with the best interests of the military. Its task was to make legally irrelevant any information that could conflict with the decision Congress made fifteen years earlier, and it succeeded. It approvingly referred to the congressional hearings on "Don't Ask, Don't Tell" as "involved," "sustained," "exhaustive," "careful," "intense," and "considered," although they were nothing of the sort. It noted that Congress made fifteen explicit findings in support of its conclusion that it was necessary to exclude gay citizens from military service—or allow them to serve only under the risk of arbitrary enforcement—to "preserve the military's effectiveness as a fighting force" and "ensure national security." It quoted the testimony of General Colin Powell, former chairman of the Joint Chiefs of Staff, as a summary of the accepted military rationale underlying the policy, one that has been repeated so often it has become military gospel for an entire new generation of enlistees since then:

> It is very difficult in a military setting, where you don't get a choice of association, where you don't get a choice of where you live, to introduce a group of individuals who are proud, brave, loyal, good Americans, but who favor a homosexual lifestyle, and put them in with heterosexuals who would prefer not to have somebody of the same sex find them sexually attractive, put them in close proximity and ask them to share the most private facilities together, the bedroom, the barracks, latrines, and showers. . . . I think it would be prejudicial to good order and discipline to try to integrate that in the current military structure.

Because Congress had once spoken by enacting a law fifteen years earlier, based on information Congress had the sole power to choose and package to support its decision by majority, *Cook* concluded that "Don't Ask, Don't Tell" had to be constitutional. What's more, because Congress had once spoken, the plaintiffs in *Cook* would not be allowed to seek evidence from the government that could undermine the assumptions behind the policy. They would not be allowed to offer evidence already in their possession demonstrating that "Don't Ask, Don't Tell" doesn't enhance military effectiveness, but instead detracts from it, and they would not be allowed to identify evidence that Congress disregarded during the 1993 debate. Their claims were dismissed without consideration of any evidence at all. In the language of legal procedure, *Cook* ruled that the plaintiffs were unable to "state a claim upon which relief can be granted,"[14] and so their claims were dismissed. The court's ruling, however, was accurate only in the most technical legal sense. The plaintiffs would have been able to state a claim that "Don't Ask, Don't Tell" was unconstitutional, but the Supreme Court's doctrine of judicial deference in matters involving the military prevented them from doing so.

There is a second way of thinking about constitutional rights in a military environment, one that is not short-circuited by judicial deference and the fear of having to openly justify military judgments that may infringe on constitutional values. Most people assume litigants who challenge the constitutionality of military personnel policies would rather talk less about the military and more about some ephemeral notion of constitutional rights. We've all been trained very well to assume there is something fundamentally incompatible between constitutional rights and military effectiveness, and so therefore anyone seeking to protect constitutional rights in a military environment must care less about military effectiveness. These assumptions are wrong. Without exception, the people who want to avoid talking about real "boots on the ground" military facts are the people who resist constitutional values as applied to the military, because they worry their arguments will not stand up under real scrutiny.

A second legal challenge to "Don't Ask, Don't Tell," *Witt v. Department of the Air Force*,[15] is still active in the federal court system. Major Margaret Witt was an Air Force Reserve flight nurse who was discharged from the military following investigation of an anonymous (and accurate) allegation she had been romantically involved with a civilian woman. One has to wonder about the judgment of Air Force officials who chose not to use the significant discretion they had under Department of Defense regulations to ignore a stray accusation like this one,[16] but they decided to discharge Major Witt, one of their most decorated medical flight officers.

The Ninth Circuit Court of Appeals handled her case very differently, however, from the First Circuit decision in *Cook*. After mildly chiding government lawyers from the Department of Justice for misrepresenting legal precedent in their briefs, the Ninth Circuit ruled that it should have more facts, not fewer facts, about the significance of sexual orientation in a military environment and whether "Don't Ask, Don't Tell" served a military interest in maintaining good order and discipline. Not only would the government need to demonstrate the rationale for the policy as a general matter—with proof of assertions about unit cohesion, preservation of privacy, esprit de corps, and the like—the government would need to justify why it was important to enforce the policy *against Major Witt as an individual*. Without that specificity, the court found, there would be little meaning to *Lawrence's* protection of constitutional dignity in one's personal relationships. The military could enforce the policy against anyone, whether or not there was any particular military justification, based on the hypothetical possibility of military justification in some other case.

This was a big decision. The ball was back in the government's court—something that had never happened before with "Don't Ask, Don't Tell"—and the case returned to the starting point for development of the evidence. *Witt* did acknowledge the existence of Justice Rehnquist's line of judicial deference cases, but it called the Supreme Court's bluff and proceeded as though judicial deference meant you needed some actual facts to defer to first, not only the government's naked insistence that it was correct. *Witt* declined to turn the lights off just because the military was the subject at hand. The government would have to demonstrate that "Don't Ask, Don't Tell" actually does significantly further military interests, and that no alternative less severe than "Don't Ask, Don't Tell"—such as a single code of proper conduct applicable to both straight and gay servicemembers—would satisfy the same interests.

I doubt anyone seriously believes the Air Force can make this showing with respect to the individual discharge of Major Witt. There was no disruption of military effectiveness at her duty station until the Air Force began the process of separating her from the service. Of greater interest will be the government's attempt to demonstrate, even as a general matter, that military effectiveness suffers from the presence of servicemembers known to be gay. To date, we've been shielded from the full answer to this question by the doctrine of judicial deference in cases concerning military affairs. It is fairly easy to convince people the military needs "Don't Ask, Don't Tell" when Congress is able to control the information they hear and courts protect the policy from serious scrutiny. Whether the argument remains convincing when all the cards are on the table is another story.

One way to imagine how different "Don't Ask, Don't Tell" would look without the protection of judicial deference is to review some of the official findings that Congress made in support of the policy and consider how well they would hold up under challenge. Congress thought so highly of its findings it enacted them into law along with the operational part of the policy, erecting what it assumed would be a bullet-proof rationale that could stand up indefinitely even if it was unconstitutional. Courts would be very unlikely to ask whether any facts or research supported the findings, and voters would also be very reluctant to second-guess any decision Congress made. When generals testify they cannot possibly do business without "Don't Ask,

Don't Tell," we don't question that assertion. We assume they are speaking knowledgeably and with the best interests of the military at heart, not out of ignorance, political partisanship, religious conviction, or personal indulgence. When a majority of the House and the Senate conclude that gay people are harmful to military effectiveness, we accept that answer without wondering whether Congress has told us only one side of the story. No one, of course, wants to look like they're not supporting the troops.

A recent book by Nathaniel Frank, *Unfriendly Fire: How the Gay Ban Undermines the Military and Weakens America*,[17] offers a more-than-comprehensive report on the misleading way "Don't Ask, Don't Tell" has been sold to the American people. No brief summary or reference can do justice to the quality and depth of his research, but even a few highlights from Frank's careful history show how painfully thin the justifications for "Don't Ask, Don't Tell" have always been. Like the doctrine of judicial deference on military subjects, this policy of exclusion and discrimination persists even though it undermines military professionalism and constitutional values. The five most important congressional findings in support of "Don't Ask, Don't Tell" appear below in italics, followed by some examples of the information we would see if we conducted an honest constitutional evaluation.

> *One of the most critical elements in combat capability is unit cohesion, that is, the bonds of trust among individual service members that make the combat effectiveness of a military unit greater than the sum of the combat effectiveness of the individual unit members.*

One of the core justifications for "Don't Ask, Don't Tell" is the assumption that straight servicemembers will not want to serve with openly gay colleagues, and their discomfort or distrust will weaken unit cohesion and therefore military effectiveness. This argument raises two very different issues. The first is whether the basic assumption underlying the argument is correct. Is there in fact evidence that the presence of openly gay servicemembers leads to breakdowns of good order and discipline within the military? A second issue arises even if we accept, for purposes of discussion, the potential for disruption within the unit. If so, should we solve the problem by enacting laws that cater to the servicemembers who insist they cannot work well with others, even when important to military effectiveness?

The first question is easier to answer. There is no evidence that the presence of openly gay servicemembers affects unit cohesion or military effectiveness in any way. Every research study conducted on the issue, including research commissioned by the Pentagon, has failed to find any justification for excluding gay people from military service. During the 1993 "Don't Ask, Don't Tell" debate, the Department of Defense asked the RAND Corporation to study the issue, but when RAND concluded gay people could serve openly without harm to good order and discipline, the military buried the report so it would not derail the plan to preserve an exclusionary policy.[18] In this report, dozens of professionals had studied the United States military, domestic police and fire departments with openly gay officers and fire-fighters, and foreign militaries around the world that have lifted their bans. It was apparently important, however, to remove from the debate any report recommending that sexual orientation be treated as "not germane to deter-mining who may serve in the military."

For researchers, when militaries change their policies concerning sexual orientation, it presents the perfect experimental research design: what hap-pened before, what happened after, and was there a difference? When our military allies lifted their bans on service by openly gay people, researchers found nothing happened. Actually, it would be more accurate to say nothing bad happened. Frank summarized the results in his book *Unfriendly Fire*:

> Militaries in Great Britain, Australia, Canada, and Israel have seen reductions in harassment, less anxiety about sexual orientation in the ranks, greater open-ness in relations between gays and straights, and less restricted access to recruitment pools as schools and universities welcomed the military back onto campus for dropping their discriminatory practices. Above all, none of the crises in recruitment, retention, resignations, morale, cohesion, readiness, or "operational effectiveness" came to pass.[19]

Before September 11, 2001, senior military officers, defense officials, and academics who supported "Don't Ask, Don't Tell" liked to make fun of mili-taries that had dropped their bans. They weren't "real" militaries like the United States military. Now that many countries who welcome gay service-members are our coalition allies in Iraq and Afghanistan, we don't do that very much anymore. But our joint-force arrangements provide another opportunity to assess the need for "Don't Ask, Don't Tell." Currently our own servicemembers are serving with foreign forces that include openly gay members, and there hasn't been a single reported problem. Even within the United States military, many junior personnel report there are gay people serving in their units despite the restrictions of "Don't Ask, Don't Tell." Researchers have found no association between knowingly serving with gay colleagues and perceptions of unit cohesion or readiness.[20]

The ultimate test case awaits the action of the president. Under federal law enacted by Congress, during a declared national emergency the president has authority to suspend by executive order any law relating to the retirement or separation of any member of the armed forces.[21] This authority is commonly known as "stop-loss" and is usually used to involuntarily extend the service of those who have reached the end of their military obligation. It could also be used, however, to prevent the separation of servicemembers who are subject to discharge but want to remain on active duty. The president has the authority to issue an executive order suspending "Don't Ask, Don't Tell" in its entirety, which would in effect create a study testing whether the policy is necessary to preserve unit cohesion and military effectiveness. During the period of suspension, gay servicemembers could live their private lives normally without fear that others would discover prohibited statements or conduct. No doubt others would become aware that these servicemembers, like everyone else, carry on private lives involving personal intimacy, and once and for all we would know whether that knowledge made a difference. The military, the president, and Congress would then have at their disposal a base of information far more credible than the exaggerated, uninformed predictions of 1993 when considering whether to permanently end "Don't Ask, Don't Tell."

Military life is fundamentally different from civilian life in that (A) the extraordinary responsibilities of the armed forces, the unique conditions of military service, and the critical role of unit cohesion, require that the military community, while subject to civilian control, exist as a specialized society; and (B) the military society is characterized by its own laws, rules, customs, and traditions, including numerous restrictions on personal behavior, that would not be acceptable in civilian society.

The second question related to the unit cohesion rationale is more difficult because the answer depends on the kind of military we would like to have. When defenders of "Don't Ask, Don't Tell" contend that straight servicemembers cannot comfortably tolerate the presence of gay people, leading to breakdowns in good order and discipline, how should we respond to that threat to military effectiveness? Do we cater to this resentment and exclude the people with whom others might refuse to work, chalking it up to the inevitable—and necessary—cultural differences between the military and civilian society? Or do we believe there are some values that are not open to compromise, and if they are important in the civilian world, they are important in the military? Most perplexing of all, is it possible we have been fooling ourselves all along, and difference just for the sake of difference harms the military more than it helps the military?

Congress cribbed the idea that the military is necessarily different, distant, and separate from civilian society directly from the Supreme Court and Justice Rehnquist's constitutional vision for our civil-military relations. Military officials and social conservatives regularly justify "Don't Ask, Don't Tell" with a statement that "the military isn't the place for social experimentation." They are rarely challenged on this assertion, but they should be, because they have things exactly backwards. The social experiment they favor is whether Congress can use military policy to create a legally and constitutionally isolated community in which civilian consensus carries no weight—and time stands still.

We rarely consider whether we are undermining the military when we strictly enforce its cultural difference from civilian society. Retired Admiral John Hutson was closely involved in the initial military discussions concerning "Don't Tell, Don't Tell," and he concedes today their decisions "were based on nothing." "It wasn't empirical, it wasn't studied, it was completely visceral, intuitive." Now Hutson worries about the long-term effects of the policy on the military's reputation at home and abroad. He said, "The real cost is the cost in human dignity, in self-respect, and in the image of the military held by the American public, the world community and itself. . . . The dignity of the armed forces is at stake."[22] The premier academic journal for the study of military affairs, *Armed Forces and Society*, published a perceptive article in 2008 posing this very question in its title: "Does the gay ban undermine the military's reputation?" The conclusion was that, yes, it does.[23]

The standards of conduct for members of the armed forces regulate a member's life for 24 hours each day beginning at the moment the member enters military status and not ending until that person is discharged or otherwise separated from the armed forces.

This finding was made in response to questions about the breathtaking scope of restrictions that "Don't Ask, Don't Tell" placed on the lives of gay servicemembers. People asked whether it was really necessary to completely prohibit gay people from having personal intimacy in their lives—or even talking about it—at any time, in any place, under any circumstances whatsoever, for as long as they serve in the military. They wondered whether a middle ground of compromise could be found in carving out some zone of private discretion in which gay servicemembers could live normal lives when not on military duty.

This congressional finding was designed to squelch these recommendations, but it's extremely disingenuous, even silly. It certainly sounds reasonable, because servicemembers are in fact subject to military law, rules, and regulations at all times and must conduct themselves accordingly. However, no one would offer the 24-hours-a-day rationale to argue that straight servicemembers shouldn't have spouses or partners, or boyfriends or girlfriends. Everyone understands, at least for heterosexual members of the military, that it is important to foster the personally intimate relationships that give them support. The military imposes great burdens of separation and stress on those relationships, but it would never consider prohibiting them because they aren't strictly part of a servicemember's duty, or because some aspects of family life would be inappropriate if brought into the military workplace.

The problem, as mentioned earlier, is that private lives are private, but they are almost never secret. Congress needed a policy consistent with the fantasy that gay people do not serve in the military, which allows straight servicemembers to pretend they live in the one place in America free from diversity in sexual orientation. The congressional finding just described was helpful because it portrayed gay servicemembers seeking space for their private lives as only wanting to break the rules. This rhetorical trick isn't new. The Supreme Court used it in *Goldman v. Weinberger* to discredit the Air Force officer who sought some constitutional flexibility in rules about uniform dress. Goldman wasn't religiously devout; instead, he was selfish and unwilling to support the larger military cause.

The worldwide deployment of United States military forces, the international responsibilities of the United States, and the potential for involvement of the armed forces in actual combat routinely make it necessary for members of the armed forces involuntarily to accept living conditions and working conditions that are often Spartan, primitive, and characterized by forced intimacy with little or no privacy.

This is the shower issue, ever present in discussions of "Don't Ask, Don't Tell." The argument has great resilience, probably because squeamishness is difficult to control and doesn't lend itself easily to rational thought. Most often, shower arguments equate the presence of gay men with the presence of women. These are the questions that always come up: "Why should the military require straight men to share showers, toilets, and sleeping accommodations with gay men, when it would never consider having men and women share those activities? Why do we care about the privacy of women but not the privacy of straight men, who have an equal interest in not being the subject of sexual interest while engaging in the most personal of activities?"

It certainly seems persuasive, until one thinks about it for a moment. In American society (or any other, for that matter) we have never segregated personal hygiene activities on the basis of sexual orientation. We are socialized to do so exclusively on the basis of sex. Males and females grow up performing these activities in the company of others of the same sex in schools, camps, locker rooms, and public bathrooms, without any expectation that gay peers will be excluded. Only in the military is there the unique expectation that it is inappropriate to perform these activities in groups of mixed sexual orientation. I have to laugh when people argue that lifting the ban will cause parents to discourage their sons and daughters from joining a "gay" military. If we assume that any activity that fails to ban gay people from participation is a "gay" activity, did the parents also discourage their children from joining "gay" high school sports teams or attending "gay" camps? The bottom line is that military privacy norms can be met by respecting the same socialized behaviors accepted in larger society.

The presence in the armed forces of persons who demonstrate a propensity or intent to engage in homosexual acts would create an unacceptable risk to the high standards of morale, good order and discipline, and unit cohesion that are the essence of military capability.

The core of the defense of "Don't Ask, Don't Tell" has always been the senior military leader who insists, based on professional military expertise, that the presence of openly gay servicemembers is incompatible with good order and discipline. One has to take into account, however, that senior military leaders who would say otherwise were not invited to the debate. For example, in 1993 Congress could have invited Steve Hall, then a submarine commander, to testify. Everyone understood Hall was gay, from the most junior members of his crew to the admirals above him. Hall said:

> I was so disappointed that Sam Nunn didn't come to my boat. . . . [H]ad Sam Nunn come to my boat with the TV cameras running, I would have said, "Senator, it's not a problem. About 10 percent of my crew is gay, sir, and it's not a problem down here."[24]

General Colin Powell dominated the debate with his firm opposition to President Clinton's proposal to allow gay Americans to serve in the military. One has to take into account, however, that a stacked political deck protected Powell from challenge even when his testimony diverged from the plausible. He testified before Congress to his belief that in three decades of service he had never knowingly served with a military colleague who was gay—except for those who were discovered and discharged. Three other service chiefs piped up after him with the same convenient answer.[25] Of course they had to say they were never aware of gay servicemembers, because otherwise they would have had to explain why they didn't report them as a risk to military effectiveness. I refuse to believe that Powell was that oblivious to his surroundings during his distinguished military career—good officers and sergeants are not oblivious to their people—but the only other explanation is that Powell was deliberately untruthful and no one cared, because truthfulness was not the point of the hearings.

Efforts to use military policy for nonmilitary purposes will eventually bend to the daily reality of military service, although it may take a significant period of time. "Don't Ask, Don't Tell" may be on the verge of that collision with military reality. However, one cautionary lesson to consider is that the Supreme Court's 1981 decision in *Rostker v. Goldberg* still directly burdens the service of military women today. The Court's doctrine of judicial deference makes it alarmingly easy to disregard reality and not be questioned. As the next chapter explains, the continued vitality of *Rostker* ensures that women will not receive full recognition for their service, and it also interferes with efforts to reduce sexual misconduct within the military.

Don't Ask, Don't Tell: August 2, 2010 Update

Although the action has been mostly circular, 2010 has been a year of significant activity for "Don't Ask, Don't Tell." There seems to be strong sentiment within the military, Congress, and the executive branch to reverse the policy, but apparently no one wants to be identified as responsible for ending it. "Don't Ask, Don't Tell" has become a political "hot potato" passed from person to person in the fervent hope someone else will make the final decision. The only thing all the players continue to agree on is that neither courts nor the Constitution should play a role.

The president declined to use "stop-loss" authority to suspend enforcement of "Don't Ask, Don't Tell," even though he has said the policy weakens our national security. Instead, he directed the Department of Defense to study the implications of repealing the law—should Congress choose to repeal it—and issue a report by the end of 2010. "Study" is a loose term, because much of the effort appears focused on polling members of the military about what they think. The answers are likely to be skewed because the Pentagon has threatened to discharge anyone revealed to be gay as a result of the study. The Pentagon did announce new regulations in March making it slightly more difficult to enforce the policy, but it has not changed its procedures to comply with the Ninth Circuit's constitutional ruling in *Witt*.

The hot potato was tossed in Congress's direction, and Congress sent it right back. In May, the House of Representatives passed a provision to repeal "Don't Ask, Don't Tell"—but repeal would take effect only after completion of the Pentagon report, and only if the president, the Secretary of Defense, and the Chairman of the Joint Chiefs all certified that repeal was consistent with military effectiveness. Even if this extremely conditional sequence of events takes place, it would not open military service to gay people. The legislation would only return the decision to the military and, presumably, to the preferences of the commander in chief, completing the potato's full circle. The Senate has yet to approve the proposal.

Chapter 10

How Long Can You Still Call
It an Experiment?

In the spring of 2006, one of the most celebrated leaders at the United States Military Academy at West Point was a civilian—and a woman. West Point had hired Maggie Dixon to coach Army's collegiate women's basketball team just eleven days before the practice season opened. She was only twenty-seven years old, with no prior experience as a head basketball coach. She had never served in the military, and she would be the only female head coach at West Point in any sport, male or female. Hiring Dixon was a tremendous leap of faith for the Army athletic department.

That basketball season became "a year of magical thinking"[1] for the Army Black Knights. After a slow start, Army reversed course and finished first in the regular-season Patriot League standings. The team then won the postseason league tournament to earn its first bid to "The Big Dance," the NCAA national championship tournament. At the end of the league tournament final against Holy Cross, hundreds of cadets rushed the court to celebrate Army's victory, and Dixon was paraded through the crowd on the shoulders of male West Pointers. The following day her appearance at the mess hall was met with a standing ovation from the entire cadet brigade. Although Army lost its opening game in the NCAA tournament to national powerhouse Tennessee, Dixon had taken her future military officers to a level far beyond what anyone could have predicted.[2]

Less than a month later, Dixon collapsed and died from an undiagnosed heart defect. She was buried at West Point Cemetery, an extraordinary honor for someone who had never served in the military and was not the wife or child of someone who had. Also extraordinary was how often academy officials talked about Dixon as "a leader" upon her death. Military officers do not lightly refer to people as leaders. Teaching leadership is the core mission of the academy, and there is no higher compliment than to be remembered as a leader within an institution of leaders. The superintendent of West Point, Lieutenant General William J. Lennox, Jr., put it this way:

> Her presence is what really struck us. That's the impact a leader can have and, in a house of leaders, she stood out. She exuberated courage, strength, caring;

she just embodied everything that we learn here at West Point. Her energy just kind of seeped into everyone else and she just—she's everything that we talk about here being a leader. She was everything and more.[3]

The reason Maggie Dixon's legacy is important to a discussion of women in military service is because the military rarely speaks of women as leaders—not this emphatically. The Army seemed truly stunned to find in its midst a woman who could lead others so effortlessly, especially one who had no prior experience with military life and culture. Dixon personified martial values of leadership that the military so often struggles—and so often fails—to foster in women. West Point's deep respect for Dixon unintentionally revealed how far the military was falling short in teaching men to appreciate military values in women. It seemed she had forced West Point to think about women and leaders in ways less mutually exclusive than they were before she arrived, but her strengths shouldn't have been that novel in an institution that prides itself as a house of leaders.

As a society, military and civilian, we remain uncomfortable when women display military virtues, and we are unsure whether we should be imposing traditional military values or expectations on them. Interestingly, people on both sides of the "women in the military" debates, regardless of whether they support an expanded or a restricted role for women, tend to agree we should not necessarily apply traditional military judgments to issues involving military women. Congress, for example, regularly takes inappropriate advantage of the deference it receives from courts. Well aware that courts are reluctant to question legislation if it even purports to rely on military judgment, Congress sometimes disregards the military's professional expertise and substitutes its own distinctly nonmilitary ideas about appropriate roles for military women. On the other hand, those who favor a larger role for women in military service often reflexively recoil from any mention of military values, because they assume all military traditions must be inherently unfriendly to women.

The military itself occupies an uneasy place in the middle. It sometimes realizes that enforcement of traditional military values is the best way to maximize both the status of women and mission readiness, but sometimes it chooses the easier path over the right path. It succumbs to the temptation offered by legal doctrine—judicial deference—that excuses the military from having to explain its decisions in terms of military necessity. The military may also bend to pressure from a Congress seeking convenient military cover for a controversial legislative policy choice. The only common ground that ever seems to join the three groups—Congress, the military, and the military's critics—is the desire to avoid talking about real military values in situations in which military judgment, properly and professionally applied, leads to inconvenient, uncomfortable, or politically incorrect conclusions.

What people most often fail to understand is that avoidance of professional military values tends to consistently disadvantage military women, and that greater reliance on military values would lead to increased respect for military women and enhanced military effectiveness. The problem, of course, is always in how we define "real" military values. Just as abusive treatment of prisoners does not become a military value just because civilian leadership encourages the military to engage in such behavior, discriminatory or disrespectful treatment of women is not a military value just because some military or civilian officials are uncomfortable with equality. The two most important issues affecting the equality of women in military service today are the assignment of women to combat duty and the control of sexual assault and harassment in a military environment. In both instances, an imperfect process of identifying and applying military values has distorted federal law and defense policy, imposing unnecessary burdens on women and unnecessary losses in military effectiveness. In some cases the damage is of constitutional proportion; in others, the result is only painfully bad and counterproductive military policy.

It is important to note, however, that a movement toward greater reliance on professional military values in law and policy is politically unpredictable. It would not uniformly favor liberal or conservative ideology. Everyone— Congress, the military, and the military's critics—would probably need to change some of the positions they have taken on strongly contested issues. The unifying principle for military law and policy would no longer be liberal versus conservative, or male versus female. Instead, decisions would be guided much more closely by reliance on traditional martial values of leadership and discipline. It could even be described as the Maggie Dixon School of Military Leadership.

In the almost thirty years since *Rostker v. Goldberg*,[4] the case that excused women from any civic responsibility to register for the draft, the clear trend within the all-volunteer force has been to expand the scope of military duties open to women and shrink the number of jobs defined as combat—or too much like combat—and therefore inappropriate for women. The most significant expansion of military duties for women took place following the first Gulf War in 1991, when it became impossible to ignore how much the military was relying on women's service. Federal laws prohibiting assignment of women to combat ships or aircraft in the Navy and Air Force were repealed. The focus of combat exclusion rules shifted to the land-based services, but even there the Department of Defense opened assignments for women that involved combat risks of hostile fire or capture, provided it was not the "primary mission" of the unit to engage in direct ground combat. On January 13, 1994, Secretary of Defense Les Aspin issued the new *Direct Ground Combat Definition and Assignment Rule*:

> Service members are eligible to be assigned to all positions for which they are qualified, except that women shall be excluded from assignment to units below the brigade level whose primary mission is to engage in direct combat on the ground, as defined below.
>
> Direct ground combat is engaging an enemy on the ground with individual or crew served weapons, while being exposed to hostile fire and to a high probability of direct physical contact with hostile force's personnel. Direct ground combat takes place well forward on the battlefield while locating and closing with the enemy to defeat them by fire, maneuver, or shock effect.

Under the new policy, the military's definition of combat duty closed to women was no longer closely tied to physical risk. Women could engage the enemy on the ground while being exposed to hostile fire—the core activity of direct ground combat—provided they were not officially filling slots in smaller units whose *primary* mission was to engage in direct ground combat. As long as ground combat itself was geographically insulated from the units providing logistical support to ground combat, the rules worked well enough. It was all a matter of degree: a bit of combat was fine, but not too much.

The individual services were also given the option to close combat support positions to women under the following additional circumstances, but they were not required to do so: (1) if the cost of providing appropriate living accommodations was too high; (2) if support units were required to physically collocate and remain with direct ground combat units; (3) if support units were involved in long-range reconnaissance or special operations; or (4) if physical requirements would exclude "the vast majority" of women. The point of the DOD policy statement, however, was to expand opportunities, not find new reasons to restrict them.

The new ground-combat definition should have signaled the final collapse of *Rostker*. In exempting women from draft registration, the Court had relied heavily on legal bans against women's service aboard combat ships and aircraft and also on defense policies that barred women even from combat *support* functions if they involved any risk of exposure to combat. By 1994, however, every significant limitation on military service by women had either been eliminated or significantly narrowed. It was difficult to make the case that men and women should be treated differently for purposes of draft registration when the remaining core of combat duties still closed to women was now only a small minority of military positions overall.[5]

Congress, however, was not deterred from holding up *Rostker* as the symbol of what it thought was the proper—and lesser—place of women as citizens responsible for our national defense. In response to the *Direct Ground Combat Definition and Assignment Rule,* Congress enacted a provision in the National Defense Authorization Act for Fiscal Year 1994 requiring the military to report to Congress ninety days before implementing any future amendment to the ground-combat exclusion policy.[6] There is nothing inappropriate, of course, as a general matter, with a congressional directive requiring the military to report on its activities. Congress has a constitutional responsibility to govern and regulate the military, and the military operates under a professional ethic of subordination to civilian control. However, there is a constitutional problem of equal protection under law when Congress usually lets the military assign its personnel without asking for permission in advance, but then micromanages whenever the troops happen to be female. Congress wanted notice in advance so it would have time to specifically prohibit whatever the military proposed to do.

The advance-notice requirement was not even the most constitutionally suspect part of the legislation. The law also strongly encouraged the military to make sure any change in policy would leave *Rostker* undisturbed: "The Secretary [of Defense] shall include . . . a detailed analysis of [the] legal implication of the proposed change with respect to the constitutionality of the application of the Military Selective Service Act to males only." In other words, for goodness sake, please don't let military women do anything that will destroy our legislative fantasy that the military doesn't really need them, because then it will be harder to justify why they shouldn't have the same obligation as men to register for the draft. It seemed extremely important to Congress to preserve the military as a refuge where constitutional standards of equal protection under law did not apply, and where Congress would always have the latitude to decide if and when military policy could be used to reinforce traditional gender roles for men and women.

It would take another war before the reality of women in combat roles became completely unavoidable. After September 11, 2001, military experts expected that men and women would fight in seamlessly integrated ground units in combat-support functions such as military police, intelligence, chemical warfare, and engineering.[7] In Iraq and Afghanistan, it soon became evident that the rules for carefully separating combat and noncombat roles were breaking down. Women were in fact serving in combat roles on the ground despite the government's insistence that they were not.

The core definition of direct ground combat was itself in question because the battlefield was not at all linear. There was no longer a clearly identifiable "enemy" or a place that was predictably "well forward on the battlefield," important terms for defining combat under the *Direct Ground Combat Definition and Assignment Rule.* Combat duty was no longer reserved only for the traditional combat arms of infantry (foot soldiers), field artillery (large projectiles), or armor (tanks). In Iraq and Afghanistan, military police units (assignments open to women) were used interchangeably with infantry units (closed to women) for restoring civil order. The similarity was so apparent that military police work became widely known as "chick infantry" because it was one of the best options for women seeking combat duty.[8] The Army had also switched to a smaller, more mobile organizational structure, which played havoc with proximity-based rules barring the assignment of women to support units that "collocate" with combat units.[9]

The Army had never taken full advantage of the flexibility for assigning women granted by the Aspin order in 1994. The Army did not amend its own assignment policies for women to expressly acknowledge the new Department of Defense guidelines, which is a level of resistance—or perhaps indecision— not often seen in the individual services. By Army regulation, women could not serve in support units below the brigade level that routinely collocated with other units having a direct combat mission, even though the Aspin memo would have allowed it.[10] In Iraq and Afghanistan, however, the Army began to realize its policies were becoming much less practical to implement under either the letter or the spirit of Army rules.

Finding itself in an uncertain legal position, the Army tended to vacillate on women-in-combat questions. Sometimes it acknowledged women did serve in combat roles, but other times it tried to paper over the reality of its assignment policies. A female combat medic was a member of the Army platoon honored as *Time's* 2003 Person of the Year, under this caption: "How a dozen soldiers—overworked, under fire, nervous, proud—chase insurgents and try to stay alive in one of Baghdad's nastiest districts." Two women—a military police sergeant and a medic—earned Silver Stars for bravery under fire (although the medic was removed from her position once her valor came to light). Female West Point graduates directed the tough but routine work of conducting foot patrols and training Iraqi soldiers. Women were assigned to convoys, checkpoints, and security details, and they responded to attacks with lethal force.[11]

Despite the occasional recognition given to women's combat performance, sometimes the inconsistency could be absolutely mind-bending. In February 2005, the Army announced a new combat honor, the Close Combat Badge (CCB), which was designed to recognize valor on a new battlefield without front lines or zones of safety in the rear.[12] The original guidelines for award of the badge read: "The CCB will be presented only to eligible soldiers who are personally present and under fire while engaged in active ground combat, to close with and destroy the enemy with direct fires." Nothing about the guidelines suggested any intent to make distinctions between men and women, except for the definition of an "eligible soldier," which just happened to track the assignments closed to women. In short, no women were allowed to receive the honor, no matter how often they were "personally present and under fire while engaged in active ground combat." The definition also made *men* automatically ineligible if they served under fire while assigned to units also open to women. It was so important to deny the honor to any woman that it was worth denying it to a much larger group of men as well.

At a military town hall meeting in Afghanistan, a female enlisted soldier asked Secretary of Defense Donald Rumsfeld why the qualifications for the CCB were tied to operational specialty alone and not an individual's actual combat experience.[13] She wanted to know "why our MPs [military police] aren't considered for the close-combat patch." For her efforts to speak up under what must have been intimidating circumstances, the soldier earned little more than laughter. Rumsfeld first passed the question to the three-star general by his side, who tried to change the subject: "You guys have got to realize that I get to do this with the Secretary every two weeks and we get lots of tough questions like that." The transcript recorded laughter in response to the general's joking and evasive answer. Rumsfeld took advantage of the diversion and asked for a new question from someone else, and the soldier never received an answer. Apparently, however, the media reports from the exchange had an effect. The Army withdrew the CCB proposal and created the similarly named Combat Action Badge, which would be awarded without regard to military occupational specialty—and without regard to sex—to all soldiers "personally present and actively engaging or being engaged by the enemy."[14]

There was no reason this had to be so difficult, unless the Department of Defense's motivation was to avoid acknowledging that women served in combat. Later in the spring of 2005, a military personnel subcommittee of the House Armed Services Committee approved a measure that would have barred women from thousands of positions in Iraq and Afghanistan in which they were already serving. The amendment would have enacted into law a longer list of positions closed to women, including a wide range of combat support jobs, despite the military's objection that combat support units used both men and women routinely and effectively.[15] This proposal could have made it difficult to assign any women to combat zones, because it barred women from serving in "forward support companies" that provided combat support "within the operational area" of a ground combat battalion.

This proposal was simply unacceptable from a military standpoint, because there were no men available to replace the women. As a matter of military expertise, there was no reason to remove women from those positions. As a matter of constitutional law, there was no justification for disqualifying women solely because they were women, because the desire to maintain traditional gender roles doesn't count as a legitimate legal justification. However, under *Rostker v. Goldberg's* doctrine of judicial defer-ence in military affairs, none of this would make a difference. Congress would have the unreviewable authority to do what it wanted, with the only limitation being the political popularity of the proposal.

The amendment was eventually withdrawn, but Congress enacted in its place yet another plea to preserve the constitutional immunity provided by *Rostker*. Congress directed the military, just as it had twelve years earlier, to give notice in advance of any future proposal to amend the combat exclusion rules. Once again, Congress also warned the military it would have to take a position on whether those proposed changes upset the holding of *Rostker*, which still rested on the obsolete assumption that women weren't very important in a time of war.[16] The provision seemed designed to make sure the military understood that preserving the illusion of *Rostker* was almost as important as the mission itself.

Legal distinctions drawn on the basis of sex in a military environment always have the potential to undermine the dignity and authority of military women, and constitutional exemptions make it difficult to distinguish between the necessary and the frivolous. After the first Gulf War, for example, the military adopted an indefensibly silly policy that military women had to wear full-length Muslim cloaks (abayas) and headscarves when traveling off base in Saudi Arabia.[17] Under these regulations, military women had to be escorted by men, they couldn't drive, and if there was more than one man in the car, women had to sit in the back seat. The rules applied only to Ameri-can military women, not American civilian women, and they were adopted at the request of the American military, not the Saudi government. The mil-itary pled "force protection" as the justification for the policy, but that was ludicrous from the outset. No one could reasonably believe Americans were safer because male servicemembers in crew cuts and western clothing were driving around in the company of abaya-clad women. Of course, military men did not have to affect a Muslim appearance. This special form of insti-tutional disrespect was only for women serving in uniform and, ironically, it operated by taking that uniform away.

One had to wonder whether the military was so comfortable with the idea of subservience in military women that it failed to understand the problem. Perhaps extremely lazy thinking prompted the military to trade away the dignity of military women as a gesture of accommodation to the host cul-ture. In any event, the abaya policy was not rescinded until a senior female Air Force officer and fighter pilot sued the Department of Defense, after years of trying to change the policy internally without success. The military still resisted, offering to settle by changing the mandatory requirement to a "strong encouragement," but finally Congress stepped in and outlawed the practice.[18] Although Congress often imposes socially conservative policies on the military, apparently there are some insults to dignity even Congress won't accept.

Military policy choices made for the purpose of preserving the proper place of women in society sometimes cause harms far more serious than a loss of dignity or authority. Sometimes they become recklessly lethal. On June 23, 2005, an attack on a convoy in Fallujah, Iraq, killed and injured more women than any other single incident in the war. The women were forced to convoy long distances on a predictable schedule each day because, unlike their male colleagues, they were not permitted to live near their duty location, where they conducted searches of Iraqi women. Collocation with a Marine combat unit, even if safer and more efficient, would have been too much like combat for military or congressional tastes.[19]

It seems incredible we would consciously choose to impose a greater risk of injury or death on military women in order to satisfy ourselves we are preserving their proper role in society. Nevertheless, the attraction of *Rostker v. Goldberg* is undeniable. It allows Congress to limit the constitutional benefit of equal protection in ways that would never be permitted in the civilian world, and without the usual checks and balances provided by courts. It is essentially a free pass to ignore the Constitution when convenient. One thing *Rostker* is not and has never been, however, is a decision that protects and affirms the value of military judgment and leadership. *Rostker* is much more likely to be used to remove military judgment and leadership from the constitutional equation, which is what happened in *Rostker* itself and again during the 2005 congressional debate on whether women should be serving in Iraq and Afghanistan. If that congressional proposal had been enacted into law, it would have happened despite military expertise, not because of military expertise. Knowing courts will not require any explanation or justification for treating military women differently invites sloppy decision making motivated by concerns often quite distant from military necessity. Even as a mainstream role for women in military service and a fundamental change in the nature of modern warfare have rendered traditional definitions of combat service obsolete, Congress continues to hide behind *Rostker* despite its deep disconnect from military reality.

Members of Congress have not been alone in their efforts to shrink the role of professional military judgment in policies concerning military women. Advocates who believe military women aren't getting enough institutional support are often just as quick to suggest military judgment doesn't need to be part of the solution. While Congress tends to ignore military input in matters related to equal protection of law, civilian advocates tend to ignore military input in addressing the serious problem of sexual misconduct in the military. Both groups see an advantage in reducing the military's role: in the case of Congress, because a military viewpoint might consider meeting mission requirements more important than maintaining traditional gender roles; in the case of some of the military's strongest critics, because they see military professionalism as the root of the sexual misconduct problem, not the solution to the problem.

The single greatest impediment to solving the problem of sexual misconduct in the military may be the assumption that military women require different principles of military leadership and different means of managing good order and discipline than men do. With all good intention, we have taught a generation of servicemembers that military leadership does not apply to women in quite the same way it applies to men. Since the infamous "Tailhook" scandal of sexual assault at a Las Vegas military aviation conference in 1991,[20] we have lived an endless Groundhog Day of repeated crises, studies, commissions, and promises of reform—but without any significant improvement. The one thing we seem to be missing is an understanding that, at its core, the problem of sexual misconduct in the military is caused by a failure of the military ethic of leadership.

A Department of Defense study on sexual assault in the military reported there were almost three thousand instances of sexual assault involving military personnel during the most recent fiscal year. The number of sexual assaults against women serving in Iraq and Afghanistan was more than 25 percent higher than the year before.[21] The military understands most sexual assaults go unreported, as they do in civilian society, and so its statistics undoubtedly understate the problem. What the military does not mention in its reports is the uncommon ability it has to control the conduct of its people. In the civilian world, all of us have varying degrees of connection or contact with employers, landlords, teachers, government officials, police officers, and other authority figures, but none of those people have overall responsibility for our day-to-day behavior. In the military, in contrast, commanders not only fill all these roles but they have the ultimate responsibility for care and discipline of their subordinates. The Army Field Manual on leadership teaches: "Command is about sacred trust. Nowhere else do superiors have to answer for how their subordinates live and act beyond duty hours."[22] Given the comprehensive influence the military has over every aspect of servicemembers' lives—especially in combat zones—the number of reported sexual assaults is disturbing. Any comparison to the frequency of sexual assault in the civilian world is spurious, because the military is in a much better position to control misconduct.

The military has no independent criminal prosecutor with a role similar to that of a civilian district attorney. The military's prosecutorial discretion is vested solely in military commanders so they can maintain good order and discipline and ensure military readiness. The same individual who is responsible for the mission and the people assigned to perform the mission also decides the manner in which misconduct will be disciplined or punished. This task requires application of military judgment and professional military values to assess "the nature of and circumstances surrounding the offense and the extent of the harm caused by the offense, including the offense's effect on morale, health, safety, welfare, and discipline."[23] The system concentrates a sobering amount of responsibility and power in the hands of commanders, but given the life-and-death decisions they make in military operations, the amount of discretion they have is not unreasonable.

Military law gives commanders great flexibility in addressing disciplinary concerns. In addition to criminal prosecution, they can impose minor administrative sanctions (reprimands, fines, or restrictions to base) or discharge the individual from the military. Perhaps more importantly, they have the ability to intervene and discipline problem behavior long before it rises to the level of a civilian criminal offense.[24] Maintenance of good order and discipline is a complex undertaking because the commander has to balance more issues than most civilians are ever asked to manage. A commander is simultaneously responsible for fulfilling mission requirements and for the health and safety of the people in the unit. Good commanders understand these are not conflicting responsibilities, except when military necessity demands that servicemembers be placed at risk. Members of the military who present a danger to their colleagues also present a danger to military readiness and effectiveness. It's very simple. People who are inclined to prey upon their colleagues can't be trusted to perform their assigned duties, and they can't be trusted to protect their fellow servicemembers should it be necessary. Good order and discipline is the glue that protects both the individual servicemember and the larger mission.

One would think the most effective way to approach the problem of sexual misconduct in the military would be to treat it as one example of a larger category of misconduct in which a servicemember has harmed or abused a colleague. Sexual assault of colleagues violates fundamental military values such as loyalty, duty, respect, selfless service, honor, integrity, and personal courage. (The Army arranged the values so the first letter of each one spells L-D-R-S-H-I-P or "leadership.")[25] Sexual assault of colleagues also undermines military discipline. Controlling criminal behavior that violates military values and undermines discipline ought to fall in the wheelhouse of a commander's professional responsibilities, and if it doesn't, then the commander isn't doing his or her job.

Surprisingly, the military rarely considers the problem of sexual assault from this perspective, and on occasion it takes the opposite approach. Sometimes the military applies civilian solutions to military problems, and then fails to understand why they don't work well. In May 2005, the *Doonesbury* comic strip ran a panel making fun of recent military policy changes designed to ensure greater privacy and confidentiality for victims of sexual assault crimes. When *Doonesbury* mocks progressive efforts, it should be a subtle warning that somebody has missed something very important. The comic-strip conversation took place between a female high-school senior, Alex, and the local Army recruiter, Sergeant Truman:

> ALEX: Sergeant Truman?
> RECRUITER: Alex! Great to see you! Finally ready to sign?
> ALEX: Not yet. I want to talk about sexual assault first.
> RECRUITER: Sexual assault? No longer a problem! We got it covered! If you get hassled, you can report it without triggering an investigation. That way you can take a deep breath before destroying a fellow soldier's career!
> ALEX: *Excuse* me?
> RECRUITER: Um . . . hold it. There might be new wording on this.[26]

Doonesbury's satire was targeted at the military's new *Confidentiality Policy for Victims of Sexual Assault*, issued on March 16, 2005.[27] Under the new policy, military victims of sexual assault could choose to report the crime in a "restricted" format, meaning they could notify a specially designated person outside the military chain of command who would help arrange medical care or counseling, but no information would be forwarded to military command authorities. Victims would be free to take the restricted reporting option if they did not want military authorities to investigate or prosecute the crime. Commanders were supposed to accept that this was a good thing. The policy memo explained: "Commanders have a responsibility to ensure community safety and due process of law, but they must also recognize the importance of protecting the privacy of victims under their command."

At the time the *Doonesbury* strip appeared, sexual assault against military women had been an especially high-profile matter for two years, since the exposure of a disciplinary disaster at the United States Air Force Academy in 2003.[28] The top four officers at the academy were relieved of duty after reports surfaced that male cadets had sexually assaulted dozens of their female classmates, yet the academy failed to investigate the complaints or punish the perpetrators. A panel appointed by the secretary of defense concluded the academy had disregarded repeated warnings of significant problems related to sexual misconduct and abuse of authority among cadets. Other reviews and investigations followed like dominoes and broadened the focus to include the combat theater in Iraq and the other federal service academies. The problem, as it so often is when military women are concerned, was a failure of leadership, all the way to the highest levels.[29]

The 2005 *Report of the Defense Task Force on Sexual Harassment and Violence at the Military Service Academies* also found a connection between sexual misconduct against military women and widespread ignorance about the role they play in military operations. One needs to look no further than Congress to discover the source of this misunderstanding. Although Congress has grudgingly tolerated the increasing integration of women into combat and combat-support duties—as a matter of military necessity, it had little choice—it has also gone out of its way to discount their contribution in order to maintain the facade that military service by women carries less constitutional weight. Many future officers apparently believed the military expanded women's roles only as a sop to political correctness, not to meet operational requirements.[30] But if law teaches us that women contribute little to military effectiveness and have no obligation as citizens to defend the nation, this is the lesson people will take away.

Even after being told in clear terms they had allowed a failure of leadership on their watch, Air Force officials did not respond in a way designed to strengthen military values. One of the first specific ideas they floated was actually to segregate and isolate female cadets in the dormitory—next to their bathrooms—so they would be better positioned to deter assaults. Representative Heather Wilson of New Mexico, an Air Force Academy graduate, explained why that was a terrible idea in terms of military professionalism: "This is not about segregating women from men. It's about segregating rapists from the Academy."[31] These kinds of solutions to the problem of sexual assault, unfortunately, are all too common in the military. We have trained a generation of servicemembers that leadership of men and leadership of women are two different things, and they should apply traditional principles of military leadership only to men. With women, the recommendation is usually a more ham-fisted idea lacking any connection to military professionalism.

For example, after more than a hundred instances of sexual misconduct by military recruiters nationwide in a single year, one state's National Guard instituted a "No One Alone Policy" prohibiting recruiters from meeting alone with applicants of the opposite sex.[32] Of course, these recruiters are the same noncommissioned officers we rely on to protect the lives of junior personnel in a combat environment. If we can't trust them when alone with another servicemember, perhaps we shouldn't trust them to do much of anything. A conference committee in Congress, however, thought the policy was such a great idea they directed the Department of Defense to consider implementing it nationwide. In Iraq, women have been ordered to travel in pairs to avoid assaults by other American soldiers. These "battle buddy" policies for women, a horrific phrase in the context of one's colleagues, have been in official use at least since the first flood of sexual abuse reports across the Army almost fifteen years ago. Female pilots in Iraq have their own version of enforced sexual segregation. They are welcome to fly combat missions in support of ground troops, but they are not allowed to socialize off duty with groups of male aviators in quarters assigned to men.[33]

In devising solutions to disciplinary problems involving the mistreatment of women, it seems the military is reluctant to respond in any way that requires individual judgment or individual responsibility. Perhaps the concern is that individual judgment can be criticized, so better to avoid the judgment entirely. This leads to simplistic policies—men must do that, women must do this—based on sex-based generalizations about men and women rather than on their commonality as professional servicemembers. It doesn't help that civilian advocates for military women tend to distrust military judgment and military professionalism, and are often satisfied if the military steps aside and gets out of the way. This is where misguided ideas like the *Confidentiality Policy for Victims of Sexual Assault*—the *Doonesbury* policy—come from.

This new policy permitting—almost encouraging—confidential reporting of sexual assault, which bypasses the professional obligations of military commanders, was a gift to those looking for an excuse not to exercise military leadership in addressing the problem. In no other circumstance would military policy grant an individual the discretion to decide, for the purpose of preserving privacy, whether a commander had a need to know about a disciplinary issue within the unit, especially when it was a serious crime. When sexual assault occurs within a military unit, the perpetrator poses a risk not only to colleagues but also to military readiness. It is incomprehensible that the military would expressly offer servicemembers a choice about whether to withhold information concerning risk to the unit's mission or to its members.

This is not to say disclosure is easy. There have been notable instances during the war in Iraq in which servicemembers disclosed criminal activity by their colleagues at great physical risk to themselves. The abuses at Abu Ghraib came to light because a fairly junior servicemember reported the conduct to military investigators. Still assigned as a military police officer, he slept with a loaded pistol: "They'd be walking around with their weapons all day long, knowing somebody has turned them in and trying to find out who. That was one of the most nervous periods of my life."[34] More recently, a private first class came forward to report his suspicions that other members of his platoon had raped a fourteen-year-old Iraqi girl and then killed her and her family. He said, "I feared for my safety. Everyone has a weapon and grenades." But he decided to make a report because "it had to be done."[35] It is not realistic to expect that servicemembers caught in such difficult circumstances will always summon the courage to report misconduct, but the military would never consider giving them the option to remain silent.

It makes a very specific statement about the status of women in military service when they are granted an exemption from the professional expectation that they may need to risk their personal safety, not to mention invasion of privacy, to protect others or ensure military readiness. This expectation of disclosure undoubtedly imposes great hardship on those who serve in the military. Many aspects of military service do. It illustrates, however, how the different values and obligations within the military profession can and should affect policy choices in matters of sexual assault. A civilian victim is under no obligation to take action for the benefit of anyone else. A military victim, harsh as it may seem, has a professional responsibility to report serious misconduct in service to a larger purpose.

Recognizing the professional obligations of military victims of sexual assault does not diminish in any way the far greater responsibilities of military leadership. It does not mean we are blaming the victim, and it does not mean we are excusing the commander. Too often we set up false and over-simplified choices that fail to reflect the causes of the problem or the difficulty of the solution. The only productive means of addressing the issue of sexual assault in the military is to hold military commanders responsible for their failures of leadership. A policy that permits reporting outside military channels directly undermines this principle.

Restricted reporting excuses failures of military leadership by taking the chain of command out of the picture, and it inflicts a number of harms on the military and on all military women. In the short term, it denies military commanders the information necessary to punish and prevent sexual assault. In the long term, it teaches military leaders that sexual assault is a problem unrelated to traditional military discipline. Finally, it diminishes and disrespects military women by assuming they are less able or less willing than men to report misconduct that sabotages military readiness. If Congress, the military, or the military's critics are dissatisfied with the performance of military leaders in punishing and preventing sexual assault—and they should be—they need to hold them accountable in exactly the same way they would in situations not involving violence against women. The answer is not to drive the responsibility underground and relieve military commanders of the obligation they have to protect the people they lead.

Military leaders and civilian defense officials have an obligation to ensure commanders take their obligation to control predatory behavior within the ranks seriously, including predatory sexual behavior disproportionately affecting women. We haven't yet reached this point, and until it is routine for commanders and subordinate military leaders—officers and NCOs—to be disciplined or relieved of their positions because they have failed to protect the servicemembers they lead, we won't make progress. If we expect victims of sexual assault to act in accordance with military values and responsibilities and in a way that enhances military effectiveness, we should expect no less from military leaders. As yet, there is no consensus that sexual misconduct reflects a failure of military leadership and a failure of command responsibility.

Greater reliance on military values—ethical standards such as loyalty, duty, respect, selfless service, honor, integrity, and personal courage—may unexpectedly offer the one neutral principle ensuring that respect for military women matches the responsibility they undertake. The Army may be the first service to see the connection between traditional military values and the prevention of sexual harassment and assault. In 2009, the Army began a new professional training program called "I. A.M. Strong,"[36] which is the first prevention program, to my knowledge, treating sexual misconduct as an assault on the military itself. It expressly assigns to soldiers a military duty to sacrifice for one another if necessary to prevent a sexual assault. It appeals to the vow they make to never leave another soldier behind, and it brilliantly melds respect for women and respect for military values. The initials stand for three obligations: to intervene, to act, and to motivate. The explanations are written from a young soldier's perspective:

> INTERVENE: When I recognize a threat to my fellow soldiers, I will have the personal courage to INTERVENE and prevent sexual assault. I will condemn acts of sexual harassment. I will not abide obscene gestures, language or behavior. . . .

> ACT: You are my brother, my sister, my fellow soldier. It is my duty to stand up for you, no matter the time or place. I will take ACTION. . . .

> MOTIVATE: We are American soldiers, MOTIVATED to keep our fellow soldiers safe. It is our mission to prevent sexual harassment and assault. . . .

Without conscious intention, the Army was beginning to repair some of the damage caused by *Rostker v. Goldberg* and its assumption that military needs, military expertise, and military values had very little to do with government policies affecting military women. Supporters of the doctrine of judicial deference—and they are the overwhelming majority of those who are aware of the doctrine—often argue courts are wrong to involve themselves in military issues. It's "out of their lane," as military people would say. The reality, however, is that a greater role for courts could be the best way to ensure an appropriate role for military expertise.

Before the Rehnquist transformation of civil-military relations following the Vietnam War, it was possible for courts to draw a straight line between constitutional values and military values and not have someone complain they were interfering with military effectiveness or disrespecting the troops. It all seems so quaint. It was possible for courts to acknowledge and reinforce the professional military ethic of political neutrality when it was important to the strength of our constitutional design. Courts no longer use that authority because they have voluntarily given it away to the elected branches and the unpredictability of majority sentiment. As the next chapter explains, during the 2000 presidential election we came very close to experiencing the worst possible thing that could happen when civilians no longer understand or respect the constitutional basis of our civil-military relations.

Chapter 11

A Cautionary Tale about Military Voting

Any ballot from a man or woman in the military who is serving this country should be counted—period. I don't care when it's dated, whether it's witnessed or anything else. If it is from someone serving this country and they made the effort to vote, count it and salute them when you do it.[1]

You might think every story that could have been written about the historic 2000 presidential election has already been written, and many times. There is one more story to tell, and it is about the military. Most people believe the conventional wisdom that partisan political forces tried to disenfranchise servicemembers voting from overseas by absentee ballot. The tale of military ballots in the 2000 election is the perfect example of what happens when our civil-military relations deteriorate, but the problem was not that military people were denied the right to vote. It was just the opposite.

The "military vote" became part of election lore when Florida's presidential vote ended in a statistical tie in the hours after the polls closed on November 7, 2000. The vote was so close that determining a winner was like "measuring bacteria with a yardstick."[2] In Florida, however, there were still more votes to be harvested after Election Day, even after news of the undecided election had been broadcast around the world. This was because Florida was one of the few states that accepted absentee ballots after Election Day from state citizens residing overseas. Under an administrative election rule, overseas absentee ballots arriving by mail in election offices within ten days after the election could still be counted provided the ballots were actually voted on or before Election Day.[3] This extra window benefited all Florida citizens living overseas, whether because of military service, civilian government service, education, retirement, or personal preference. Overseas voters were often referred to as "military voters," but only a small percentage of eligible overseas voters were servicemembers or spouses of servicemembers, fewer than 10 percent.[4]

Within a few days after Election Day, it became clear the most important questions concerning the postelection overseas ballots would be (1) whether the ballots had actually been mailed from overseas, because ballots mailed from within the United States had to arrive by Election Day; and (2) whether the ballots had actually been voted on or before Election Day, because votes cast after the election are, of course, invalid. Verification of overseas origin and timely voting had never been controversial in Florida before. Postmarking was the most certain and objective measure for both, and Florida election officials had always invalidated ballots lacking overseas postmarks with a date on or before Election Day. In 2000, news reports early in the ten-day window, including from the *Stars and Stripes*, a military newspaper, referenced the universal assumption that ballots arriving late would have to bear a valid postmark.[5]

Under the spotlight of an unresolved presidential election, however, the clarity of prior practice unraveled. It would be fair to say that on Friday, November 17, the day Florida counties began to count the overseas absentee ballots received after Election Day, election hell broke loose. An unexpectedly high percentage of ballots from purported overseas voters had arrived with postmarks dated after Election Day, with postmarks of domestic origin, or without postmarks of any kind. Numerous ballots had other disqualifying defects such as missing signatures and witness certifications, and some were from individuals who had not registered to vote or who had not requested absentee ballots. Some counties canvassed ballots like they always had before, rejecting those without postmarks confirming origin and date, but others devised their own rules on an ad hoc basis, giving an extra benefit of the doubt to absentee voters. Overall, election officials invalidated about 40 percent of overseas absentee ballots arriving after Election Day.[6]

It was at this point that the overseas absentee ballots became "military ballots" and enforcement of Florida election law became a referendum on patriotism and support for the military. Spokespersons for Governor George Bush charged that the Democratic Party was encouraging election officials to throw out ballots from servicemembers. The statements were merciless in linking enforcement of Florida election law to hostility against those serving in uniform. For example, Montana governor Mark Racicot, a Bush spokesperson, charged that Vice President Al Gore's lawyers "have gone to war, in my judgment, against the men and women who serve in our armed forces."[7] Republicans cited a legal memo drafted by a lawyer for the Democratic Party as evidence of intent to suppress the military vote, but the memo was nothing more than a list of federal and Florida election law provisions that apply to all overseas voters, military and civilian, with a check sheet for recording the reason or reasons a particular ballot did not qualify under law.[8] Apparently the federal government and the state of Florida had also "gone to war" against the military, because the memo contained nothing but the laws themselves.

The pressure to reconsider and count previously rejected ballots was relentless. Republicans obtained a letter from an officer with the Military

Postal Service Agency stating it was hypothetically possible for military mail to leave a ship at sea without a postmark if a mailbag was hurriedly tossed aboard a departing aircraft before the ship's crew had a chance to postmark the contents. Within days, the Pentagon was retreating from the accuracy of that statement.[9] It was possible, defense officials speculated, that a single piece of mail might escape postmarking if it went through the machine stuck to another piece of mail, but they were no longer standing behind the mailbag story. Regardless, neither explanation could possibly account for the number of ballots arriving in Florida without proper overseas postmarks, but by then it was too late. The story of the dramatic shipboard departure had mutated into reports that all branches of the military "frequently" fail to postmark mail, even though Department of Defense regulations require postmarking of all military mail. The popular talking point was the unfairness of penalizing servicemembers whose votes were rejected through no fault of their own.

The Democratic Party abandoned any effort to ensure that overseas absentee ballots complied with federal and Florida election law when Senator Joe Lieberman, the Democratic vice-presidential candidate, appeared on *Meet the Press* on November 19. He encouraged county election officials to "go back and take another look" and "give the benefit of the doubt to ballots coming in from military personnel, generally."[10] Democrats conceded the validity of any overseas ballot arriving after Election Day, no matter how egregious the flaws. Florida attorney general Robert Butterworth issued a statement the next day also urging officials to reconsider rejected ballots, basing his recommendation on the common, but false, belief that the military often failed to postmark its mail properly.[11]

Despite heavy criticism that overseas ballots were being invalidated for politically partisan and antimilitary reasons, some county election officials continued to stand by their original ballot counts. On November 22, Governor Bush filed a lawsuit against election officials in thirteen counties, seeking a court order to count ballots even if they bore a postmark after Election Day, a postmark within the United States, or no postmark at all. He also asked that ballots be counted even if they came from people who were not registered to vote or who had not requested an absentee ballot. The lawsuit took the pressure to another level, and many of the named counties immediately recanvassed their overseas ballots under more generous standards.[12]

Republicans were very successful in equating legal disqualification of a ballot with antimilitary sentiment, and county officials were quickly losing interest in explaining the law. No one wanted to defend Florida election law when Medal of Honor winners made public appearances on behalf of the Republican Party to criticize the state of Florida and Democrats for denying servicemembers the right to vote.[13] Counties did not send lawyers to defend the lawsuits, and so the briefs and hearings were usually one-sided affairs. The line separating valid from invalid ballots soon evaporated. Additional ballots were counted even if they were postmarked after Election Day, postmarked in the United States, or not postmarked at all—and, in some cases, even if they arrived after the end of the ten-day window. Ballots were counted even if they were sent by unregistered voters or by voters who did not ask to vote absentee. It was an absolute free for all. Some voters voted twice. Clay County, Florida, even counted two ballots sent from a fax machine in Maryland as valid overseas votes. One sailor reported mailing his ballot six days after the election: "I was just seeing if it would count or not." It did.[14]

Following the election, a *New York Times* investigation of overseas absentee ballots found numerous servicemembers willing to admit they had voted after Election Day. One has to assume this was the tip of the iceberg, because few people are going to confess to committing a felony.

> Aboard the George Washington, an aircraft carrier then in the Adriatic Sea, Michael J. Kohrt recalled fellow crew members gathering around television sets on the morning of Nov. 8. "We saw Florida was deadlocked, and everyone on the ship said, 'Whoa, I have to get my ballot in,'" he said. "A lot of guys voted late."[15]

Seven months after *Bush v. Gore*,[16] the Supreme Court decision that ended the vote recount in Florida, the inspector general of the Department of Defense released a report entitled *Overseas Absentee Ballot Handling in DOD*.[17] The report found no systemic problems in the military postal system that could explain the irregularities in ballots sent by overseas voters. A few months later, in September 2001, an investigation conducted by the General Accounting Office, *Voting Assistance to Military and Overseas Citizens Should Be Improved*,[18] reached the same conclusion. These two investigations revealed that the most important factual assertion underlying the overseas ballot controversy in Florida—that the military postal system often failed to postmark mail correctly—was false.

Both the inspector general and the GAO found military post offices overseas followed Department of Defense requirements to postmark mail with a date and place of origin. Military mail sent from overseas is postmarked overseas, even if the mail originates from a ship deployed at sea and even if the mail does not require a stamp. The inspector general conceded the possibility that some random piece of military mail could escape postmarking, but it definitively rejected the idea that military post offices routinely, systematically, or even frequently fail to postmark mail. The GAO conducted spot checks of mail inbound to United States military mail gateways and found no problems with postmarking. GAO investigators were apparently mystified when, during their visits to local election offices, they were shown ballot envelopes purportedly sent from overseas but bearing domestic post-marks or no postmarks at all.[19]

Over the course of the *Bush v. Gore* election dispute, Department of Defense officials offered a shifting variety of explanations about military postal procedures and absentee balloting. On November 7, 2000, Election Day, when no one could have foreseen a result so close that absentee ballots would decide the election, DOD dismissed any concern that servicemembers overseas were having any trouble with voting. Kenneth Bacon, the assistant secretary of defense for public affairs, told reporters that naval personnel at sea, for example, would have registered to vote and requested absentee ballots months ago, before leaving the United States. Bacon also clarified that military voters never have to wait for their mail to catch up with them in order to vote. Once a servicemember files a request with his or her home state to vote by absentee ballot, if the official state ballot fails to arrive promptly, federal law offers an easy substitute. Standard Form 186, the Federal Write-In Absentee Ballot, is a fill-in-the-blank form kept on hand by the military and by American civilian agencies overseas. However, Bacon said there had been no reports of any delays requiring significant use of the write-in ballots.[20]

Two days later, on November 9, postmarking was beginning to crystallize as a important issue affecting absentee ballots arriving after Election Day. Assistant Secretary Bacon was unprepared for a reporter's question about how Florida's postmarking requirement might affect deployed naval personnel, but Bacon's staff in attendance at the news conference assured him that ships postmark their own mail.[21] By November 28, however, after large numbers of overseas ballots arrived without overseas postmarks, the story had changed. Bacon was now taking the position that military mail was not necessarily postmarked, and in fact was *frequently not postmarked*. He had somehow come to believe that the only purpose of a postmark was to prevent people from reusing the stamp. Bacon decided that if ballots could be mailed postage-free, then there was no need to postmark them, because, in his words, "there is not a stamp to cancel."[22]

If this DOD spokesperson had checked military postal regulations, he would have discovered that cancellation and postmarking are two different things. Cancelling a piece of mail means to render the stamp unusable; postmarking identifies date and place of origin. Military postal regulations explain that the presence or absence of a stamp is unrelated to postmarking requirements.[23] The only possible source for Bacon's statement was one of the lawsuits just filed by Governor Bush. Using very much the same language, Bush's lawyers incorrectly alleged that postage-free ballots were not postmarked because "there is no postage to cancel."[24]

In the overseas balloting debate, the tail had begun to wag the dog. Bush's lawyers could not have been relying on information obtained from the military or the Department of Defense in support of their client's claims, because the military's own postal procedures would have proved them wrong. However, it seemed that DOD was relying on allegations made in the Bush lawsuits in order to explain military policy and procedure to the public. In essence, the allegations of the lawyers were transformed into fact by cycling them through military press briefings.

Upon release of the June 2001 inspector general report, Charles Abell, assistant secretary of defense for force management policy, and Navy Captain Eugene DuCom, deputy director of the Military Postal Service Agency, discussed its findings at a Department of Defense news conference. They attempted to explain why there was in fact *no* problem with an issue that was presented as the *central* problem during the overseas ballot controversy—the supposed failure of the military to postmark its mail correctly. Captain DuCom confirmed that the military requires all mail to be postmarked, and he was at a loss to explain why a large number of ballots arrived in Florida without overseas postmarks, or with postmarks dated after Election Day:

> And we would require that the ballots be postmarked. We do require that all the mail be postmarked. There have been—obviously some were not postmarked that arrived. I don't know the reasons for that. . . .
> I think there had been some misunderstandings throughout since November about postmarking mail. . . . But we postmark everything.[25]

Of course, back in November 2000, Captain DuCom was one of the principal sources of that misunderstanding. He authored the story of the dramatic shipboard transfer of the unpostmarked bag of mail, the story that expanded to fill all military contingencies on land or at sea. You could not blame reporters at this news conference for being baffled at a report finding that overseas military mail was in fact postmarked with regularity. One asked:

> QUESTION: Mr. Abell, I'm a little confused. Wasn't one of the major problems with the election in November that members of the military were disenfranchised because their ballots arrived without postmarks?
> ABELL: I'm not prepared to talk about that. It's not part of the audit.

The elephant in the room that no one would ever dare to discuss was the possibility that servicemembers were using the special election assistance provided to them—write-in ballot forms on hand and the military postal system—to stuff the ballot box after Election Day. No one was going to touch it.

Perhaps the most compelling evidence that overseas voters were marking and mailing ballots after Election Day was the disproportionate number of ballots that arrived in Florida during the last few days of the ten-day, post-election window. The extended window was only a safety valve for ballots that were mailed ahead of Election Day but then unexpectedly delayed in transit. In most instances, it wasn't needed. Florida sent ballots to overseas voters forty-five days ahead of the election,[26] and most were returned before Election Day and counted with all the domestic ballots. In any event, both military and civilian overseas voters had the option to vote and mail a write-in ballot if they had any concern that waiting for the state ballot might cause them to miss the deadline. There is simply no reasonable scenario in which large numbers of overseas voters are holding their ballots for mailing on or just before Election Day. As a result, "late" ballots normally arrive in the first few days of the ten-day window, followed by declining numbers over the remaining days. By the tenth day, it's usually down to "a trickle."[27]

Florida election officials did not keep records of how many absentee ballots arrived each day during the postelection window. However, it is possible to estimate those figures from daily newspaper accounts, particularly in four counties with large military installations: Duval (Jacksonville Naval Air Station), Escambia (Pensacola Naval Air Station), Hillsborough (MacDill Air Force Base), and Okaloosa (Eglin Air Force Base). There was intense interest in how many absentee ballots were arriving from overseas because that number exceeded the margin of votes, and so county election officials sometimes provided newspapers with running tallies of ballots received. The day-by-day ballot numbers are sometimes imprecise because of differences in the time of day the tally was made, but the numbers are consistent enough to illustrate the trend.

During the 2000 election in Florida, ballots arrived in the expected pattern at the beginning of the ten-day window. A fair number of ballots—still a small fraction of those received by Election Day—arrived within a day or two of the election. The number of ballots received each day then steadily declined. However, between the seventh day and the tenth day of the window, an unexpectedly large number of overseas absentee ballots were delivered to county election officials. A declining curve had shifted abruptly into a sudden increase in arriving ballots.

In Escambia County,[28] for example, 89 ballots arrived in the first two days of the postelection period, and another 47 had arrived by noon of the sixth day. Between days seven and ten, however, the total number of ballots doubled. In Hillsborough County,[29] 22 ballots arrived in the first two days, and another 36 over the next six days. In the last two days, 78 more ballots arrived. In Okaloosa County,[30] the number of ballots received more than tripled between days seven and ten; in Duval County,[31] it almost quadrupled. Florida-wide tallies showed the same trend. A total of 1,873 overseas absentee ballots had arrived in Florida's sixty-seven counties during the first eight days of the postelection window. More than 1,000 additional ballots arrived on the ninth day alone, followed by approximately 800 more on the tenth day. The last two days doubled the count.[32]

It was no coincidence that the sudden upturn in ballots began on or shortly after the seventh day of the postelection window. Ballots voted after the election, once it became known the result was a virtual tie, would have arrived at that time. The GAO found in its postelection review of the military's postal system that 74 percent of first-class mail was delivered from domestic mail gateways to overseas military locations within seven days. The DOD inspector general made similar findings, estimating that transit time from the United States to overseas military locations averages, at most, five days longer than normal domestic mail delivery. Neither were there delays in the other direction, from overseas military locations to the United States. A DOD spokesman said: "It could take anywhere from three to six days. . . . Even if you're in the Indian Ocean somewhere, it shouldn't take more than six days."[33]

Overseas civilians who did not have access to the military postal service system, however, faced much longer mailing times and more unreliable service. The GAO estimated that diplomatic pouch mail and regular international mail could take from two to five weeks for delivery, depending on the country of origin.[34] It would not have been possible for civilian overseas voters to wake up on November 8, learn the election was still in play, and mail ballots that could arrive in Florida before the end of the ten-day window.

We play a very dangerous game with civilian control of the military when we deliberately inject political partisanship and political resentment into the relationship between the military and civilian society. In November 2000, civilians were successful in selling a story—unsupported by fact or law but devastatingly effective—that military voters had been discriminated against because they were military. Civilians were successful in fueling a sense of resentment among servicemembers that their votes had been discarded for reasons of raw political partisanship or even distaste for the military. The resentment got so out of hand that senior military leadership had to warn its officers against violating a provision of the Uniform Code of Military Justice prohibiting contemptuous statements against civilian leadership.[35] The resentment fanned by the Florida absentee ballot count continues today, and every time we hold an election, someone, somewhere, alleges servicemembers are at risk of disenfranchisement.

An episode like this became entirely foreseeable, however, when the Supreme Court began to teach civilians thirty-five years ago that the military was supposed to be different from, and better than, the rest of us. We learned it was not our place to question the facts we were given if they had anything to do with the military. We learned that following the law was much less important—sometimes it was even subversive—when the law ran counter to something that could be sold as the military's best interest. We became less and less capable of noticing when civilians made assertions about the military that were not true. Our duty as citizens was to go along with it, because to be skeptical was to be unpatriotic. Many Florida election officials tried to do the right thing in identifying suspicious ballots, but they were bowled over by the force of what the Supreme Court had put in motion. These officials were unfairly painted as hostile to the military, and it was done for short-term political advantage.

This cautionary tale about military voting is, for the most part, not about the military, although we should have had the civil-military courage to acknowledge significant evidence of fraudulent voting by servicemembers. This cautionary tale is primarily about civilians who used the military in a way that violated its proper constitutional bounds. They used the military to bully other civilians, and it worked, placing at risk the political neutrality that is at the core of civilian control of the military.

Chapter 12

A Part of America, Not Apart from America

After more than three decades of a widening civil-military gap, it's not realistic to think we can eliminate the divide easily or quickly. We have grown comfortable with the unexamined assumption that the best way to maintain the strength of an all-volunteer military is to underscore its difference from civilian America. But we have a responsibility to do something to reverse this trend, because a divide of experience, ideology, and culture between the military and civilian society is tremendously corrosive to healthy civilian control of the military, to constitutional fidelity, and to military professionalism. The civil-military gap is not sustainable over the long term. The nature of the problem, however, tends to push the solution further out of reach. With the civil-military gap in place, we are much less likely to understand why it is a problem, and we are much less likely to care. Distance causes indifference and resentment, and indifference and resentment cause more distance, making it very difficult to stop the cycle. This final chapter offers three recommendations for reversing the direction of our civil-military relations and restoring a new sense of shared constitutional bond between military and civilian communities.

1. *We need Supreme Court justices who understand how judicial deference undermines the military.*

It might be tempting to dismiss the doctrine of judicial deference in military affairs as an innocuous intellectual exercise—an egghead way of thinking about the military—but judicial deference has not been good for the military's institutional health. This doctrine has changed the military and, interestingly, it has changed America. Deference now characterizes the American way of talking about the military, for civilians and military people alike.

Judicial deference became an indispensible part of a new civil-military dynamic that took hold in the post-Vietnam, postdraft era. Without a military draft, a less representative range of civilian society circulated through the military, and we lost some of the natural check we once had on the ability of government to shade or misrepresent military values and military needs. The rise of judicial deference ensured courts would not become an independent, alternate forum for airing evidence about the nature of military service and the importance of constitutional values in a military environment. Congress would be able to create its own reality by majority vote without opportunity for challenge or review, even when Congress clearly had a conflict of interest in the matter. Congress quickly learned it had unlimited discretion to define the military in ways that seemed to make the Constitution less important— and sometimes even a burden to the military—and courts would reinforce the result by deeming conflicting information irrelevant.

Judicial deference relied on a host of damaging assumptions about the relationship between the military and civilian America. It taught us that public debate of military issues was often inappropriate or unnecessary, because civilians were generally incapable of contributing to the discussion. It taught us that asking questions about military affairs was unpatriotic and disrespectful of people serving in uniform. It taught members of the military that they were of higher moral character than civilians and therefore above the lower, pedestrian requirements of law or the Constitution. It taught both Congress and the military that decisions involving the military would not have to withstand public scrutiny the same way other decisions of govern-ment did. The effect was to excuse and encourage poorly considered and poorly justified decisions. Judicial deference announced to America that facts, evidence, and truth were no longer very important, at least not when military issues were on the table.

How do we begin to reverse this understanding? Judicial deference is now the law of the land in terms of Supreme Court precedent, but judges do have more discretion than they typically exercise to think honestly about what judicial deference should mean when applied to military cases. When courts "defer" to an institution, they ought to be deferring to some identifi-able professional expertise, not simply to the result the institution would like to see. Courts should be deferring, if at all, to hard-earned experience and lessons learned, not bare assertions or opinions. For example, when generals testify that good order and discipline suffer when members of a unit become aware some of their colleagues are gay, but they also insist they have never knowingly served with a gay person, should that qualify as pro-fessional expertise? It seems much closer to a statement of professional ignorance. It doesn't make sense for courts to accept assertions from the military when it lacks any informed experience and then reject research demonstrating the assertions are inaccurate. "Don't Ask, Don't Tell" is a par-ticularly good illustration of this problem, because courts have been defer-ring to the personal opinions of senior officers on a subject that by law is invisible and by culture is a taboo subject of conversation—particularly in the age range of those officers.

Courts can also be much more discerning about the scope of deference when it touches on matters related to legal expertise. It is unclear why courts should defer to congressional interpretations of the Constitution, and they generally don't, except when the interpretation concerns the military clauses of the Constitution. It's also unclear why courts should feel bound to defer to any finding that constitutional values are inconsistent with military values, or to any conclusion that constitutional values must automatically give way. That's certainly not the military's call to make, and it's not Congress's call to make either, at least not without the prospect of serious review by courts. Congress does not have sole authority to decide the meaning and scope of constitutional rights, even under pressing circumstances. Ironically, in constitutional controversies of a military nature, there is almost always a resolution to the dilemma that respects both constitutional values and military values, because both arise from a common respect for the rule of law. We shouldn't be working so hard to avoid finding this resolution.

There is an appropriate role for judicial deference in military affairs, but it needs to be much smaller and more focused on the reasons one institution of government should defer to another. Courts should have discretion to defer to military experience and expertise, for example, on matters in which the military actually has some experience and expertise. That may seem self-evident, but in practice it has been anything but self-evident. Sometimes courts defer under circumstances in which Congress and the military have made little or no effort to educate themselves before taking action. When Congress enacted the Solomon Amendment, it had no idea whether law school interviewing policies were affecting JAG officer recruiting, and it had no idea whether introducing financial coercion into the mix would make things worse. To Congress, it didn't really matter, because the military's needs weren't the issue. The point was to punish what it considered disrespectful behavior toward the military.

The best way to determine if the military does have relevant experience and expertise—and to ensure it will be heard fairly, completely, and unedited—is to require the government to produce evidence of those military facts when military policies are challenged as unconstitutional. The legally warped version of judicial deference we often follow today is much more likely to hide the presence or absence of military expertise than it is to hear and respect it. When government relies on judicial deference today, more often than not it is a sign little evidence exists to support the government's position. In addition, any practice of deference needs to have a reasonable shelf life to avoid reliance on stale information. It makes little sense to bar plaintiffs challenging the constitutionality of "Don't Ask, Don't Tell," for example, from introducing on-point, persuasive research conducted today on the basis that the research didn't exist fifteen years ago when Congress first made its decision. Judicial deference should never be interpreted in a way that requires the government to be willfully oblivious to relevant information.

In the more narrow range of circumstances in which it is appropriate for courts to defer to an informed explanation of military needs or circumstances, it's important to remember this is only half of the constitutional equation. Even if courts defer to the accuracy of a military assessment, courts still have an obligation to determine, with all due respect to the military, if that assessment really matters in the context of a larger question. Consider, for example, what should happen if either the military or Congress made a factually informed judgment that religious diversity within the military was causing breakdowns in good order and discipline. Assume that some servicemembers had questioned the loyalty of others who held religious beliefs associated with the enemy, and either the military or Congress chose to address the problem by making certain religious beliefs a disqualification for enlistment. Courts should not defer to that finding on good order and discipline no matter how accurate it might be, because a larger principle of the right to free exercise of religion is at stake. Faithfulness to the Constitution requires the court to invalidate the policy and tell the military to solve its good order and discipline problem in another way.

One of the most direct ways of introducing some rationality into the doctrine of judicial deference would be to appoint more federal judges—and especially new justices of the Supreme Court—who have an understanding of judicial deference consistent with healthy civil-military relations and strong civilian control. Professing strong support for the military, without any awareness of how judicial rulings can undermine military professionalism, should not be enough. During Senate confirmation hearings for Supreme Court justices, we generally don't hear questions on the subject of civil-military relations and judicial deference, but this may be because each institution has a vested interest in reducing the role of federal courts in civilian control of the military. Congress protects the doctrine because it radically increases congressional power in matters involving the military. The Supreme Court first developed the doctrine as a way of changing our basic understanding of civil-military relations and weakening the military's connection to law. After thirty-five years of judicial deference, however, this may also be the only way of thinking about military affairs any of the participants has ever known. With time, it becomes very easy to follow the crowd and pretend judicial deference is supportive of the military, avoiding the harder truth that courts are imposing real consequences on the military and on civil-military relations when they shirk their constitutional obligation for civilian control.

2. We need to change the way we think about military advice.

One of the ways the doctrine of judicial deference has left a scar on civil-military relations is by changing how civilian government manages the military advice it receives. I don't meant to suggest this is a new problem for civilian control of the military—President Harry Truman certainly struggled to manage the military advice offered by General Douglas MacArthur during the Korean War[1]—but judicial deference has contributed to a more pervasive problem broadly affecting the way civilians engage with information from military sources.

Strictly speaking, judicial deference in military affairs applies only when constitutional or legal issues are in play. When the question is whether a particular military policy or plan of action is a wise or prudent thing to do, and not whether it is constitutional or lawful, courts have no role in answering the question and judicial deference is irrelevant. However, because judicial deference has expanded beyond an abstract legal theory into a more general way of thinking about military affairs, it has come to have an indirect effect on all forms of military decision making by civilian officials. Deference in a strictly legal sense is only a part of the broad cultural deference on military issues we have adopted since the end of the Vietnam War.

We consistently discourage civilians from serious engagement with military issues. We assume most civilians are incapable of understanding the military and have little to add to the conversation. We suspect they have not earned the right to speak about military affairs, even though at some level we must know civilian engagement is necessary in a system built on civilian control of the military. There is always a risk that asking too many questions will be interpreted as a lack of support for the military, and so the easier path is often to endorse whatever appears to be the consensus "military" position on an issue, whether or not the consensus position is actually helpful to the military.

Our inclination toward deference in matters involving the military is so strong that military advice can sometimes carry the power of a military veto when the advice becomes part of public debate. Few government officials want to be in the position of asking for the military's viewpoint on an issue and then choosing a policy direction inconsistent with that viewpoint. As a result, civilians may package or present military advice in a way that misleadingly removes any conflict with civilian policy preference, ensuring at least the appearance of a deferential attitude. The "Don't Ask, Don't Tell" debate offered a good example of this phenomenon. Congress put on what were essentially "show hearings" to create the appearance of unified military opposition to gay citizens in military service. I don't doubt that in 1993 military opposition outweighed military support, but the hearings were carefully scrubbed of any military expertise from the minority viewpoint.

The military's increasing political partisanship also plays an important role in how we characterize and respond to military advice, and there may be no better example of why political partisanship is damaging to military professionalism. At the same time civilians have an incentive to package military opinion selectively for favorable effect, the military may also feel an obligation to shape the advice it gives (or to withhold contrary opinions) in an effort to be loyal to a particular political interest. Political partisanship within the military imposes great pressure on military professionals to produce advice supportive of its political allegiance. At the very least, there will always be an air of uncertainty as to whether military advice has been tainted by a desire to either support or undercut the commander in chief or the Congress.

Even the general public responds to military advice differently depending on whether the advice matches expectations about the military's presumed political allegiance. When military officials were uncooperative to the point of being insubordinate and refused to seriously consider how to implement President Clinton's proposal to end sexual orientation discrimination in the military, most people believed they were simply following their professional obligation to give civilian leaders candid military advice. We are so comfortable with the idea of military testimony running counter to policy preferences of the Democratic Party that no one objected when General Colin Powell gave a speech at the Naval Academy encouraging midshipmen to resign if they believed they could not morally serve in a military that also permitted gay people to serve.[2] That's not advice, that's insubordination.

On the other hand, when military advice upsets the careful civil-military consensus we usually construct for public consumption and also runs counter to the military's expected political allegiances, people take notice and ask whether the military has violated its ethical obligation of subordination to civilian control. The recent example of note occurred when General Eric Shinseki, the Army chief of staff, responded to a question during a Senate hearing asking how large a force would be necessary to maintain public order in Iraq following an invasion. This was information Congress needed to know in order to carry out its constitutional responsibilities to declare war and fund military operations. Shinseki responded with a significantly higher number than the administration's party line, and it began a debate among civil-military experts that continues today. A series of essays in the professional journal *Armed Forces and Society* examined the controversy,[3] and one author seriously argued Shinseki had a professional obligation to answer in a way that would protect the president from the perception he might be acting against military advice, or at least without a consensus military opinion.[4] Our system of civilian control of the military included, according to this argument, an obligation on the part of military professionals to adjust their advice to shore up civilian policy preferences. I have a feeling, however, the same ethical argument would not have been made on behalf of a Democratic Party commander in chief.

The solution is both simple to understand and difficult to achieve. If we were more comfortable with open engagement and conversation about military advice—if we were more comfortable with robust, messy debate about military issues—it would not be so important to shape or distort military advice to match civilian preferences. If we were more comfortable with military viewpoints, and believed we could invite them, consider them, weigh their strengths and weaknesses, balance them against other nonmilitary concerns, and then, if necessary, make a decision inconsistent with those viewpoints, our civil-military relations would be much healthier. This is the same dynamic that inhibits a healthy civil-military exchange in judicial settings. We believe the system cannot tolerate the complexity or the inconvenience of real information, and so we construct a system specifically designed to generate a false consensus—the doctrine of judicial deference—so we can all feel better about making military decisions.

One of the most pressing concerns in the military profession today is whether its leaders lack candor in their dealings with civilian authority. The most notorious statement of that concern came in "A Failure in Generalship," a fearless article published in *Armed Forces Journal* in 2007 and widely distributed throughout the military.[5] The author, Lieutenant Colonel Paul Yingling, was willing to state openly what was apparently clear to many, but voiced by few. Senior military officers, he wrote, "never explained to the president the magnitude of the challenges inherent in stabilizing postwar Iraq," "failed to provide Congress with an accurate assessment of security conditions," and "did not accurately portray the intensity of the insurgency to the American public." Interestingly, an important part of the solution he suggested was to demand that members of Congress ask more questions and insist on answers, even if, and especially if, the answers made the ultimate decision more difficult: "Some of the answers will be shocking, which is perhaps why Congress has not asked and the generals have not told."

Some, and perhaps many or most, senior military officers would say that public disagreement with civilian leadership is inappropriate and unprofessional. Military advice should generally remain within the chain of command, and if the next level of leadership in the chain disagrees, then that's the end of it. The issue received a great deal of attention when a handful of general officers who had commanded forces in Iraq publicly criticized the planning and execution of the war after they retired.[6] What the senior officers who counsel staying within the chain of command may be missing, however, is the impact of our political culture of deference on this important issue of military ethics.

Military officials may have a professional obligation to speak publicly if disclosure is necessary to avoid being complicit in the misrepresentation of military advice. If civilians take advantage of our culture of timidity and deference with respect to military affairs and falsely represent that they are acting in reliance on military advice—knowing, of course, this will have the effect of discouraging further debate—the military should not have an obligation to assist government in concealing that misrepresentation. If civilian government erects a facade of military expertise to justify policy preferences, it may in fact be the obligation of military officers to correct the record.

It is telling that officers like Lt. Col. Yingling identify the artificial nature of our public conversations about the military as one of the primary problems in achieving military success. Judicial deference in a legal setting presents issues that are perfectly parallel to the much larger question of how civilians should request and digest military advice. In both cases, the problem is usually a lack of transparency and a system that encourages artificial consensus and exaggerated simplicity. In both cases, we wrongly assume that transparency is damaging to the military, when reality is exactly the opposite.

3. *We need to change the incentives for military service and appeal to a new kind of volunteer.*

This may be the most difficult transformation of all because, unlike proposals to reform the legal rules for deciding military cases or improve the transparency of military information in government policy, this change affects the way the military views itself from top to bottom. This many years after the creation of an all-volunteer military, no one remembers the inherent constitutional strength of a military that is more culturally and politically representative of civilian society. We now see civil-military distance and difference as a measure of strength, not weakness, despite increasing evidence of declining quality in military recruitment. The government goes to great lengths to defend a civil-military gap that leaves civic responsibility for military service in the hands of a smaller number of people, even though the uneven burden generates frustration and resentment that the obligation is not more fairly shared.

If we want to reverse this trend and instill an expectation that military service should be a responsibility for the many and not only the few, things have to change. I'm not suggesting we should introduce a mandatory obligation for national service—a draft—although there are strong arguments to be made that it is difficult to have a constitutionally healthy military without one. But we do need to make a fundamentally different appeal to potential volunteers and redefine the incentives for military service. Only then do we have any hope of reestablishing a candid civil-military dialog and finding a ready pool of competitively qualified personnel. We cannot continue to dig deeper within a dwindling base under the guise of preserving an artificial sense of military values.

It does not help military recruiting when the military narrowly defines itself in terms of social conservatism, religious fundamentalism, political partisanship, or resistance to constitutional ideals. The military cannot significantly expand its base for recruitment without taking concrete steps to convince young people it will be welcoming and respectful of women, of political diversity, of religious diversity and, yes, of gay people. The military must decouple itself from stances on social issues that divide Americans unless it can demonstrate that taking a particular position is necessary for military effectiveness. Treating military service like a social club for like-minded people is a luxury the military can no longer afford. The military must make absolutely clear its commitment to the same constitutional ideals respected and relied upon in the civilian world, and it must vow it will never disregard those ideals without strong justification, fully explained.

Because young people are very attuned to inconsistency, Congress and the military need to understand that arguments sufficient to pass muster under a standard of judicial deference will often not make sense to prospective recruits. For example, when the military argues the First Amendment has no relevance in a military environment when a gay servicemember speaks of a personal life back home, but then it trumpets the First Amendment to protect a general who rails against the Muslim religion in uniform, putting servicemembers at risk, young people notice.[7] When the military looks the other way when a general pleads the Fifth Amendment to avoid responsibility for Abu Ghraib, but then it prosecutes junior enlisted personnel who commit the acts of abuse encouraged by government policy, young people notice.[8] A consistent respect for the Constitution and for the rule of law is essential.

Once the military reestablishes its traditional bond to constitutional ideals, it becomes possible to devise incentives with appeal for college-bound youth. We need to be imaginative. Military service doesn't necessarily require a long-term commitment or obligation from either side of the all-volunteer contract. There is work to be done that doesn't require a long period of enlistment, and on the other hand, the military always has discretion to carry out a reduction in force. The military doesn't owe anyone a twenty-year career.

The military mission requires a wide variety of skills, talents, and interests. This fact tends to be hidden by our extensive use of civilian contractors,[9] whom we hire in an effort to conceal that the military is much too small for all the missions we ask it to perform. We could circulate a much wider variety of Americans through military service if the military profession accurately reflected the military's true needs. What if, for example, the military offered some of the most sought-after internships in agriculture, anthropology, computers, engineering, government and civil affairs, international studies, journalism, languages, medicine, meteorology, veterinary science, or women's studies, to name a few? Don't laugh. Civilian anthropologists have been very closely involved, on the ground, with the military's counterinsurgency operations.[10] Harvard University's Carr Center for Human Rights Policy helped General David Petraeus revise the counterinsurgency field manual.[11] Senior Airman Ashton Goodman, who was killed in Afghanistan by an improvised explosive device, was a college-age woman who mentored female Afghan leaders and worked to advance the economic and social development of women.[12]

Many young adults far outside the military's usual recruiting focus are looking for opportunities larger than themselves, even if the work is challenging and the compensation is less than they could receive in the private sector. They include graduates of our most prestigious universities, the "elite" who are often the subject of scorn in military circles. Teach for America, a program recruiting new graduates for service in public schools that are difficult to staff, has been the largest employer of graduates at Duke, Emory, George Washington, Georgetown, New York University, and Spelman.[13] I don't intend to equate teaching in urban schools with the sacrifices required for combat service, but the high level of competition for slots in the Teach for America program does suggest many graduates are seeking an opportunity to serve, even if the conditions are unglamorous and difficult. Many of these individuals would be open to military service, I believe, if they thought they could be part of something that mattered. The military only needs to ask.

Notes

INTRODUCTION

1. Frank Newport, "Americans' Confidence in Congress at All-Time Low," *Gallup News Service*, June 21, 2007.

2. Professor Elizabeth Hillman of Hastings College of the Law was an Air Force space operations officer. She is also the author of *Defending America: Military Culture and the Cold War Court-Martial* (Princeton, NJ: Princeton University Press, 2005).

3. John Hechinger, "At Ivy League Schools, ROTC, Long Banned, Plots a Comeback," *Wall Street Journal*, December 16, 2004.

4. For a typical example, see Michael Winerip, "The R.O.T.C. Dilemma," *New York Times*, November 1, 2009.

5. Marc Lindemann, "Storming the Ivory Tower: The Military's Return to American Campuses," *Parameters*, Winter 2006-7. A publication from the Veterans of Foreign Wars splashed the word "Banned!" across a recent cover article on ROTC. Ken Harbaugh, "Bring Back ROTC," *VFW Magazine*, September 2009.

6. 10 U.S.C. § 983(a).

7. Transcript of the MSNBC Democratic debate in Las Vegas, *Federal News Service*, January 15, 2008; Patrick Healy, "Candidates Take Break, of Sorts, to Mark 7th Anniversary of the 9/11 Attacks," *New York Times*, September 12, 2008.

8. Michael S. Neiberg, *Making Citizen-Soldiers: ROTC and the Ideology of American Military Service* (Cambridge, MA: Harvard University Press, 2000).

9. Neiberg, *Making Citizen-Soldiers*, 4.

10. Neiberg, *Making Citizen-Soldiers*, 123-28.

11. Neiberg, *Making Citizen-Soldiers*, 117-19.

12. Peter M. Shane, "ROTC: Is It Coming Back?" *Harvard Crimson*, September 1, 1973; Gregg J. Kilday, "Army Plans to Terminate Harvard ROTC in 1970; Air Force Stays Until '71," *Harvard Crimson*, August 12, 1969.

13. Neiberg, *Making Citizen-Soldiers*, 121.

14. The *Wall Street Journal* published a report on the Army's decision to reduce its ROTC footprint in northern, urban areas and relocate elsewhere. Greg Jaffe, "A Retreat From Big Cities Hurts ROTC Recruiting," *Wall Street Journal*, February 22, 2007.

15. *Rumsfeld v. Forum for Academic and Institutional Rights*, 547 U.S. 47 (2006).

16. Natalie Patton, "'Don't Ask, Don't Tell': Law School Dean Apologizes," *Las Vegas Review-Journal*, December 8, 2001; Karen W. Arenson, "After 22 Years, N.Y.U. Allows an Army Recruiter to Visit," *New York Times*, October 17, 2000 (reporting that faculty members joined protestors who chanted and hooted at military recruiters).

17. Michael S. Neiberg, "Different Beat, Same Drummer," *Newsday*, December 27, 2002.

18. Nancy Gibbs, "Wings of Desire," *Time*, June 2, 1997.

19. Marvine Howe, "U.S. Acts to Improve Air Base in Turkey," *New York Times*, March 5, 1981; Dexter Filkins, "U.S. Demands for Help Roil Turkey's Government," *New York Times*, December 21, 2002; Dexter Filkins, "In Iraqi No-Flight Zones, 12 Years of Containment May End in Bombardment," *New York Times*, January 25, 2003; David S. Cloud, "Military Seeks Alternatives in Case Turkey Limits Access," *New York Times*, October 11, 2007.

CHAPTER 1 SLAM-DUNKED LAW PROFESSORS

1. *Rumsfeld v. Forum for Academic and Institutional Rights*, 547 U.S. 47 (2006). All pleadings and briefs in the *Rumsfeld v. FAIR* litigation are available at http://www.law.georgetown.edu/solomon.

2. 10 U.S.C. § 983(b). The Solomon Amendment denies federal funding to universities having a policy or practice "that either prohibits, or in effect prevents . . . access to campuses, or access to students . . . for purposes of military recruiting in a manner that is at least equal in quality and scope to the access to campuses and to students that is provided to any other employer."

3. Brief for the Respondents, 1.

4. The Association of American Law Schools (AALS), an educational association representing 171 law schools (including every nationally prominent law school), requires its member institutions to follow a policy of nondiscrimination in career-placement programs. AALS Bylaws, § 6-3(b), http://aals.org/about_handbook_bylaws.php.

5. 10 U.S.C. § 654.

6. Second Amended Complaint, Preliminary Statement ¶ 1, *Forum for Academic and Institutional Rights v. Rumsfeld*, 291 F. Supp. 2d 269 (D.N.J. 2003). Rumsfeld is listed first in the title of the Supreme Court decision because the government was the appealing party, having lost in the Third Circuit.

7. Brief for the Petitioners, 17.

8. Charles Moskos, "Patriotism-Lite Meets the Citizen-Soldier," in *United We Serve: National Service and the Future of Citizenship*, ed. E. J. Dionne, Jr., Kayla Meltzer Drogosz, and Robert E. Litan (Washington, DC: Brookings Institution Press, 2003), 33–42; Robin Toner, "Who's This 'We,' Non-Soldier Boy?" *New York Times*, June 25, 2006; Thom Shanker, "Military Memo; All Quiet on the Home Front, and Some Soldiers Are Asking Why," *New York Times*, July 24, 2005.

9. *Wooley v. Maynard*, 430 U.S. 705 (1977).

10. *Speiser v. Randall*, 357 U.S. 513 (1958).

11. Richard A. Posner, "A Note on Rumsfeld v. FAIR and the Legal Academy," *Supreme Court Review*, 2006, 52.

12. *Boy Scouts of America v. Dale*, 530 U.S. 640 (2000).

13. *Forum for Academic and Institutional Rights v. Rumsfeld*, 291 F. Supp. 2d 269, 278 n.2 (D.N.J. 2003).

14. *Congressional Record* 140 (May 23, 1994): H3863 (statement of Rep. Richard Pombo of California).

15. "U.S. Judge: No Yale Law Clerks," *National Law Journal*, February 21, 2005.

16. *Forum for Academic and Institutional Rights v. Rumsfeld*, 390 F.3d 219 (3d. Cir. 2004).

17. Since the 1993 congressional debates that led to "Don't Ask, Don't Tell," the *New York Times* editorial pages have called for ending the ban over a dozen times, most recently in "A Stronger Military," May 26, 2010.

18. Adam Liptak, "Supreme Court Smackdown!" *New York Times*, March 12, 2006. Conservatives, of course, joined in heckling the hapless law professors. George F. Will, "Professors of Pretense," *Washington Post*, March 8, 2006; Peter Berkowitz, "U.S. Military: 8, Elite Law Schools: 0; How Did So Many Professors Misunderstand the Law?" *Weekly Standard*, March 20, 2006.

19. It is inaccurate to address the solicitor general of the United States as "General" because, in this context, "General" is an adjective (describing the scope of his duties), not a noun (a person of a particular rank). William Safire, "On Language; General, No," *New York Times*, July 20, 2003.

20. Oral Argument, 12–13, *Rumsfeld v. Forum for Academic and Institutional Rights*, 547 U.S. 47 (2006).

21. U.S. Constitution, art. 1, § 8, cl. 1.

22. Congress has the power "to raise and support armies," "to provide and maintain a navy," and "to make rules for the government and regulation of the land and naval forces." U.S. Constitution, art. 1, § 8, cls. 12–14.

23. Oral Argument, 43.

CHAPTER 2 A CANARY IN THE CIVIL-MILITARY MINE

1. Brief of the UCLAW Veterans Society et al. as Amici Curiae in Support of Appellees, *FAIR v. Rumsfeld*, 390 F.3d 219 (3d. Cir. 2004).

2. Joint Appendix, 169–70, 173–74. In letters to New York University's dean for career placement, the Army tried to comfort rejected JAG candidates: "Unfortunately, [keen competition] means that some very qualified applicants will not be selected for a position. Please convey this information to your students and assure them that non-selection does not reflect negatively on their qualifications."

3. U.S. Army Judge Advocate General's Corps, *Judge Advocate Recruiting Office*, https://www.jagcnet.army.mil/JARO.

4. Draft Brief of the UCLAW Veterans Society as Amicus Curiae in Support of Appellees and Affirmance of the District Court (on file with the author).

5. The toned-down, final version of the brief alleged that military law students would be "implicitly marked by their schools' action as linked to an employer whose conduct was so reprehensible as to be undeserving to set foot on campus."

6. 10 U.S.C. § 12305. See also chapter 9.

7. *Policy Concerning Homosexuality in the Armed Forces: Hearings before the Senate Committee on Armed Services*, 103rd Congress (1993), 615 (testimony that it was "a definite possibility" that "straight males would probably murder gays"); *Policy Implications of Lifting the Ban on Homosexuals in the Military: Hearings before the House Committee on Armed Services*, 103rd Congress (1993), 171 (testimony that "on a number of occasions," gay men were thrown overboard at sea; but "I can't think of a way that we could specifically control or decrease the things that might happen").

8. 5 U.S.C. § 3331 (commissioned officers); 10 U.S.C. § 502 (enlisted personnel).

CHAPTER 3 INVENTING THE CIVIL-MILITARY DIVIDE

1. *Orloff v. Willoughby*, 345 U.S. 83 (1953).
2. The Uniform Code of Military Justice was originally enacted as Pub. L. No. 81-506 in 1950 and is codified in federal law today at 10 U.S.C. §§ 801–947.
3. Frank I. Michelman, "Forward: Traces of Self-Government," *Harvard Law Review* 100 (1986): 8.
4. *Flower v. United States*, 407 U.S. 197 (1972).
5. *Frontiero v. Richardson*, 411 U.S. 677 (1973).
6. *United States v. Flower*, 452 F.2d 80, 90 (5th Cir. 1971) (dissenting opinion).
7. *Frontiero v. Laird*, 341 F. Supp. 201, 207-08 (M.D. Ala. 1972).
8. *Gilligan v. Morgan*, 413 U.S. 1 (1973).

CHAPTER 4 JUSTICE REHNQUIST'S VIETNAM WAR

1. *Reid v. Covert*, 354 U.S. 1 (1957).
2. *United States ex rel. Toth v. Quarles*, 350 U.S. 11 (1955).
3. *Solorio v. United States*, 483 U.S. 435 (1987). In an opinion written by Justice Rehnquist, the Court overruled eighteen years of precedent that limited court-martial prosecutions to "service-connected" offenses. *O'Callahan v. Parker*, 395 U.S. 258 (1969).
4. *Feres v. United States*, 340 U.S. 135 (1950) (negligence causing death in a barracks fire; medical malpractice); *Chappell v. Wallace*, 462 U.S. 296 (1983) (racial discrimination).
5. For arguments that the military's legal control over servicemembers has grown beyond reasonable bounds, see Jonathan Turley, "Pax Militaris: The *Feres* Doctrine and the Retention of Sovereign Immunity in the Military System of Governance," *George Washington Law Review* 71 (2003): 1; Jonathan Turley, "Tribunals and Tribulations: The Antithetical Elements of Military Governance in a Madisonian Democracy," *George Washington Law Review* 70 (2002): 649.
6. *Parker v. Levy*, 417 U.S. 733 (1974); *Rostker v. Goldberg*, 453 U.S. 57 (1981); *Goldman v. Weinberger*, 475 U.S. 503 (1986).
7. Hawkeye Pierce was the lead character in the movie and television show *M*A*S*H*, a sensitive comedy set in an Army surgical unit during the Korean War. Hawkeye was a drafted surgeon who always chafed at the military side of his medical duties.
8. Profiles of Captain Levy appear in James Finn, "Personal Testimony: Howard Levy, M.D.," in *Conscience and Command: Justice and Discipline in the Military*, ed. James Finn (New York: Random House, 1971), and Robert Sherrill, *Military Justice Is to Justice as Military Music Is to Music* (New York: Harper and Row, 1970).
9. 10 U.S.C. §§ 933, 934. Captain Levy was also convicted for willfully disobeying a lawful command under Article 90 of the UCMJ.
10. *City of Chicago v. Morales*, 527 U.S. 41 (1999) (invalidating a law against "loitering" because it was unconstitutionally vague).
11. *Houston v. Hill*, 482 U.S. 451 (1987) (invalidating a law against "interrupting" a police officer because it was unconstitutionally overbroad).
12. *Pickering v. Board of Education*, 391 U.S. 563 (1968).
13. *Orloff v. Willoughby*, 345 U.S. 83, 94 (1953).

14. *Parker v. Levy*, 417 U.S. 733, 743–44 (1974).

15. *Burns v. Wilson*, 346 U.S. 137, 140 (1953) (drawing an analogy between state law and military law, each separate and apart from federal law).

16. Samuel P. Huntington, *The Soldier and the State: The Theory and Politics of Civil-Military Relations* (Cambridge, MA: Harvard University Press, 1957), 226–29.

17. The Court itself (pre-Rehnquist, of course) has recognized the citizen-soldier's contribution to important reforms in military law, particularly following World War II. *Burns v. Wilson*, 346 U.S. 137 (1953); *Reid v. Covert*, 354 U.S. 1 (1957).

18. As early as 1851, the Supreme Court recognized that servicemembers have a duty to disobey illegal orders. *Mitchell v. Harmony*, 54 U.S. 115 (1851).

19. Rules for Courts-Martial 916(d), in *Manual for Courts-Martial, United States* (2008), II-109.

20. *Rostker v. Goldberg*, 453 U.S. 57 (1981).

21. *Williamson v. Lee Optical*, 348 U.S. 483 (1955) (upholding a law that discriminated against opticians by prohibiting them from duplicating or fitting eyeglass lenses without a prescription from an optometrist or an ophthalmologist).

22. *Grutter v. Bollinger*, 539 U.S. 306 (2003) (law school admissions); *Regents of the Univ. of Cal. v. Bakke*, 438 U.S. 265 (1978) (medical school admissions) (opinion by Justice Powell).

23. *Craig v. Boren*, 429 U.S. 190 (1976) (invalidating an Oklahoma law allowing women, but not men, to buy beer at the age of eighteen; men had to wait until they were twenty-one).

24. The classic Supreme Court opinion, *Marbury v. Madison*, 5 U.S. 137, 177 (1803) reads: "It is emphatically the province and duty of the judicial department to say what the law is."

25. The Court quoted Senator Sam Nunn of Georgia, who would later make his mark in 1993 as the senator most invested in the exclusion of gay citizens from military service. Coincidentally, it was Senator Nunn's great-uncle, Representative Carl Vinson, who led the legislative effort more than thirty years earlier to exclude Navy women from service at sea. Jean Zimmerman, *Tailspin: Women at War in the Wake of Tailhook* (New York: Doubleday, 1995), 155, 161–62.

26. *Rostker v. Goldberg*, 453 U.S. 57, 84 (1981) (Justices White and Brennan dissenting).

27. Jeanne Holm, *Women in the Military: An Unfinished Revolution*, rev. ed. (Novato, CA: Presidio Press, 1992), 274.

28. *Congressional Record* 126 (June 10, 1980): S13881-82; Linda Greenhouse, "Bork Nomination Is Rejected, 58–42; Reagan 'Saddened,'" *New York Times*, October 24, 1987.

29. *Goldman v. Weinberger*, 475 U.S. 503 (1986).

30. At the time *Goldman v. Weinberger* was decided, laws that had the effect of restricting free exercise of religion were subject to strict scrutiny. *Sherbert v. Verner*, 374 U.S. 398 (1963). Almost thirty years later, *Employment Division v. Smith*, 494 U.S. 872 (1990) eased that standard, approving laws that interfered with religious observance provided they applied to everyone and were not intended to burden free exercise.

31. Air Force Instruction 36-2903, *Dress and Personal Appearance of Air Force Personnel*, available at http://www.e-publishing.af.mil, is the current version of the regulation cited in *Goldman v. Weinberger*.

32. 10 U.S.C. § 774.

33. Rehnquist remained consistent on this point. In a later book he wrote on the relationship between law and war, he asserted that the military is "not entrusted with the protection of anyone's civil liberties." William H. Rehnquist, *All the Laws but One: Civil Liberties in Wartime* (New York: Alfred A. Knopf, 1998), 204. What a sad thing to say about the military's responsibility to treat people—including its own members—in accordance with our national values and the military's own professional ethic.

CHAPTER 5 CONSTITUTIONAL BARGAINS AND MILITARY ETHICS

1. Department of Defense Directive 1344.10, *Political Activities by Members of the Armed Forces* (February 19, 2008), replacing earlier version dated August 2, 2004. Department of Defense publications are available at http://www.dtic.mil/whs/directives.

2. Thomas E. Ricks, *Making the Corps* (New York: Scribner, 1997); Thomas E. Ricks, "The Widening Gap between the Military and Society," *Atlantic Monthly*, July 1997; Thomas E. Ricks, "Separation Anxiety: 'New' Marines Illustrate Growing Gap between Military and Society," *Wall Street Journal*, July 27, 1995. Ricks is also the author of two influential books about the war in Iraq, *Fiasco: The American Military Adventure in Iraq* (New York: Penguin Press, 2006) and *The Gamble: General David Petraeus and the American Military Adventure in Iraq, 2006–2008* (New York: Penguin Press, 2009).

3. Ricks, *Making the Corps*, 23.

4. Ricks later joined the *Washington Post* as a Pentagon reporter, and he now writes for *Foreign Policy*.

5. Stanley R. Arthur, "The American Military: Some Thoughts on Who We Are and What We Are," in *Civil-Military Relations and the Not-Quite Wars of the Present and Future*, ed. Vincent Davis (Carlisle, PA: U.S. Army War College Strategic Studies Institute, 1996), 15.

6. Andrew J. Bacevich and Richard H. Kohn, "Has the U.S. Military Become a Partisan Force?" *New Republic*, December 8, 1997, 25. Professor Bacevich, a West Point graduate and Vietnam veteran, has written several books on the military and international relations, including *The New American Militarism: How Americans Are Seduced by War* (New York: Oxford University Press, 2005). Professor Kohn, former chief historian of the Air Force and now a professor in military history and civil-military relations, was the editor of an important work on military-legal history, *The United States Military under the Constitution of the United States, 1789–1989* (New York: New York University Press, 1991).

7. Richard H. Kohn, "Out of Control: The Crisis in Civil-Military Relations," *The National Interest* 35 (Spring 1994).

8. John Lancaster, "Air Force General Demands Tight Formation for Commander in Chief," *Washington Post*, April 22, 1993; Charles Moskos, "Solving Clinton's Military Problem," *Chicago Tribune*, April 20, 1993 ("In 30 years of studying civil-military affairs, I have never before heard members of the armed forces express such ill will toward their commander"); Barton Gellman, "Warship Gives Clinton a Not-So-Hail to the Chief," *Washington Post*, March 12, 1993. Article 88 of the Uniform Code of Military Justice prohibits officers from using "contemptuous words" against the president,

vice president, Congress, the secretary of defense, and a number of other government officials and institutions. *Political Activities by Members of the Armed Forces* prohibits the same behavior by enlisted personnel, and violations are criminally punishable under Article 92 as a failure to obey orders.

9. Michael R. Gordon, "General Ousted for Derisive Remarks about President," *New York Times*, June 19, 1993; Steven Greenhouse, "Helms Takes New Swipe at Clinton, and Then Calls It Mistake," *New York Times*, November 23, 1994. General Campbell was reprimanded, fined, and forced to retire.

10. Nadine Cohodas, *Strom Thurmond and the Politics of Southern Change* (New York: Simon and Schuster, 1993).

11. U.S. Department of Defense news release, "Remarks as Delivered by Secretary of Defense William S. Cohen, Yale University, New Haven, Connecticut," September 26, 1997. Secretary Cohen had an odd way of describing the civil-military gap, one that put all the blame on civilians and none on the military. He said, with all apparent seriousness: "So one of the challenges for me is to somehow prevent a chasm from developing between the military and civilian worlds, where the civilian world doesn't fully grasp the mission of the military, and the military doesn't understand why the memories of our citizens and civilian policy makers are so short, or why the criticism is so quick and so unrelenting." In other words, we have a civil-military gap of knowledge and experience because, first, civilians can't understand the military and, second, the military can't understand why civilians have to be so ignorant.

12. Ricks, *Making the Corps*, 286.

13. Ole R. Holsti, "A Widening Gap between the U.S. Military and Civilian Society? Some Evidence, 1976-1996," *International Security* 23 (1998): 5; Thomas E. Ricks, "Military Is Becoming More Conservative, Study Says," *Wall Street Journal*, November 11, 1997; Adam Clymer, "Sharp Divergence Is Found in Views of Military and Civilians," *New York Times*, September 9, 1999.

14. Samuel P. Huntington, *The Soldier and the State: The Theory and Politics of Civil-Military Relations* (Cambridge, MA: Harvard University Press, 1957), 71, 83.

15. Morris Janowitz, *The Professional Soldier: A Social and Political Portrait* (Glencoe, IL: Free Press, 1960), 233.

16. 18 U.S.C. § 592. This law can have the effect of preventing local election officials from using military facilities as voting locations. Voting locations on military installations that local election officials have designated as official polling places on or before December 31, 2000, or that have been used as official polling places since January 1, 1996, are grandfathered into use. 10 U.S.C. § 2670.

17. 18 U.S.C. §§ 593, 609. Although servicemembers cannot use their rank to influence military subordinates, the law contains this proviso: "Nothing in this section shall prohibit free discussion of political issues or candidates for public office."

18. 18 U.S.C. § 596.

19. *Greer v. Spock*, 424 U.S. 828 (1976).

20. Sasha Issenberg, "Army Personnel Spoke at McCain Rally: Military Bars Such Political Displays," *Boston Globe*, September 28, 2007.

21. "President Bush Meets with Military Personnel at Fort Campbell," March 18, 2004 (transcript of remarks), http://georgewbush-whitehouse.archives.gov/news/releases/2004/03/20040318-3.html.

22. David Stout, "Bush Hails Returning Troops on Eve of Iraq Anniversary," *New York Times*, March 18, 2004.

23. Ricks, *Making the Corps*, 280–81.

24. Secretary of Defense Robert M. Gates, "United States Naval Academy Commencement Remarks," May 25, 2007. Gates gave the same lesson to Air Force Academy graduates on May 30, 2007.

25. Jonathan Weisman, "Lawmakers Describe 'Being Slimed in the Green Zone,'" *Washington Post*, August 31, 2007.

26. Bryan Bender, "Soldiers Warned Not to Forward Bogus Chain E-Mail Using Military Computers," *Boston Globe*, January 20, 2008.

27. Admiral Michael G. Mullen, "From the Chairman: Military Must Stay Apolitical," *Joint Force Quarterly* 50 (2008): 2–3; Thom Shanker, "Military Chief Warns Troops about Politics," *New York Times*, May 26, 2008.

28. Studies based on this huge database of responses were published in *Soldiers and Civilians: The Civil-Military Gap and American National Security*, ed. Peter D. Feaver and Richard H. Kohn (Cambridge, MA: MIT Press, 2001).

29. Ole R. Holsti, "Of Chasms and Convergences: Attitudes and Beliefs of Civilians and Military Elites at the Start of a New Millennium," in Feaver and Kohn, *Soldiers and Civilians*, 15.

30. John Lehman, "An Exchange on Civil-Military Relations," *The National Interest* (Summer 1994): 23–24.

31. David M. Halbfinger and Steven A. Holmes, "Military Mirrors a Working-Class America," *New York Times*, March 30, 2003; Michael C. Desch, "Explaining the Gap: Vietnam, the Republicanization of the South, and the End of the Mass Army," in Feaver and Kohn, *Soldiers and Civilians*, 289, 308–12.

32. Ricks, *Making the Corps*, 278–79.

33. Major Tom Bryant, "Vice Chief of Staff Designates West Point Center of Excellence for Ethics," *Army News Service*, August 22, 2007.

34. Paul Gronke and Peter D. Feaver, "Uncertain Confidence: Civilian and Military Attitudes about Civil-Military Relations," in Feaver and Kohn, *Soldiers and Civilians*, 129, 148.

35. Phillip Carter, "Extraordinary Acts of Valor," *Los Angeles Times*, November 11, 2006.

36. Holsti, "Of Chasms and Convergences," 62.

CHAPTER 6 FACING THE CONSEQUENCES

1. James Key, "Politics Aside, a Day to Thank Our Troops," *USA Today*, November 23, 2007.

2. Luke 17: 11–19.

3. Dana Priest and Anne Hull, "Soldiers Face Neglect, Frustration at Army's Top Medical Facility," *Washington Post*, February 18, 2007; Anne Hull and Dana Priest, "The Hotel Aftermath," *Washington Post*, February 19, 2007. The entire *Washington Post* coverage of the Walter Reed investigation is available at "Walter Reed and Beyond," http://www.washingtonpost.com/wp-srv/nation/walter-reed/index.html.

4. Steve Vogel and William Branigin, "Army Fires Commander of Walter Reed," *Washington Post*, March 2, 2007; Michael Abramowitz and Steve Vogel, "Army

Secretary Ousted," *Washington Post*, March 3, 2007; Josh White, "Surgeon General of the Army Steps Down," *Washington Post*, March 13, 2007; Michael Abramowitz and Steve Vogel, "Apologies, Anger at Walter Reed Hearing," *Washington Post*, March 6, 2007; Paul D. Eaton, "Casualties of the Budget Wars," *New York Times*, March 6, 2007.

5. Robert Pear, "President's Military Medical Care Panel Hears Frustrations of Soldiers Wounded in Iraq," *New York Times*, April 15, 2007.

6. *Serve, Support, Simplify: Report of the President's Commission on Care for America's Returning Wounded Warriors* (July 2007); *Rebuilding the Trust: Independent Review Group, Report on Rehabilitative Care and Administrative Processes at Walter Reed Army Medical Center and National Naval Medical Center* (April 2007); Scott Shane, "Panel on Walter Reed Issues Strong Rebuke," *New York Times*, April 12, 2007.

7. Lt. Col. Randolph C. White, Jr., Infantry One Station Unit Training Graduation Remarks, Fort Benning, Georgia, July 7, 2006, http://www.youtube.com/watch?v=kbOcJ6kqJAA (video).

8. Bruce Fleming, "Why I Love Conservatives," *Antioch Review*, Spring 2004. Apparently the feeling hasn't changed. According to another report, just thirteen weeks of basic training produced Marines who were disgusted with their former peer group. Civilian behavior as innocuous as gum chewing irritated them; civilians were "lazy," "unkempt," and "a waste of time." Kristin Henderson, "Their War," *Washington Post*, July 22, 2007.

9. Rick Hampson, "In This War, Troops Get a Rousing Welcome Home," *USA Today*, July 3, 2008.

10. Democratic Party Response by Kansas Governor Kathleen Sebelius to the State of the Union Address, January 28, 2008.

11. For a typical example, see Michael Winerip, "Guard Families, on Their Own for the Holidays, Dig Deep," *New York Times*, December 11, 2008 (reporting an Army master sergeant's observation that Americans who oppose the war in Iraq "have not taken those feelings out on the soldiers, as they did in the Vietnam era").

12. Javier C. Hernandez, "A Trip to New York Gives Wounded Veterans a Break from a Patient's Dull Routine," *New York Times*, August 4, 2008. For other examples, see William M. Arkin, "Early Warning: The Troops Also Need to Support the American People," *Washington Post*, January 30, 2007; Jonathan Darman, Richard Wolffe, and Evan Thomas, "Iraq: Friends at War," *Newsweek*, January 15, 2007; Steve Vogel, "Incoming Troops, Outgoing Vets," *Washington Post*, November 11, 2003; Clyde Haberman, "McCain Eases the Stigma of Vietnam," *New York Times*, February 29, 2000; Kathy Roth-Douquet and Frank Schaeffer, *AWOL: The Unexcused Absence of America's Upper Classes from Military Service—and How It Hurts Our Country* (New York: Collins, 2006), 125-26.

13. Jerry Lembcke, *The Spitting Image: Myth, Memory, and the Legacy of Vietnam* (New York: New York University Press, 1998); Jerry Lembcke, "Debunking a Spitting Image," *Boston Globe*, April 30, 2005.

14. For more on the spitting controversy, see a series of articles by Jack Shafer that close with "Delmar Pickett Jr. Stands by His Spit Story," *Slate*, March 7, 2007, compiled at http://www.slate.com/id/2161383, and a series of posts at *The Volokh Conspiracy* blog written by law professor Jim Lindgren during February 2007, compiled at http://www.volokh.com/posts/1170519427.shtml.

15. Lembcke, *The Spitting Image*, 75.

16. Lembke, *The Spitting Image*, 78.

17. Founding Principle, Vietnam Veterans of America, http://www.vva.org/who.html.

18. Tom Philpott, "Transition Chief Vows to Protect Wounded Veterans," *Stars and Stripes*, September 5, 2009. See also Knight Ridder, "VFW Halls Close as Memberships Decline," January 28, 2008 (quoting a Vietnam veteran who said the older VFW members shunned them, saying "they didn't fight in a real war").

19. Knight Ridder, "Report: Airport Didn't Snub Marines," February 1, 2008.

20. Arkin, "Early Warning."

21. Ruth Holladay, "Professor Enmeshed in Flap over Collegiality," *Indianapolis Star*, June 26, 2005; "Potentially Troubling, but Hard to Figure Out without More Information," *Volokh Conspiracy*, June 27, 2005, http://volokh.com/posts/1119854297.shtml.

22. Ruth Holladay, "Truth Comes Out about Professor's Background," *Indianapolis Star*, December 4, 2005; "A Remarkable Turn of Events in the Professor Bradford (Indiana University Law School) Matter," *Volokh Conspiracy*, December 6, 2005, http://www.volokh.com/posts/1133910368.shtml; David Epstein, "Web of Lies," *Inside Higher Ed*, December 6, 2005. Professor Bradford's web site, http://williamcbradford.com, attempts to reconcile the inconsistencies in his record.

23. B. G. Burkett and Glenna Whitley, *Stolen Valor: How the Vietnam Generation Was Robbed of Its Heroes and Its History* (Dallas: Verity Press, 1998). The Stolen Valor Act, 18 U.S.C. § 704, makes false claims about receipt of military decorations or medals a crime, punishable by fine or imprisonment.

24. John Renehan, "Who Says the Elite Aren't Fit to Serve?" *Washington Post*, March 16, 2008.

25. David S. Cloud, "Army Misses Its June Goal for New Recruits," *New York Times*, July 10, 2007. See also chapter 8.

26. *Brown v. Glines*, 586 F.2d 675, 677 (9th Cir. 1978), *reversed*, 444 U.S. 348, 351 (1980). The legal wheels sometimes turn slowly, six years having passed between the original incident and the final court decision.

27. Mark Nichol and Andrew Chapman, "Harry's Band of Brothers," *Mail on Sunday* (United Kingdom), March 2, 2008.

28. James Brooke, "Pentagon Tells Troops in Afghanistan: Shape Up and Dress Right," *New York Times*, September 12, 2002.

29. Jane McHugh, "Baldness Is Authorized," *Army Times*, January 21, 2002; Sean Gill, "Being All They Can Be, but with Individuality," *Los Angeles Times*, January 27, 2002.

30. According to an undated Army memorandum, the ACU "is issued as a combat uniform and is not intended for wear as an all-purpose uniform when other uniforms (Class A or B, dress, and mess uniform) are more appropriate." Headquarters, U.S. Department of the Army, *Change to the Army Combat Uniform (ACU), Battle Dress Uniform (BDU), and Desert Battle Dress Uniform (DBDU) Wear Policy*. In January 2010, Secretary of Defense Robert Gates ordered his military aides to stop wearing ACUs to work at the Pentagon. Thom Shanker and Eric Schmitt, "For Gates Aides, No Fatigues at Work," *New York Times*, January 19, 2010.

31. Charles M. Sennott, "General Tells Cambridge Crowd U.S. Has Not Failed in Iraq," *Boston Globe*, November 18, 2006. For another example, the Army chief of staff

wore ACUs and desert combat boots to give a formal address to the Brookings Institution in Washington, DC. Video of the event highlights the jarring contrast between the speaker and the mostly civilian audience dressed in traditional business suits. Brookings Institution, "Maintaining Quality in the Force: A Briefing by General George W. Casey, Jr.," December 4, 2007, http://www.brookings.edu/events/2007/1204casey.aspx.

32. William Safire, "On Language: Warrior," *New York Times*, August 26, 2007.

33. William Glaberson, "Panel Convicts bin Laden Driver in Split Verdict," *New York Times*, August 7, 2008.

34. "Army Changes PLDC to Warrior Leader Course," *Army News Service*, October 12, 2005. "A true warrior ethos must underpin the Army's enduring traditions and values." U.S. Department of the Army, FM 6-22, *Army Leadership: Competent, Confident, and Agile*, ¶ 4–46.

35. U.S. Army Reserve, *2010 Posture Statement*, 5, 23, 28.

36. Wounded Warrior Act, Pub. L. No. 110-181, §§ 1601-76 (2008 National Defense Authorization Act). I suspect that "warrior" jargon leads us to treat wounded servicemembers more like warriors and less like patients who need care. U.S. Government Accountability Office, *Army Health Care: Progress Made in Staffing and Monitoring Units That Provide Outpatient Case Management, but Additional Steps Needed* (2009) (documenting problems in implementing new "Warrior Transition Units," the Army's idea for improving follow-up medical care).

37. Kristin Henderson, "Their War," *Washington Post*, July 22, 2007.

38. "Nike Launches New Army and Navy Football 'Enforcer' Uniforms," *Army Athletics News Release*, December 6, 2008.

39. Mitch Gettle, "Airman's Creed Exemplifies Warfighting Ethos," *Air Force News*, April 18, 2007.

40. Matt Grills, "Next Generation of Navy Uniform Arrives," *Navy News*, June 21, 2008; Mitch Gettle, "Airman Battle Uniform Finalized, Ready for Production," *Air Force News*, March 17, 2006.

41. Seth G. Jones and Martin C. Libicki, RAND Corporation, *How Terrorist Groups End: Lessons for Countering al Qa'ida* (2008), xvi–xvii.

42. "Rumsfeld Praises Army General Who Ridicules Islam as 'Satan,'" *New York Times*, October 17, 2003; U.S. Department of Defense, Office of the Inspector General, *Alleged Improprieties Related to Public Speaking: Lieutenant General William G. Boykin, U.S. Army Deputy Under Secretary of Defense for Intelligence* (2004).

43. Brigadier Nigel Aylwin-Foster, "Changing the Army for Counterinsurgency Operations," *Military Review* (November–December 2005).

44. George Packer, "Letter from Iraq: The Lesson of Tal Afar," *New Yorker*, April 10, 2006 (quoting Aylwin-Foster). This article profiled Colonel (now General) H. R. McMaster, a member of Petraeus's inner intellectual circle and the author of a classic work on military professionalism, *Dereliction of Duty: Lyndon Johnson, Robert McNamara, the Joint Chiefs of Staff, and the Lies That Led to Vietnam* (New York: HarperCollins, 1997). McMaster was one of the very few who understood the importance of ordering his soldiers not to call Iraqis "hajis." Even Charles Moskos, a highly respected military academic, returned from a research visit to Iraq naively convinced that soldiers used "haji" as a term of endearment for the local population: "It seems to have no special negative meaning." Memo from Charles Moskos to Acting Secretary of the

Army Les Brownlee, *Preliminary Report on Operation Iraq Freedom (OIF)*, December 14, 2003.

CHAPTER 7 A DANGEROUS DISREGARD FOR LAW

1. William Glaberson, "In Detainee Trial, System Is Tested," *New York Times*, July 28, 2008; William Glaberson and Eric Lichtblau, "Military Trial Begins for Guantánamo Detainee," *New York Times*, July 22, 2008.

2. *Rasul v. Bush*, 542 U.S. 466 (2004); *Boumediene v. Bush*, 128 S. Ct. 2229 (2008); Linda Greenhouse, "Justices, 5-4, Back Detainee Appeals for Guantánamo," *New York Times*, June 13, 2008; William Glaberson, "Detention Camp Remains, but Not Its Rationale," *New York Times*, June 13, 2008.

3. *Hamdan v. Rumsfeld*, 548 U.S. 557 (2006).

4. The single individual captured by the United States military was Omar Kahdr, a fifteen-year-old Canadian citizen. Mark Denbeaux, Joshua Denbeaux, and R. David Gratz, *The Meaning of "Battlefield": An Analysis of the Government's Representations of "Battlefield" Capture and "Recidivism" of the Guantánamo Detainees* (2007); Mark Denbeaux and Joshua Denbeaux, *Report on Guantánamo Detainees: A Profile of 517 Detainees through Analysis of Department of Defense Data* (2006). These reports are available from the Seton Hall School of Law's Center for Policy and Research, at http://law.shu.edu/ProgramsCenters/PublicIntGovServ/policyresearch/Guantanamo-Reports.cfm. The Combating Terrorism Center at West Point, http://ctc.usma.edu, published a response to the 2006 report at the request of the Department of Defense, *An Assessment of 516 Combatant Status Review Tribunal (CSRT) Unclassified Summaries* (2007), but it did not contest the near-total absence of battlefield captures.

5. Memorandum for the secretary of the Navy, *Implementation of Combatant Status Review Tribunal Procedures for Enemy Combatants Detained at Guantanamo Bay Naval Base, Cuba*, July 29, 2004.

6. "The privilege of the writ of habeas corpus shall not be suspended, unless when in cases of rebellion or invasion the public safety may require it." U.S. Constitution, art. 1, § 9, cl. 2.

7. Declaration of Stephen Abraham, Appendix to Petitioners' Reply to Opposition to Petition for Rehearing, *Al Odah v. United States* (U.S. June 22, 2007).

8. Not surprisingly, the admiral in charge of the CSRT process strongly disagreed with Abraham's characterization. The government filed an objection arguing that Abraham's role was too small for him to understand the big picture of how CSRTs were intended to operate. Government's Opposition to Motion to File Declaration, *Bismullah v. Gates* and *Parhat v. Gates* (D.C. Cir. July 6, 2007). Abraham had the last word. It is commonly believed his affidavit was responsible for convincing the Supreme Court to grant review in *Boumediene v. Bush*, the case holding that CSRTs were not constitutionally adequate substitutes for habeas corpus proceedings. William Glaberson, "Unlikely Adversary Arises to Criticize Detainee Hearings," *New York Times*, July 23, 2007.

9. Declaration of William J. Teesdale, Esq. (Redacted), *Hamad v. Bush* (D.D.C. October 5, 2007). Mr. Teesdale was the civilian lawyer who recorded the military lawyer's statement.

10. Under the Detainee Treatment Act of 2005, Pub. L. No. 109-148 (2005), Congress gave one specific federal court, the Court of Appeals for the District of Columbia Circuit, a limited ability to review CSRT decisions. The idea was to give this court enough of a role to satisfy any constitutional complaints about the process, but not so much that the court strayed from rubber-stamp approvals. Congress would not even concede that the Constitution or other laws of the United States might pose limits, cautioning the court to consider this question only "to the extent the Constitution and laws of the United States are applicable."

11. *Parhat v. Gates*, 532 F.3d 834 (D.C. Cir. 2008).

12. Edward Wong, "Clashes in China Shed Light on Ethnic Divide," *New York Times*, July 8, 2009.

13. William Glaberson, "Evidence Faulted in Detainee Case," *New York Times*, July 1, 2008. Commander Glenn M. Sulmasy, a professor at the Coast Guard Academy, coauthored an article on civil-military relations and law with Professor John Yoo, a former Justice Department lawyer and infamous writer of several of the so-called "torture memos" that offered strained legal justifications for the torture and abuse of detainees. In "Challenges to Civilian Control of the Military: A Rational Choice Approach to the War on Terror," *UCLA Law Review* 54 (2007): 1815, they argued the war on terror was being hampered not by a failure to abide by law, but by too much attention to following the law.

14. Notice of Status, *In re Guantanamo Bay Detainee Litigation* (D.D.C. September 30, 2008); Del Quentin Wilber, "Judge Orders Release of Chinese Muslims into U.S.," *Washington Post*, October 7, 2008; William Glaberson, "Judge Orders 17 Detainees at Guantánamo Freed," *New York Times*, October 7, 2008.

15. *Kiyemba v. Obama*, 555 F.3d 1022 (D.C. Cir. 2009), vacated and remanded, 130 S. Ct. 1235 (2010); David Johnston, "Uighurs Leave Guantánamo for Palau," *New York Times*, November 1, 2009.

16. Darrel J. Vandeveld, "I Was Slow to Recognize the Stain of Guantanamo," *Washington Post*, January 18, 2009; Gordon Corera, "Guantanamo 'A Stain on U.S. Military,'" *BBC News*, December 2, 2008; Josh Meyer, "For Lawyer, Trial Was Tribulation," *Los Angeles Times*, October 12, 2008; Jess Bravin, "The Conscience of the Colonel," *Wall Street Journal*, March 31, 2007. One of the officers who resigned was the chief prosecutor for the military commissions system, Air Force Colonel Morris Davis. He later testified that senior Pentagon officials, both civilian and military, pressured him to try cases with "strategic political value" in time for the 2008 elections. William Glaberson, "Ex-Prosecutor Tells of Push by Pentagon on Detainees," *New York Times*, April 29, 2008.

17. Detainee Treatment Act of 2005, § 1002(a), 10 U.S.C. § 801 note.

18. Daniel Engber, "What Are Army Field Manuals? How-To Guides for Interrogation, Laser Injury Prevention, and Other Useful Skills," *Slate*, November 16, 2005.

19. U.S. Department of the Army, FM 34-52, *Intelligence Interrogation*. FM 34-52 was revised, renumbered, and renamed in 2006. The new manual incorporated lessons learned, including the importance of command responsibility and the obligations of soldiers to report abuse, but the basic principles remained the same. U.S. Department of the Army, FM 2-22.3, *Human Intelligence Collector Operations*. FM 2-22.3 also lengthened the list of specifically prohibited conduct after the publicized abuses at Abu Ghraib, including "forcing the detainee to be naked, perform sexual acts, or pose in a sexual manner."

20. Evan Wallach, "Waterboarding Used to Be a Crime," *Washington Post*, November 4, 2007.

21. The JAG Memos (Air Force, Navy, Marine Corps, and Army), February–March 2003, http://balkin.blogspot.com/jag.memos.pdf.

22. Peter Finn, "Retired Officers Meet with Obama Aides on Interrogation Policy," *Washington Post*, December 4, 2008 (quoting John Hutson, a retired Navy admiral).

23. Peter Finn and Joby Warrick, "In 2002, Military Agency Warned against 'Torture,'" *Washington Post*, April 25, 2009. In a memo entitled *Operational Issues Pertaining to the Use of Physical/Psychological Coercion in Interrogation*, the military's Joint Personnel Recovery Agency warned senior officials in the Department of Defense that coercive interrogation produced unreliable information and put American servicemembers at risk. The assumption that everyone was making—that physical or psychological duress will produce accurate information more quickly—was always false.

24. Petula Dvorak, "Fort Hunt's Quiet Men Break Silence on WWII," *Washington Post*, October 6, 2007.

25. Colin Freeze, "What Would Jack Bauer Do?" *Globe and Mail* (Toronto), June 16, 2007; Colin Freeze, "Top U.S. Jurist's Ruling on Torture Scrutiny: Judge Not," *Globe and Mail* (Toronto), June 30, 2007.

26. Senate Armed Services Committee, *Inquiry into the Treatment of Detainees in U.S. Custody* (November 20, 2008), xii.

CHAPTER 8 RECRUITING FOR A CONSTITUTIONALLY FRAGILE MILITARY

1. *Universal National Service Act of 2003*, H.R. 163, 108th Congress (2003).

2. Charles B. Rangel, "Bring Back the Draft," *New York Times*, December 31, 2002.

3. Thom Shanker, "Who Will Fight This War?" *New York Times*, September 30, 2001.

4. U.S. Department of Defense news briefing, "Secretary Rumsfeld and General Myers," January 7, 2003.

5. Current laws and regulations on the military draft are contained in the Military Selective Service Act, 50 U.S.C. appendix §§ 451–71a, and the Selective Service System, 32 C.F.R. §§ 1602–99.

6. Amendments to the Military Selective Service Act of 1967, Pub. L. No. 92–129, §§ 101(a)(17)-(18), (20) (1971).

7. Sandra Jontz and Lisa Burgess, "Marines Enact Stop-Loss Plan for All; Some GIs Also Held in Place," *Stars and Stripes*, January 9, 2003.

8. Vernon Loeb, "Rumsfeld Apologizes for Remarks on Draftees," *Washington Post*, January 22, 2003.

9. Peter F. Ramsberger and D. Bruce Bell, U.S. Army Research Institute, *What We Know about AWOL and Desertion: A Review of the Professional Literature for Policy Makers and Commanders* (2002), 6.

10. George Q. Flynn, *The Draft: 1940–1973* (Lawrence, KS: University Press of Kansas, 1993), 235.

11. Loeb, "Rumsfeld Apologizes."

12. Richard J. Buddin, RAND Arroyo Center, *Success of First-Term Soldiers: The Effects of Recruiting Practices and Recruit Characteristics* (2005), 2.

13. Steven M. Kosiak, Center for Strategic and Budgetary Assessments, *Military Manpower for the Long Haul* (2008), 6.

14. Charles Moskos, "A New Kind of Draft for the 21st Century," *Boston Globe*, February 9, 2003.

15. U.S. Department of Defense, Office of the Under Secretary of Defense (Personnel and Readiness), *Conscription Threatens Hard-Won Achievements and Military Readiness* (2003).

16. Rangel, "Bring Back the Draft." On the same topic, see David M. Halbfinger and Steven A. Holmes, "Military Mirrors a Working-Class America," *New York Times*, March 30, 2003.

17. Kathy Roth-Douquet and Frank Schaeffer, *AWOL: The Unexcused Absence of America's Upper Classes from Military Service—and How It Hurts Our Country* (New York: Collins, 2006).

18. A former secretary of defense also chimed in with the bizarre claim that Rangel was unhappy because there were "too many patriotic blacks." Caspar W. Weinberger, "Dodgy Drafters," *Wall Street Journal*, January 10, 2003.

19. Charles B. Rangel, letter to the editor, "You're Not in the Army, Mr. J. Worthington III," *Wall Street Journal*, January 17, 2003.

20. U.S. Department of Defense news briefing, "Background Briefing on the All-Volunteer Force," January 13, 2003.

21. Steven D. Levitt, "Restore the Draft? What a Bad Idea," *New York Times*, August 14, 2007. Levitt is the author, with Stephen J. Dubner, of *Freakonomics: A Rogue Economist Explores the Hidden Side of Everything* (New York: William Morrow, 2005).

22. The final tally was 402-2, with 29 present and not voting. Rep. John Murtha of Pennsylvania and Rep. Pete Stark of California voted in favor of the bill.

23. U.S. Department of Defense news briefing, "Who Is Volunteering for Today's Military? Myths Versus Facts," December 13, 2005.

24. Mission: Readiness, *Ready, Willing, and Unable to Serve* (2009); "Recruiting the Best," *New York Times*, December 28, 2008.

25. Charles Moskos, the prominent military sociologist, called it a "baloney number." Pauline Jelinek, Associated Press, "Uncle Sam Doesn't Want You," *Chicago Tribune*, March 13, 2006. It is possible, disturbing as the proposition might be, that the people who calculated this number fail to understand that you can't just add together the percentages of the population with disqualifying characteristics, such as lack of a high school degree, obesity, asthma, etc., to arrive at an overall percentage of ineligibility. For example, see the statement by Curtis Gilroy, undersecretary of defense for personnel and readiness, before the House Armed Services Personnel Subcommittee (March 3, 2009) (offering a pie chart using this statistically faulty method). These factors are statistically dependent, not independent: a single individual, for example, could have dropped out of school, be obese, and have asthma. You can't count that person three times. A recent government report confirmed this suspicion. The private group that generated the percentage conceded it had a problem with overlapping, dependent factors, but did not specify the extent of the inaccuracy or reveal the bases for its calculations. U.S. Government Accountability Office, *Military Personnel: Army Needs to Focus on Cost-Effective Use of Financial Incentives*

and Quality Standards in Managing Force Growth (2009), 27 n. 25. The "Mission: Readiness" group of generals and admirals was no better. They based their estimate on the unsubstantiated assertions of a single DOD research analyst.

26. Josh White, "Army Off Target on Recruits," *Washington Post*, January 23, 2008; National Priorities Project, *Military Recruiting 2007: Army Misses Benchmarks by Greater Margin*. The Army also employs accounting tricks to exclude large numbers of dropouts from its year-end calculation of graduation rates. Kelly Kennedy, "Finessing the Dropout Count," *Army Times*, August 14, 2006.

27. Steven Lee Myers, "Good Times Mean Hard Sell for the Military," *New York Times*, November 3, 1998; Greg Jaffe, "The Price of Power: No Sir! The Military Wages Uphill Battle to Find the Willing and Able," *Wall Street Journal*, September 23, 1999.

28. Damien Cave, "For Army Recruiters, a Hard Toll from a Hard Sell," *New York Times*, March 27, 2005; Damien Cave, "For Army Recruiters, a Day of Rules, and Little Else," *New York Times*, May 21, 2005; Lindsay Wise, "Army Recruiters Describe Nightmare of Job," *Houston Chronicle*, February 12, 2009; U.S. Government Accountability Office, *DOD and Services Need Better Data to Enhance Visibility over Recruiter Irregularities* (2006).

29. James Kitfield, *Prodigal Soldiers: How the Generation of Officers Born of Vietnam Revolutionized the American Style of War* (New York: Simon and Schuster, 1995).

30. Flynn, *The Draft*, 234–35, 277.

31. Beth J. Asch, M. Rebecca Kilburn, and Jacob A. Klerman, RAND Corporation, *Attracting College-Bound Youth into the Military: Toward the Development of New Recruiting Policy Options* (1999); Charles Moskos and Paul Glastris, "Now Do You Believe We Need a Draft?" *Washington Monthly* (November 2001).

32. National Call to Service Act, 10 U.S.C. § 510; U.S. Department of Defense, Office of the Under Secretary of Defense (Personnel and Readiness), "National Call to Service: Department of Defense Implementation," April 21, 2003.

33. Sheila Nataraj Kirby and Harry J. Thie, RAND Corporation, *Enlisted Personnel Management: A Historical Perspective* (1996), 1.

34. Kitfield, *Prodigal Soldiers*, 149–51.

35. *Perpich v. Department of Defense*, 496 U.S. 334 (1990).

36. Joseph Williams and Kevin Baron, "Military Sees Big Decline in Black Enlistees," *Boston Globe*, October 7, 2007; Josh White, "Steady Drop in Black Army Recruits," *Washington Post*, March 9, 2005; Benjamin O. Fordham, "Military Interests and Civilian Politics: The Influence of the Civil-Military 'Gap' on Peacetime Military Policy," in *Soldiers and Civilians: The Civil-Military Gap and American National Security*, ed. Peter D. Feaver and Richard H. Kohn (Cambridge, MA: MIT Press, 2001), 353 (relationship between economic decline and propensity to enlist for black and white youth).

37. 10 U.S.C. § 504; Ann Scott Tyson, "Military Waivers for Ex-Convicts Increase," *Washington Post*, April 22, 2008. The raw data on felonies is available from the House Committee on Oversight and Government Reform, http://oversight.house.gov/ images/stories/documents/20080421104349.pdf. See also special report, "Suspect Soldiers," *Sacramento Bee*, July 13–16, 27, 2008 (a yearlong study of criminal histories of recent military recruits).

38. U.S. General Accounting Office, *Military Recruiting: New Initiatives Could Improve Criminal Screening History* (1999), 10–13.

39. Gerry J. Gilmore, "General Cites Challenging Recruiting Environment," *American Forces Press Service*, June 19, 2008.

40. National Gang Intelligence Center, *Gang-Related Activity in the U.S. Armed Forces Increasing* (2007), 4.

41. National Defense Authorization Act for Fiscal Year 2008, Pub. L. No. 110-181, § 544 (2008).

42. Army Regulation 601-210, *Active and Reserve Components Enlistment Program* (June 7, 2007), § 4-2(e)(1)(a)(9). The Southern Poverty Law Center, an organization that tracks hate groups, issued a report estimating the number of neo-Nazis and white supremacists in the military could number in the thousands, citing Department of Defense sources and data. John Kifner, "Hate Groups Are Infiltrating the Military, Group Asserts," *New York Times*, July 7, 2006.

43. 10 U.S.C. § 505 (minimum age for enlistment); Tom Vanden Brook, "Military on Pace to Meet Recruiting Goals for This Year," *USA Today*, July 10, 2006; Susanne M. Schafer, Associated Press, "Army Teaches School Dropouts," *Washington Times*, August 28, 2008; Gordon Lubold, "To Boost Recruits, U.S. Army Relaxes Weight Rules," *Christian Science Monitor*, January 5, 2009; Associated Press, "Army Mulls Weight-Loss Camp for New Recruits," January 12, 2009; Dan Vierria, "Think Before You Ink," *Sacramento Bee*, January 2, 2008.

44. Julia Preston, "U.S. Military Will Offer Path to Citizenship," *New York Times*, February 15, 2009.

45. Bryan M. Johnson, "How the Navy Changed My Life," *Newsweek*, August 2, 1999.

46. U.S. Government Accountability Office, *DOD Needs to Improve the Transparency and Reassess the Reasonableness, Appropriateness, Affordability, and Sustainability of Its Military Compensation System* (2005), 6.

47. U.S. Department of Defense, Office of the Secretary of Defense, *Military Compensation*, http://www.defenselink.mil/militarypay.

48. For an anecdotal example, see Michael Leahy, "The Last Resort," *Washington Post*, November 18, 2007 (telling the desperate story of an overweight forty-year-old who joins the Army along with both parents of his new wife's infant grandchild, all enlisting in search of a steady income and medical care for themselves and their children).

49. Phillip Carter and Brad Flora, "I Want You . . . Badly: A Complete Guide to Uncle Sam's Recruiting Incentives," *Slate*, November 7, 2007; Josh White, "Many Take Army's 'Quick Ship' Bonus," *Washington Post*, August 27, 2007; Seth Schiesel, "Facing the Horrors of Distant Battlefields with a TV and Console," *New York Times*, March 19, 2008; John Leland, "Urban Tool in Recruiting by the Army: An Arcade," *New York Times*, January 5, 2009.

50. Tom Vanden Brook, "Army Surpassing Year's Retention Goal by 15%," *USA Today*, April 10, 2006.

51. Terri Tanielian and Lisa H. Jaycox, eds., RAND Center for Military Health Policy Research, *Invisible Wounds of War: Psychological and Cognitive Injuries, Their Consequences, and Services to Assist Recovery* (2008); Lisa Foderaro, "Military Kin Struggle with Loss and a Windfall," *New York Times*, March 22, 2008; Thom Shanker, "Army Is Worried by Rising Stress of Return Tours to Iraq," *New York Times*, April 6, 2008; Leslie Kaufman, "After War, Love Can Be a Battlefield," *New York Times*, April 6,

2008; Mark Thompson, "America's Medicated Army," *Time*, June 5, 2008; Lizette Alvarez, "After the Battle, Fighting the Bottle at Home," *New York Times*, July 8, 2008; Lizette Alvarez, "Army Data Show Rise in Number of Suicides," *New York Times*, February 5, 2009.

52. James Risen, "Use of Iraq Contractors Costs Billions, Report Says," *New York Times*, August 11, 2008; Bradley Brooks, Associated Press, "Iraq Rewards Trump Risks for Job Seekers," *USA Today*, February 28, 2008.

53. Ralph Blumenthal, "Army Acts to Curb Abuses of Injured Recruits," *New York Times*, May 12, 2006; Lizette Alvarez, "Despite Army's Assurances, Violence at Home," *New York Times*, November 22, 2008. An important factor in the military's lukewarm response to domestic violence is the Lautenberg Amendment, a federal law directing that persons convicted of domestic violence, including members of the military, cannot possess guns. 10 U.S.C. § 922(g)(9).

54. Post-9/11 Veterans Educational Assistance Act of 2008, Pub. L. No. 110-252, §§ 5001-6 (2008); Steven Lee Meyers, "Fear of Troop Exodus Fuels Debate on G.I. Bill," *New York Times*, May 22, 2008.

55. Aaron Glantz, "The Soldier and the Student," *Nation*, November 27, 2007; Knight-Ridder, "Texas Wants Its Vets to Finish College," August 12, 2008.

56. Diana Jean Schemo, "At 2 Year Colleges, Students Eager but Unready," *New York Times*, September 2, 2006. See also Strong American Schools, *Diploma to Nowhere* (2008) (data on the extent of remedial education in colleges).

CHAPTER 9 IT NEVER WAS ABOUT THE MISSION

1. "An Expectation of 'Less Reliance' on Guard, Reserve," *USA Today*, May 5, 2005.

2. A study estimates that only one-fourth of the personnel losses caused by the policy are the result of formal discharges. Gary J. Gates, Williams Institute, *Effects of "Don't Ask, Don't Tell" on Retention among Lesbian, Gay, and Bisexual Military Personnel* (2007).

3. Oral Argument, *Pleasant Grove City v. Summum*, 129 S. Ct. 1125 (2009), 23-25.

4. It is very difficult to determine the number of gay people serving in the military when law requires they remain invisible, but a statistical analysis estimated there are 65,000 gay people serving in uniform today and 1,000,000 gay veterans. Gary J. Gates, Urban Institute, *Gay Men and Lesbians in the U.S. Military: Estimates from Census 2000* (2004).

5. Department of Defense Instruction 1332.14, *Enlisted Administrative Separations*, Enclosure 3, § 8(a)(1) (March 29, 2010), 18.

6. The current "Don't Ask, Don't Tell" law is codified at 10 U.S.C. § 654. The earlier Department of Defense policy it replaced, 32 C.F.R., chapter 1, part 41 (1993), is available in a Stanford Law School database of "Don't Ask, Don't Tell" legal materials, http://dont.stanford.edu/regulations/32cfr41.pdf.

7. Mike Allen, "McCain Says He Can Identify Gays by Behavior, Attitudes," *Washington Post*, January 18, 2000; Alison Mitchell, "McCain Plans Strategy for Long Haul," *New York Times*, January 21, 2000.

8. *Cook v. Gates*, 528 F.3d 42 (1st Cir. 2008).

9. *Lawrence v. Texas*, 539 U.S. 558 (2003).

10. *Sodomy* is a term sometimes mistakenly defined as sexual relations between men, but in law it usually means nonprocreative forms of sexual relations, such as oral sex, whether engaged in by same-sex or opposite-sex partners, male or female. The military prohibits "unnatural carnal copulation" in the same equal opportunity way and allows no exceptions, not even for heterosexual married couples. 10 U.S.C. § 925.

11. *Romer v. Evans*, 517 U.S. 620 (1996).

12. Complaint, *Cook v. Rumsfeld* (D. Mass. December 6, 2004).

13. *Rostker v. Goldberg*, 453 U.S. 57 (1981).

14. Federal Rule of Civil Procedure 12(b)(6).

15. *Witt v. Department of the Air Force*, 527 F.3d 806 (9th Cir. 2008).

16. "[Commanders] shall examine the information . . . and decide whether an inquiry is warranted or whether no action should be taken." *Enlisted Administrative Separations*, Enclosure 5, § 3(b), 40.

17. Nathaniel Frank, *Unfriendly Fire: How the Gay Ban Undermines the Military and Weakens America* (New York: Thomas Dunne/St. Martin's Press, 2009).

18. RAND National Defense Research Institute, *Sexual Orientation and U.S. Military Personnel Policy: Options and Assessment* (1993); Eric Schmitt, "Pentagon Keeps Silent on Rejected Gay Troop Plan," *New York Times*, July 23, 1993.

19. Frank, *Unfriendly Fire*, 145; Nathaniel Frank, Palm Center, *Gays in Foreign Militaries 2010: A Global Primer* (2010), http://www.palmcenter.org.

20. Bonnie Moradi and Laura Miller, "Attitudes of Iraq and Afghanistan War Veterans toward Gay and Lesbian Service Members," *Armed Forces and Society* 36 (2010): 397.

21. 10 U.S.C. § 12305 (Authority of the President to Suspend Certain Laws Relating to Promotion, Retirement, and Separation).

22. Frank, *Unfriendly Fire*, 122; Josh White, "'Don't Ask' Costs More Than Expected," *Washington Post*, February 14, 2006.

23. Aaron Belkin, "'Don't Ask, Don't Tell': Does the Gay Ban Undermine the Military's Reputation?" *Armed Forces and Society* 34 (2008): 276.

24. Steve Estes, *Ask and Tell: Gay and Lesbian Veterans Speak Out* (Chapel Hill: University of North Carolina Press, 2007), 109.

25. *Assessment of the Plan to Lift the Ban on Homosexuals in the Military: Hearings before the Military Forces and Personnel Subcommittee of the House Committee on Armed Services*, 103rd Congress (1993), 62.

CHAPTER 10 HOW LONG CAN YOU STILL CALL IT AN EXPERIMENT?

1. Selena Roberts, "Dixon's Civility Lightened Load at West Point," *New York Times*, April 16, 2006.

2. Ira Berkow, "West Point Is Standing at Attention for Army Women's Coach," *New York Times*, March 15, 2006; Frank Litsky, "Maggie Dixon, 28, Who Led Army Women to Tournament," *New York Times*, April 8, 2006; Ira Berkow, "Memory Softens a Brother's Sadness," *New York Times*, April 24, 2006.

3. *SportsCenter* (ESPN television broadcast), April 10, 2006.

4. *Rostker v. Goldberg*, 453 U.S. 57 (1981).

5. Lory Manning, *Women in the Military: Where They Stand*, 5th ed. (Washington, DC: Women's Research and Education Institute, 2005), 13, figure 2.

6. National Defense Authorization Act for Fiscal Year 1994, Pub. L. No. 103-60, § 542(b)(3) (1993).

7. Phillip Carter, "War Dames," *Washington Monthly*, December 2002, 32.

8. Erin Solaro, *Women in the Line of Fire: What You Should Know about Women in the Military* (Emeryville, CA: Seal Press, 2006), 117.

9. Margaret C. Harrell et al., RAND National Defense Research Institute, *Assessing the Assignment Policy for Army Women* (2007).

10. Army Regulation 600-13, *Army Policy for the Assignment of Female Soldiers* (March 27, 1992). Army publications are available at http://www.army.mil/usapa.

11. Romesh Ratnesar and Michael Weisskopf, "Portrait of a Platoon," *Time*, December 29, 2003; Eric Schmitt, "Female M.P. Wins Silver Star for Bravery in Iraq Firefight," *New York Times*, June 17, 2005; Ann Scott Tyson, "Woman Gains Silver Star—and Removal from Combat," *Washington Post*, May 1, 2008; Kirk Semple, "A Captain's Journey from Hope to Just Getting Her Unit Home," *New York Times*, November 19, 2006; Ann Scott Tyson, "For Female GIs, Combat Is a Fact," *Washington Post*, May 13, 2005; Lizette Alvarez, "G.I. Jane Breaks the Combat Barrier," *New York Times*, August 16, 2009.

12. News release, U.S. Army Public Affairs, "Army Announces Close Combat Badge," February 11, 2005.

13. U.S. Department of Defense news transcript, "Secretary Rumsfeld Townhall Meeting in Kandahar, Afghanistan," April 13, 2005.

14. U.S. Army, Combat Action Badge, http://www.army.mil/symbols/combatbadges/Action.html.

15. Ann Scott Tyson, "Panel Votes to Ban Women from Combat," *Washington Post*, May 12, 2005; Thom Shanker, "House Bill Would Preserve, and Limit, the Role of Women in Combat Zones," *New York Times*, May 20, 2005; Thom Shanker, "Military Bill Backtracks on Women," *New York Times*, May 26, 2005.

16. National Defense Authorization Act for Fiscal Year 2006, Pub. L. No. 109-163, § 541 (2006).

17. Amended Complaint for Deprivation of Constitutional and Statutory Rights, *McSally v. Rumsfeld* (D.D.C. May 3, 2002); Ann Gerhart, "The Air Force Flier in the Ointment; Martha McSally's Garb in Saudi Arabia Chafed, So She Pressed a Lawsuit," *Washington Post*, January 7, 2002.

18. National Defense Authorization Act for Fiscal Year 2003, Pub. L. No. 107-314, § 563 (2002).

19. Michael Moss, "A Mission That Ended in Inferno for 3 Women," *New York Times*, December 20, 2005.

20. Jean Zimmerman, *Tailspin: Women at War in the Wake of Tailhook* (New York: Doubleday, 1995).

21. U.S. Department of Defense, Office of the Under Secretary of Defense (Personnel and Readiness), *FY08 Report on Sexual Assault in the Military* (2009).

22. U.S. Department of the Army, FM 6-22, *Army Leadership: Competent, Confident, and Agile*, ¶ 2-11.

23. Rules for Courts-Martial 306(b) discussion, in *Manual for Courts-Martial, United States* (2008), II-25.

24. *Parker v. Levy*, 417 U.S. 733, 749-50 (1974), explained that the Uniform Code of Military Justice "regulates aspects of the conduct of members of the military which

in the civilian sphere are left unregulated," but it balances that intrusiveness with flexible levels of correction or punishment "which are below the threshold of what would normally be considered a criminal sanction."

25. *Army Leadership*, ¶ 4-7.

26. Gary B. Trudeau, *Doonesbury*, May 25, 2005.

27. Memorandum from Paul Wolfowitz, deputy secretary of defense, to the secretaries of the military departments et al., *Confidentiality Policy for Victims of Sexual Assault*, JTF-SAPR-009, March 16, 2005.

28. Diana Jean Schemo, "4 Top Officers at Air Force Academy Are Replaced in Wake of Rape Scandal," *New York Times*, March 26, 2003.

29. U.S. Department of Defense, *Report of the Panel to Review Sexual Misconduct Allegations at the U.S. Air Force Academy* (2003); U.S. Department of Defense, *Task Force Report on Care for Victims of Sexual Assault* (2004); U.S. Department of Defense, *Report of the Defense Task Force on Sexual Harassment and Violence at the Military Service Academies* (2005).

30. *Report of the Panel to Review Sexual Misconduct Allegations at the U.S. Air Force Academy*, 8.

31. U.S. Air Force Academy, *Agenda for Change* (2003); Diana Jean Schemo, "Air Force Secretary Says Academy's Leaders Could Be Punished in Rape Scandal," *New York Times*, April 2, 2005.

32. Martha Mendoza, Associated Press, "AP Probe Looks at Recruiters' Misconduct," *Washington Post*, August 19, 2006.

33. *John Warner National Defense Authorization Act for Fiscal Year 2007*, Conference Report H. Rep. 109-702, 109th Congress (2006), 707; Ann Scott Tyson, "Reported Cases of Sexual Assault in Military Increase," *Washington Post*, May 7, 2005; Peter T. Kilborn, "Sex Abuse Cases Sting Pentagon, but the Problem Has Deep Roots," *New York Times*, February 10, 1997; Ann Scott Tyson, "Female Pilots Get Their Shot in the Iraqi Skies," *Washington Post*, February 27, 2006.

34. Richard Pyle, Associated Press, "GI Who Exposed Abu Ghraib Feared Revenge," *San Francisco Chronicle*, August 10, 2006.

35. Paul Von Zielbauer, "Soldier Who Testified on Killings Says He Feared for His Life," *New York Times*, August 8, 2006.

36. U.S. Army Public Affairs, "Army Sending 'I A.M. Strong' Kits to Battalions," February 6, 2009; U.S. Army Sexual Assault Prevention and Response Program, *Annual Report–Fiscal Year 2008* (2009), 8-10; http://www.preventsexualassault.army.mil.

CHAPTER 11 A CAUTIONARY TALE ABOUT MILITARY VOTING

1. Susan Schmidt, "Military Ballot Review Is Urged," *Washington Post*, November 21, 2000 (quoting Senator Zell Miller of Georgia).

2. John Allen Paulos, "We're Measuring Bacteria with a Yardstick," *New York Times*, November 22, 2000.

3. Absentee Ballots to Overseas Electors, Fla. Admin. Code. Ann., rule 1S-2.013. Unless otherwise noted, all references in this chapter are to laws and regulations as they existed at the time of the 2000 election.

4. U.S. General Accounting Office, *Voting Assistance to Military and Overseas Citizens Should Be Improved* (2001), 17.

5. "Close Vote, Absentees' Influence Provide Lesson in Politics," *Stars and Stripes*, November 10, 2000.

6. Richard Perez-Pena, "The Overseas Ballots; Floridians Abroad Are Counted, or Not, as Counties Interpret 'Rules' Differently," *New York Times*, November 18, 2000; David Barstow and Don Van Natta, Jr., "How Bush Took Florida: Mining the Overseas Absentee Vote," *New York Times*, July 15, 2001.

7. Bush campaign briefing, Austin, Texas, November 18, 2000 (Karen Hughes and Mark Racicot).

8. Memorandum from Mark Herron, Overseas Absentee Ballot Review and Protest (November 15, 2000), Appendix A to Motion for Emergency Injunctive Relief, *Bush v. Bay County Canvassing Board* (Fla. 2d Cir. November 22, 2000). Legal documents related to the 2000 presidential election controversy are compiled in a Stanford University database, http://election2000.stanford.edu.

9. Susan Schmidt, "Republican Officials Complain about Military Vote Challenges," *Washington Post*, November 19, 2000; "GOP Seeks to Reinstate Many Rejected Absentee Votes," *Wall Street Journal*, November 22, 2000.

10. Richard Perez-Pena, "Military Ballots Merit a Review, Lieberman Says," *New York Times*, November 20, 2000.

11. Memorandum from Robert A. Butterworth, Florida attorney general, to all county supervisors of elections and all county canvassing boards (November 20, 2000).

12. *Bush v. Bay County Canvassing Board* (Fla. 2d Cir. November 22, 2000); Michael Cooper, "Lawyers for Bush Want a Judge to Reinstate Military Ballots That Were Disqualified," *New York Times*, November 25, 2000.

13. Lucy Morgan and Linda Gibson, "Bush Picks Up 45 Overseas Military Votes," *St. Petersburg Times*, November 26, 2000.

14. John Mintz and Peter Slevin, "Human Factor Was at Core of Vote Fiasco; Decisions and Leadership Were Erratic, Arbitrary," *Washington Post*, June 1, 2001.

15. Barstow and Van Natta, "How Bush Took Florida."

16. *Bush v. Gore*, 531 U.S. 98 (2000).

17. U.S. Department of Defense, Office of the Inspector General, *Overseas Absentee Ballot Handling in DOD* (2001).

18. GAO, *Voting Assistance*.

19. Office of the Inspector General, *Overseas Absentee Ballot*, 44; GAO, *Voting Assistance*, 71, 74.

20. U.S. Department of Defense news briefing, Office of the Assistant Secretary of Defense (Public Affairs), November 7, 2000.

21. U.S. Department of Defense news briefing, Office of the Assistant Secretary of Defense (Public Affairs), November 9, 2000.

22. U.S. Department of Defense news briefing, Office of the Assistant Secretary of Defense (Public Affairs), November 28, 2000.

23. The military generally follows United States Postal Service procedures for postmarking. Office of the Deputy Under Secretary of Defense (Logistics and Materiel Readiness), *Department of Defense Postal Manual* (2002).

24. Complaint, *Bush v. Bay County Canvassing Board*, 6.

25. U.S. Department of Defense news briefing, "Overseas Absentee Voting," June 22, 2001.

26. 1989 Florida Laws, chapter 89-338.

27. Meg Laughlin, "Overseas Ballots: Military Vote Drive May Benefit Republicans," *Miami Herald*, November 17, 2000.

28. David Wasson, "Lawyers Move to Front Lines for Election 2000 Maneuvers," *Tampa Tribune*, November 10, 2000; Paige St. John et al., "Ballot Fight Goes to Court; Bush May Have Edge in Overseas Balloting," *Tallahassee Democrat*, November 14, 2000; Stephen Hegarty, "Count of Ballots Ruled by Minutiae," *St. Petersburg Times*, November 18, 2000.

29. Wasson, "Lawyers Move to Front Lines"; William March, "Absentee Ballots' Day Has Arrived: Today," *Tampa Tribune*, November 17, 2000; Kathy Steele and Carlos Moncada, "Area Overseas Vote Tilts toward Bush," *Tampa Tribune*, November 18, 2000.

30. St. John et al., "Ballot Fight Goes to Court"; Paul Brinkley-Rogers, "Military Ballots: Rejected Votes Not Unusual," *Miami Herald*, November 21, 2000.

31. Bryan Gilmer et al., "300 and Counting; for Gore, Overseas Votes a Long Shot," *St. Petersburg Times*, November 15, 2000; Tyler Bridges, "Duval County Overseas Ballots Favor Bush, 318-151," *Miami Herald*, November 19, 2000.

32. Eric Bailey and Scott Martelle, "In Political Game of Inches, an Everest of 1,850 Absentee Votes," *Los Angeles Times*, November 16, 2000; Laughlin, "Overseas Ballots: Military Vote Drive May Benefit Republicans." A total of 3,704 overseas ballots were received after Election Day. Barstow and Van Natta, "How Bush Took Florida."

33. GAO, *Voting Assistance*, 72-73; Office of the Inspector General, *Overseas Absentee Ballot*, 43-44; Stephen Hegarty, "Military Ballots Brook Varying Rules," *St. Petersburg Times*, November 22, 2000 (quoting DOD spokesperson).

34. GAO, *Voting Assistance*, 48, 73-74.

35. Thomas E. Ricks, "Military Personnel Warned on Politics," *Washington Post*, November 30, 2000.

CHAPTER 12 A PART OF AMERICA, NOT APART FROM AMERICA

1. David Halberstam, *The Coldest Winter: America and the Korean War* (New York: Hyperion, 2007).

2. Todd Spangler, "Angry Midshipmen Fear Violence if Military Accepts Homosexuals," *Washington Times*, January 28, 1993. Richard Kohn, an expert in civil-military relations, once wrote that General Powell's resistance to military intervention in the Balkans was "the most explicit intrusion into policy since MacArthur's conflict with Truman." Richard H. Kohn, "Out of Control: The Crisis in Civil-Military Relations," *The National Interest* 35 (Spring 1994).

3. Damon Coletta, "Courage in the Service of Virtue," *Armed Forces and Society* 34 (2007): 109; Paul R. Camacho and William Locke Hauser, "Civil-Military Relations—Who Are the Real Principals?" *Armed Forces and Society* 34 (2007): 122; Damon Coletta, "There Are Several Principals—Each One Worthy of Research," *Armed Forces and Society* 34 (2008): 503.

4. Coletta, "Courage in the Service of Virtue," 110 (urging delicate treatment of "military truth," with quotation marks in the original).

5. Paul Yingling, "A Failure in Generalship," *Armed Forces Journal*, May 2007; Fred Kaplan, "Challenging the Generals," *New York Times*, August 26, 2007.

6. David S. Cloud and Eric Schmitt, "More Retired Generals Call for Rumsfeld's Resignation," *New York Times*, April 14, 2006.

7. "Rumsfeld Praises Army General Who Ridicules Islam as 'Satan,'" *New York Times*, October 17, 2003.

8. Anthony Lagouranis, "Tortured Logic," *New York Times*, February 28, 2006.

9. James Risen, "Use of Iraq Contractors Costs Billions, Report Says," *New York Times*, August 11, 2008.

10. Montgomery McFate, "Anthropology and Counterinsurgency: The Strange Story of Their Curious Relationship," *Military Review*, March-April 2005; David Rohde, "Army Enlists Anthropology in War Zones," *New York Times*, October 5, 2007.

11. Patricia Cohen, "Scholars and the Military Share a Foxhole, Uneasily," *New York Times*, December 22, 2007.

12. Capt. Stacie N. Shafran, "A Tribute to Ashton Goodman," *Air Force News*, May 29, 2009; Elisabeth Bumiller, "Letting Women Reach Women in Afghan War," *New York Times*, March 7, 2010.

13. Sam Dillon, "Teach for America Sees Surge in Popularity," *New York Times*, May 14, 2008.

Index